Trade Financing

Co-ordinated
by
Charles J. Gmür

Published by Euromoney Publications

Published by
Euromoney Publications Limited,
Nestor House, Playhouse Yard,
London, EC4

Text set in 10/11 pt Linotron 202 Times,
printed and bound in Great Britain at
The Pitman Press, Bath

Acknowledgements

Euromoney Publications is most grateful to Mr. Charles J. Gmür for co-ordinating, as well as contributing to, this book on techniques and practice in trade finance. We are also grateful to the other authors for their contributions.

Contents

List of exhibits

Introduction

We know that in the region of the Euphrates and Tigris, in present day Iraq, a substantial volume of trade was already taking place around 4000 BC. What was previously a direct exchange of two goods, i.e., barter, was evolving to include an intermediary—a third person—who exchanged desired goods for ones with no immediate market. This form of commodity switch finally led to exchange on credit. Farmers bought seed for a price—at the time of sowing—and paid for it after the harvest. Since the grain was then worth less, they were paying a form of interest to their financier. Written records of such transactions date from the time of King Hammurabi (c. 2000 BC).

Elements of such early exchange on credit—the first form of export finance—still exist today in compensation and cooperation transactions which have experienced a renaissance in the last 10 to 15 years, primarily in trade with countries possessing little foreign exchange. In Chapter I, C. Raemy-Dirks of Crédit Suisse, Zurich, deals with her experience of this revived, original form of trade finance. Where cross-border trade existed, money took on importance. We know from the Bible that Abraham (c. 2000 BC) carried out substantial trade with other countries, and in his time slaves, for example, were bought with money. At the time of King Solomon (c. 970–930 BC), barley and wine were supplied in large quantities by the Jews to neighbouring countries. Maritime trade with Africa and India brought plentiful gold and silver to the Near East and gave these precious metals a monetary status. In India, as early as c. 1000 BC, metal coins were stamped with officially controlled weights. Metal coinage was reported in China as early as the time of Hsia (2200–1766 BC).

Where money existed in the form of durable metal, lending against instruments of credit, e.g. against bills, soon developed. The long trade routes made it essential to finance such cross-border trade exchanges. The Assyrians developed a system whereby an agent would make the voyage in place of the merchant. The agent received the money for the purchases against the issue of a written promissory note in which the agent committed himself to pay penal interest should he cause any delay in payment. These promissory notes were also traded among the merchants and served, among other things, to refinance trade which had already been completed.

With the further passage of time, the bill became obsolete. Although the Greeks had a cashless giro or credit system in the 4th century BC, bills were not used in trade. Reports of the use of bills in trading appear again at the time of the Islamic invasion of the Byzantine Empire. The use of the trade bill only really spread in the later middle ages, with the rise of the Medici banking family in Florence and the Fugger family of merchants in southern Germany.

Increasingly, from 1300 on, merchants began to conduct their business from an office, thereby separating the trading function from the transportation function; and so the documentary aspect of commerce developed.

In 1697, in England, inland bills were made legal and from then on became widely used in domestic trade and as a refinancing instrument by endorsement. In the 19th century, the bill was recognized throughout Europe as a means of payment, and in England this was embodied in the Bills of Exchange Act of 1882. With the disruption in international trade following World War I, the bill as an international financing instrument declined in importance. Since the fixing of international currency parities by the Bretton Woods agreement and by the international legal codification of 1930, the bill has once again come into widespread use. N.P. Soskin of Gillet Brothers, London, presents a detailed study of the bill of exchange in Chapter II.

The widening of trade, both in terms of turnover and distance, entails an increase in the risks. While the early travelling agent used letters of recommendation and letters of credit as his credentials, modern payment transfers through international banks necessitate an alternative form of protection against risks. The documentary credit has been developed, whereby the buyer gives his bank instructions to make payment to the seller only on presentation of certain documents evidencing dispatch of the goods ordered. An explanation of the various aspects of a documentary collection and of documentary credits in international trade is provided in Chapter III by P. O'Hanlon of Citicorp, London.

In the history of trading, consumer goods predominated. Exports of capital goods only began to gain importance at the time of the industrial revolution. In Chapter IV, I look at the ways of financing international trade in consumer goods.

Investment goods have an important share of world trade today, and R. H. Miller of Finanz AG London Limited, London, has written on the subject of financing investment goods transactions in Chapter V.

The exporter is not always in a position to offer financing to the buyer. A large trade turnover could lead to country risks which could not be borne by the exporter. The subject of buyer credits is dealt with by T. Teichman of Crédit Suisse, London, in Chapter VI.

An alternative to supplier credit and buyer credit is leasing. Although tenancy and rental contracts are a form of leasing, leasing in the corporate sense is a relatively recent form of financing. In Chapter VII, I discuss developments that have taken place in leasing, and the way it is handled by specialist companies.

Another recent form of trade financing is forfaiting. This is not a real credit transaction because the forfaiter purchases the bills and the risk from the exporter. He takes the place of the creditor, without a contract between him and the debtor. I discuss forfaiting as a modern way of financing export transactions in Chapter VIII.

In the 1960s, a new market developed for credit financing—the Euromarket, a parallel to the domestic markets. This market has expanded rapidly to become an independent credit market in the main international currencies. G. Clarke of Credit Suisse First Boston, London, describes the use of bonds, private placements and Eurocredits in Chapter IX.

With the arrival of multinational project financing, importers and exporters became conscious of new risks. The internationalism in today's transactions means it is not always possible for contracting partners to know and assess one another. In Chapter X, L. Beckers of Citibank, Paris, discusses how bid bonds and performance bonds, as well as other guarantees, can be used.

Lastly, in Chapter XI, R. Davies and A. Grabiner, both barristers, examine the legal aspects of international trade financing, a field which is becoming ever more complex to the layman. International legal agreements and recognized arbitration committees have already led the way to a furthering and expansion of international trade transactions.

December 1980   **C. J. Gmür**
                                                                                 Zurich

16

CHAPTER ONE
Countertrade: linked purchases in international trade

Christine Raemy-Dirks

1. Introduction

The strengthened presence of Socialist and Third World countries in a world market previously dominated by the industrialized nations has, since the early 1970s, brought with it a rapidly increasing balance of payments disequilibrium. The indebtedness of developing countries between 1967 and 1980 leapt from about US$ 45 billion to around US$ 450 billion (without adjusting for inflation), and that of Eastern Europe in the same period from some US$ 13 billion to about US$ 65 billion. The Comecon countries in particular made an early attempt to restrain this development by obtaining countertrade commitments from their trading partners. Countertrade or linked purchases today imply predominantly the many forms which modern trade deals with Comecon have taken.

No country *has to engage* in countertrade. In Switzerland, for example, countertrade transactions account for no more than 10% of their exports to Eastern Europe, and in West Germany, a major trading partner with East European countries, the percentage is not appreciably higher. However, certain industries are more likely than others to participate in countertrade; and certain countries with high countertrade quotas can sometimes distort an analysis of this form of trade.

The abundance of forms taken by these modern trade deals necessitates a clear distinction of terms. There is no convention, either in Eastern or Western Europe, about an internationally binding nomenclature for individual types of transaction. Before a businessman, financier or academic enters into a deep discussion of countertrade, he (or she) should make themselves aware of the counterparty's understanding of the term.

2. Definitions

Transactions with compensation or countertrade character mean foreign trade deals in which deliveries to a foreign country are intimately linked to imports from that country: this includes the individual transaction, even when it is carried out within the framework of an intergovernmental agreement or, as is usual with large contracts, is negotiated at government level. Bilateral trade agreements between two countries with fixed, balanced yearly quotas do not fall under the heading of compensation deals or countertrade.

2.1. Barter

The expression barter has found its way into many languages as a term for the earliest form of exchange: the exchange of goods for goods without the medium of cash payments. In the U.S.S.R. however, it is also used for exchange transactions in the form of compensation and counterpurchase. The following are the characteristics of barter transactions:
- The exchange of goods is set out in a single contract.
- The goods to be exchanged are specified in quantity and quality, without any value being given to them, either in total or individually, in any unit of currency.
- Payment is made exclusively by the countersupply of the agreed products. There is no financing in money.
- The exchange of goods takes place between two trading partners. No provision is made for the intervention of a third.
- The exchange of goods usually happens simultaneously. Between delivery and counter-delivery there is seldom a delay of more than one year.

Barter transactions are concluded only in the rarest cases today (see section 4.1.1).

2.2. Compensation deals

The term compensation has long been used, particularly among German-speakers, as a generic term for all countertrade transactions with Eastern Europe. Today, this term is used in a narrower sense. Compensation deals have the following features:
— Delivery and counterdelivery are covered by one contract.
— The exchanged products have no technical dependence on one another, i.e., do not come into existence as a result of the primary delivery. They do, however, often come from the same industry.
— The goods, in contrast to barter transactions, are priced in money value. Delivery and counterdelivery are invoiced in an agreed currency.
— To each flow of goods there is a corresponding flow of payments. In certain cases, payments are credited to a clearing account, in others payments reach each supplier in his own country.
— The compensation contract usually provides that the counterparty's purchase commitment is transferable to third parties.
— The deliveries do not have to take place simultaneously. The time limit for completion of the countercommitment is about three years.
— Two or more contracting parties can participate in compensation. One speaks of triangular compensation, for example, when the counterdelivery is made to a third country, e.g., in Eastern Europe or in the Third World, and the Western exporter is paid from there.

Compensation transactions, unlike barter deals, need not provide for 100% counterdelivery (see section 4.1.2). The options include:

2.2.1. Partial compensation
A specified fraction of the Western export must be compensated by the purchase of goods, the balance being exempt from counterpurchase commitments.

2.2.2. Full compensation
The agreed compensation purchases make up 100% or even more of the Western export. The expression compensation transaction as defined here matches the usage employed in most Western literature on the practice of countertrade. The U.S. Department of Commerce, however, employs the term counterpurchase for this type of business, whilst compensation is used to describe transactions generally denoted by cooperation. The East European and Third World countries follow Western Europe and use compensation and cooperation in the sense used in this chapter.

2.3. Counterpurchase

This differs in an important respect from compensation deals, in that it contains two contracts. Since the exchanged goods are technically independent of one another, this may be considered as a developed form of a compensation deal.
Counterpurchase has the following characteristics:
— Delivery and counterdelivery are embodied in two legally self-contained contracts.
— Invoicing is carried out in an agreed currency.
— Each delivery is paid for independently of the other.
— The goods often belong to different industries, but can originate through the same foreign trade organization, and therefore belong to a related category of goods. They are not, however, a result of the primary delivery.
— The intervention of a third party, i.e., a transfer of the counterpurchase commitment, is possible as a result of separated supply contracts.
— Delivery and counterdelivery can extend over a medium-term time span, but in most cases take place within five years of each other.

The following transaction types are recognized as special forms of counterpurchase:

2.3.1. Parallel deals
This is the usual form of counterpurchase. It developed from the compensation deals in order to take advantage, owing to the separated purchase contracts, of state export assistance schemes or other financing and insurance possibilities in the West (see section 4.2.1).

2.3.2 Linked deals (*Junctim*)
This form has the characteristics of counterpurchase, and was used when only compensation deals existed. In a linked deal, the sequence of sales is reversed: a Western importer first buys goods from an East European or Third World supplier, on condition that his purchase will be allowed to him or

to another Western exporter as a fulfilled counterpurchase commitment on future exports (see section 4.2.2).

2.3.3. Gentlemen's agreement
A further type of counterpurchase deal is where no legally binding counterpurchase commitment exists. However, when Western goods are sold, a gentlemen's agreement is entered into to look for possibilities of buying East European or Third World goods. No sanctions are agreed upon in the event of non-fulfilment of the commitment, but usually in subsequent transactions the counter-purchase commitment is formulated in a legally binding way.

2.4. Cooperation

This form of business is distinguished from all the aforementioned forms of countertrade by the long-term contracts of economic collaboration which are concluded (partnership contracts). The countercommitment does not entail a one-off purchase of compensation goods, but is extended over a long period by the continuing purchase of goods which have some technical connection with the Western goods supplied. Alternatively, the cooperation entails collaboration in joint ventures and in projects in other markets (see section 4.3).

2.4.1. Industrial cooperation or buy-back arrangements
Arrangements of this nature involve the supply of complexes of machines or installations from a Western country, and the continuous supply of the goods produced by these machines or installations from Eastern Europe or the Third World. A similar procedure applies under licence arrangements or sales of licences. The Western supplier balances the credit supplied for the intervening period out of the sale proceeds of the goods.

The features of industrial cooperation are:
— Cooperation contracts are most common, with sales of Western production plants, from large machines to the installation of whole factories, to East European or developing country importers.
— Delivery and counterdelivery are linked through the production process. The buy-back goods are usually produced or processed by the installation. Sometimes, because of the long installation and production periods, similar products from an existing plant are supplied instead.
— For reasons similar to those in parallel deals, separate contracts are often drawn up for the purchase of the Western installation and for the supply of East European or Third World goods.
— All transactions are denominated in units of an agreed currency.
— A long period usually elapses between primary delivery and the first counterdelivery. As much as 10 years or more may elapse before all deliveries are completed.
— Credit is agreed upon for the bridging period. Cash deals with subsequent purchases of goods by the West are rare; buy-back deals involve payment by produced goods in place of money.
— The buy-back products may constitute a fraction of the Western supply value, may equal it or may even amount to more than 100%, in order to cover financing costs and local costs connected with the installation of the plant.

In the U.S.S.R., China and the U.S., this type of industrial cooperation is called compensation while in Eastern and Western Europe and in the Third World the term cooperation has been adopted.

2.4.2. Joint ventures
In certain cases, Western exporters to Eastern Europe or the Third World participate in the production and sales risk, and enter into a form of equity participation with the importing company. The capital provided, be it in the form of know-how or of production equipment, is repaid through participation in the sales proceeds. This solution exists where there are no precisely defined markets for the goods produced with Western help, or when a forward sale of the buy-back goods cannot be arranged in advance.

Joint ventures do not necessarily have to take the form of reluctant participation in an East European or Third World company. While the aforementioned forms of countertrade have the flavour of a compulsory exchange, forced by the shortage of foreign exchange in the importing country, joint ventures may be positively sought by Western enterprises because of their low-cost production, and not be introduced merely as a makeshift solution to trade financing problems. Joint ventures are, therefore, not included in most Western literature on countertrade, but are placed alongside countertrade as an independent species.

3. Why and when countertrade?

In what circumstances is a Western exporter confronted with a request for countertrade? When should he himself make such an offer? In most cases the East European or Third World buyer will indicate an interest in a counterdelivery of his own products at the latest during contract negotiations. It is, however, often possible to foresee when such demands could be made upon the Western exporter, since linked purchases serve specific objectives.

The East European state-trading nations adhere to a system of country-by-country bilateralism. In the absence of intergovernmental trade agreements, the overriding principle is to maintain a balance between exports and imports with each trading partner. The urgent need to import expensive investment goods has, in recent years, frequently rendered it impossible to uphold this principle. Exporters from countries which show a persistent balance of trade surplus *vis-à-vis* an East European importing country will more readily countenance counterpurchase commitments than exporters from countries with no difficulty importing equal quantities of East European goods.

Demands for countertrade are directed particularly at any Western suppliers who already have a *long-standing business relationship* with an East European trading partner, and at those who have undertaken counterpurchase commitments with earlier deliveries. New business partners, however, are also confronted with counterpurchase suggestions. These occur, on the one hand, when *competition* among Western suppliers makes it easier to impose such a demand; on the other, when *unplanned imports* force the East European buyer, in the absence of foreign exchange, to make payment in goods or, alternatively, to first earn the foreign exchange through his own exports.

Countertrade is seen as the ideal solution to the problem of importing from the West goods which fall outside a five-year plan. In a few socialist countries it is possible to achieve unplanned imports by linking them with unplanned national exports, thereby giving individual enterprises a certain measure of economic freedom. Western suppliers, however, should determine to what extent this import is provided for in the economic plan of their East European partner.

In the U.S.S.R. and other Comecon countries import requirements are prescribed in long-term five-year plans, providing details for the production companies. Import requirements are often divided into priority imports and normal planned imports. Unplanned imports can be accommodated, on condition that no foreign exchange allocated to the plan is used. For priority imports, foreign exchange is generally freely available, so that the Western supplier can transact a cash deal. While with unplanned imports, countertrade is the rule, with planned imports it may also, in certain circumstances, be demanded. The extent of counterpurchase commitments depends on the demand for a given import, the competition among suppliers and the availability of the required foreign exchange.

The *size of the Western delivery* will affect the demand for counterpurchase commitments. The greater the volume of an individual transaction, the more likely it is that at least a part will be linked to counterpurchases. The installation of large plants usually occurs on the basis of industrial cooperation, i.e., as buy-back deals, particularly in trade with the U.S.S.R. There, the large-scale developments intended for the Asian region represent a considerable economic burden. There seems to be a broad opinion in the East European countries that linked deals are a suitable means of obtaining better credit conditions and larger amounts of credit. If the loan repayment depends on the free sale of the products produced by the project, then the sales prospects of the goods, and the soundness of the borrower, are more carefully assessed by the lenders. Conversely, the guaranteed transfer of goods reduces the risk margin and permits cheaper financing. Linked deals thus fulfil the purpose of carrying through large schemes without self-financing, or with a reduced need for it, thereby securing long-term economic provisions, at the same time as increasing the volume of Western exports.

4. Countertrade: the execution of transactions

4.1. Barter and compensation

4.1.1. Barter

These deals are so seldom encountered nowadays that an exhaustive discussion of this form of business is unnecessary. The direct exchange of two unpriced goods is usually carried out on trust, without the introduction of bank guarantees or letters of credit. It stands apart from the monetary system, and therefore does not make use of its security mechanisms. Barter can, for example, be transacted in such a way that the transportation used for the primary goods also carries back the countergoods. Or, a later counterdelivery is promised, and the commencement of production of these goods provides a certain security for the primary delivery.

Barter can be represented schematically, as shown in Exhibit 101.

Exhibit 101: Barter/exchange contract

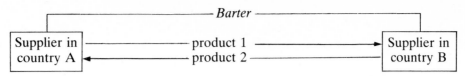

4.1.2. Compensation

This also involves an exchange by means of a single contract. However, here each flow of goods is valued in monetary units and has, in principle, a counterflow of finance. This financial flow can consist of the clearing of claims, and does not necessarily mean a transfer of foreign exchange. It is precisely to avoid this foreign exchange transfer that compensation transactions are often concluded. Payment for the primary delivery is allowed on credit by the supplier, his claims for payment on the delivery are registered on a clearing account in the East European country, and are liquidated by the counterdelivery. Thus, his claims for repayment of the credit are cancelled by the counterdeliveries.

A Western delivery does not always take place first. It is also possible for a purchase to be made first in an East European country. When the Western exporter has found compensation goods available from his buyer or from another company, he can either take them himself or, insofar as a right of assignment has been agreed, sell them to a trader at a reduced price, i.e., paying him a countertrade premium. Both deliveries can now be carried out. The trader pays the Western exporter the value of the goods, less the compensation premium, while an internal clearing arrangement exists if necessary between the exporter and East European importer (see Exhibit 102).

Exhibit 102: Compensation with assignment

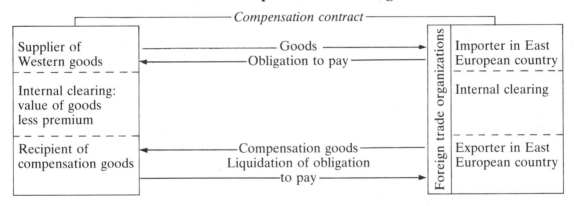

Should it not be possible for the goods to be delivered simultaneously, it is feasible for the counterparty to issue a guarantee of delivery (performance bond) issued or guaranteed by a bank. It is also possible in such cases to use a letter of credit, though this is not common.

Compensation may be transacted as partial or full compensation (see Exhibits 103 and 104), although the former predominates, especially when dealing with small Western exporting companies.

Exhibit 103: Partial compensation

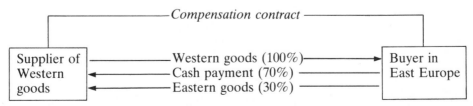

21

Exhibit 104: Full compensation

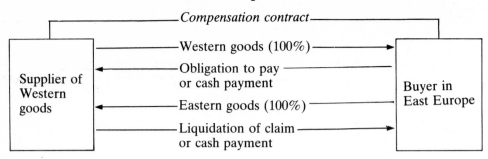

In most cases of *partial compensation* the East European or Third World company makes no payment for the compensated portion. Should the Western exporter succeed in selling the expected compensation goods in advance to a third party, e.g., a trading company, he can then turn the transaction into a cash deal with the deduction of a support payment to the third party. In partial compensation, East European foreign trade organizations prefer the supplier to take up the compensation goods, so that no support costs enter the cost to be passed on to them. Consequently, the East European side is glad to restrict the transferability of compensation commitments.

Compensation contracts may be concluded between more than two parties. Triangular compensation, for example, is possible, whereby the compensation goods are not taken by the Western exporter, but are passed on to a buyer in another country. The latter then pays the Western exporter. A schematic representation is shown in Exhibit 105.

Exhibit 105: Triangular compensation: Compensation contract between three partners, A, B, C

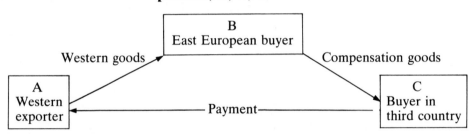

Triangular compensation may create *switch-deals*. In these, a bilateral payment agreement exists between a third country and an East European country, involving clearing currency. The buyer of Western goods pays by delivering goods to the third country, which thereby enters into a commitment to pay the Western exporter in hard currency. The switch dealer acquires the clearing currency and passes on hard currency to the primary supplier after deducting a disagio or fee (see Exhibit 106). A switch deal does not need to be a triangular deal. The Western exporter could accept directly a payment claim in a clearing currency, which he then exchanges for hard currency through a switch dealer. In all cases, switch dealers will take on only clearing credits which they can use for their own purchases, or sell on. The disagio is determined by the negotiability of the clearing currency.

Exhibit 106: Triangular compensation with switch

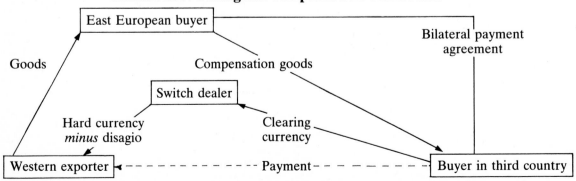

Compensation transactions have now been extensively replaced by counterpurchase transactions. These have the advantage, through the formulation of a separate contract for each delivery, of being clearer and more unequivocable about the claims and obligations of each side. Otherwise, however, many of the problems and risks of countertrade apply equally to compensation and counterpurchase transactions.

4.2. Counterpurchase

4.2.1. Parallel deals
These involve two trade transactions for which separate contracts are drawn up. Each delivery results in a commitment to pay, which must be satisfied irrespective of the performance of the counterdeal. These two trading agreements are linked by a skeleton contract, which sets out the commitment of the Western supplier to make a counterpurchase or arrange for one to be made within a certain fixed time. A further link exists on the East European side, where the currency proceeds of the counterdelivery are credited to the importing company. Such internal clearing between two East European companies, which do not always belong to the same foreign trade organization, may involve a payment of an acknowledgement premium by the importer to the exporter for the release of his foreign exchange holdings.

As a rule, the two trade agreements are no different to any other export or import deal. The Western supplier, in granting credit terms to his buyer, is using available financing, be it state credit insurance and financing, or commercial bank financing (see Chapters IV and V).

4.2.2. Linked deals
The linked deal, often known by its Latin name *Junctim*, is like a reversed parallel deal. A Western importer demands from an East European or Third World party the right to link subsequent Western sales with his purchase, i.e., to connect them contractually and have them set off as counterpurchases. This right may be conceded to him if, during negotiations, he does not bargain for too low a price. He will then look for Western exporters who are committed to counterpurchase, and are prepared to pay him a subsidy for taking over the commitment. He will thus achieve the desired price reduction in arrears for his import, but must meanwhile put up with a degree of uncertainty.

4.3. Industrial cooperation: buy-back deals

There is little to be said by way of generalization about these operations; owing to their size, they are governed by very rigorously negotiated, specific contracts. When they are of a long-term nature, short-term trade financing is out of the question. They are often transacted, therefore, with state support or even, in certain circumstances, concluded at government level, and have the characteristics of *project financing*. Smaller buy-back deals are occasionally carried out within intergovernmental skeleton agreements, with the risk being assumed by export-assistance programmes; these also make long-term finance more easily available through banks in the exporting country. However, industrial cooperation can be considered as a form of investment abroad by Western companies, yielding income only after a certain time lapse. Buy-back deals, however, entail a great number of problems and risks.

5. Problems and risks in countertrade

The problems and risks in countertrade are mainly connected with buy-back goods and concern choice, availability, punctuality of delivery and quality of the compensation goods. Other contractual commitments, such as punctual repayment and the accrual of penalties, as well as the problems and risks on the refinancing side, are closely connected with them. In general, East European and Third World nations are reliable debtors, taking pains to adhere strictly to contractual agreements. The difficulties which occur arise from the inadequacy of a planned economic system and are seldom the responsibility of any individual enterprise.

5.1. Selection of buy-back goods

The choice of goods in buy-back arrangements is straightforward, since the product to be purchased is produced by the plant supplied with, for instance, Western machinery. In compensation and parallel deals, however, the selection of products is more complex.

In a few Comecon countries, the choice of buy-back goods is restricted to the domain of the foreign trade organization, or a specialist ministry. An in-house compensation deal occurs when an internal costing procedure for the foreign exchange proceeds from the counterdelivery is legally impossible, protracted or costly. Furthermore, the remuneration of the persons concerned sometimes depends on the export quotas achieved. Poland, Czechoslovakia, Hungary and Romania often prescribe in-house compensation. In Poland, an offer can also be obtained from other Polish enterprises through the intervention of the firm DAL in Warsaw, but this possibility must be insisted upon in contract negotiations with the East European importer. Usually, a package of goods, consisting of machines and general goods, is offered for compensation.

In Czechoslovakia, goods from other foreign trade enterprises can, in exceptional cases, also be offered for the counterpurchase commitment, although this is sometimes paid for with a higher compensation quota which may exceed the value of the Western goods supplied.

In Hungary, to avoid in-house compensation, the Hungarian import company must reach an agreement with the Hungarian exporter about the foreign exchange transfer. In contrast to other Comecon countries this is an entrepreneurial issue between two production concerns, rather than a central economic problem.

The East European countries will, as a rule, attempt to offer as buy-back goods those products which are difficult to dispose of in the market. Just as priorities underlie imports, so the choice of buy-back goods is determined by a *priority list for Comecon exports*. In principle, three groupings are recognized: free currency goods, buy-back goods and unplanned goods. In the first group are those goods for which export orders or traditional sales channels already exist. These are predominantly raw materials and high-quality products. They are available as compensation goods only in exceptional cases. Buy-back goods are, as a rule, the residue of goods which have been planned for export but which have proved difficult to dispose of. Such selling difficulties may be the result of world market conditions, the competition in Western industrialized countries, or false assessments of the market. Unplanned goods are the result of over achievement of planned targets or of reciprocal imports from developing countries under bilateral trade and payment agreements. In the absence of a planned domestic use for such products, they are offered for countertrade. The Western supplier should not place long-term reliance on the availability of any compensation goods which have been offered. A further limitation on the choice of buy-back goods arises from the East European policy of offering the Western supplier products within his own field of manufacture. It is assumed that his own sales channels for these products make it easiest for him to market them. In accepting such products a Western firm may be creating competition for itself in conflict with its own market interests. Nevertheless, provided that a broader range of specialized goods is offered, a Western firm will sometimes welcome a few East European buy-back goods in order to widen its range on offer in the Western market, and marketing will be easier than for unfamiliar products.

A Western exporter should retain as much free choice as possible over the buy-back goods. With an unrestricted choice of goods, the support payment to compensation dealers is appreciably smaller than when less saleable goods must be accepted and one must depend on foreign trade organizations, which have a reputation among compensation dealers of being difficult.

5.2. Availability and punctuality of buy-back goods

Certain East European bloc countries willingly supply extensive lists of buy-back goods, but the goods are not always available. The lists may be out of date, or may contain a few interesting buy-back goods which are quickly exhausted; the lists are often distributed to all Western exporters and not just to the one supplier.

When a concrete countertrade deal for specified goods is agreed with a foreign trade organization, the availability of the goods is, in most cases, guaranteed. However, certain of the smaller Comecon countries (particularly Bulgaria and Romania) repeatedly experience supply difficulties, and the compensation quota is subsequently reduced by non-delivery.

Smaller quantities of buy-back goods are more readily available than large orders, which must be provided for in the production plan. Large Western companies thus complain more about punctual delivery than small Western suppliers. However, the countersale, like all exports from countries with a weak foreign exchange, will be important and will be treated with relative priority.

If the Eastern supplier breaks his contract by not making available, or not being punctual in supplying, the goods within a specified time limit, the Western exporter might nonetheless have to pay a *penalty fee* for not meeting his commitment. This penalty payment is prescribed in the skeleton agreement for parallel deals, as it is in compensation contracts, and the Western supplier should pay some attention to it. Determining the size of the penalty payment can be of importance when transacting countertrade deals. If it is small, the supplier could evade a troublesome counterpurchase commitment by paying the penalty fee as a form of price rebate. However, should he ever wish to do business there again, the penalty fee will be considerably higher. On the other hand, a very high penalty might encourage the East European enterprise to obstruct the counterdelivery, since the payment represents an attractive rebate for the East European importer. The penalty payment should, therefore, lie somewhere between 10 and 15%, especially as compensation dealers are seldom prepared to accept penalties amounting to more than their subsidy payment.

In buy-back operations, there is a risk that the goods may not be available. Under a planned economy, in which supplies are not freely available, new production can run into problems which are not resolvable by an individual enterprise. The non-availability of a component can set back an entire production run for a five-year planning period. In certain circumstances, a Western company may feel obliged to relieve such shortages by making the supplies itself, without the certainty of any compensation or payment. The size of the countertrade operation is thus unintentionally increased and the buy-back period prolonged.

5.3. Quality of buy-back goods

The generally prevailing opinion is that East European and Third World products are of inferior quality, and many goods do not come up to Western standards of design, packaging and finishing. This is especially true where finished articles compete with comparable Western products, and even a small price advantage may not make their sale easy.

With raw materials and semi-finished goods, the exporter could encounter products which, because of their low quality, have proved unsaleable on the free export market and have therefore been added to the list of buy-back goods. Such action damages the reputation of the Comecon nations, and gives compensation and countertrade a bad name.

Quality also presents a problem in buy-back operations. Although it should be possible to adhere to a standard of quality, Western companies repeatedly complain that buy-back goods do not match the standard of samples. Precise contractual agreements attempt to secure a comprehensive technical specification of the goods to be produced, and clauses for minimum fulfilment of the guarantee obligation. Certain companies have had satisfactory experiences with interim technical inspections and acceptance checks before loading at an East European enterprise. Large companies can also afford to carry out education and training courses for East European technical personnel. But these measures merely emphasize that a Western company must check closely the quality of buy-back goods.

6. Costs of countertrade

It is more difficult to reach a generalized conclusion on the costs of countertrade than of other forms of trade finance. Refinancing costs for the credit period depend on the type of trade finance employed, and the market conditions for credit. But these are objective costs; they also apply to exports without countertrade. The special costs associated with countertrade, arising from the marketing of products taken up under counterpurchase commitments, are less easily assessable.

If a Western supplier accepts the buy-back goods for his own business, he must calculate the price of an alternative purchase to determine his costs. Accepting office furniture, for example, could work out cheaper or more expensive than comparable Western fittings. Alternatively, there may be no comparison, since the design does not come up to Western expectations. Such subjective costs cannot be formally quantified; the costs of marketing are also tied up with business conditions, and therefore cannot be generally determined. If the buy-back goods fit into the company's product range without competing with its own products, then existing sales outlets can be used without any great additional costs. Conversely, if unfamiliar products are to be marketed, the costs will be incurred in introducing the products and opening new outlets. In such cases, many companies would prefer to avoid unknown costs and the risk that the product cannot be marketed, by paying a fixed subsidy to a trading house.

The *price subsidy* demanded by compensation dealers in the trading houses is composed of a transaction fee and a charge estimated to cover price differences. The transaction fee is determined by the dealer's experiences with the country in question and the foreign trade organization concerned, as well as the choice of products available. If there is a free choice of products, and experience of business in the vendor country is easy, then this will serve to reduce the subsidy. Nevertheless, the dealer must judge the quality and saleability of the buy-back goods. New products require subsidies before arriving on Western markets. If the range of possible countries for distribution is limited (as specified, for example, in contracts with Russia), then the risk of non-saleability of the product is increased. The same is true of large buy-back operations, since smaller quantities are easier to sell. To cover the risk of being left with the goods, the dealer also charges a premium, which comprises the third element of the subsidy.

The costs for a company which transacts an industrial cooperation deal are difficult to evaluate.

Since the buy-back product rarely has a price which can be calculated several years in advance for the Western market, the company runs the risk of making a loss when it comes to disposing of the buy-back goods. The length of many cooperation agreements gives rise to the additional danger that the product no longer meets market demand, and has been overtaken by competing products. These potential costs of falsely assessing the market must be classed as entrepreneurial risks which accompany any long-term investment. Other costs can arise from the quality control, but are more readily assessable in advance. A lump sum should be set aside to cover unexpected journeys to resolve production difficulties connected with the machine or installation.

The other costs of industrial cooperation are connected with the financing, which can be carried out by bank consortia, with or without state assistance, and risk participation. These traditional financing costs are not connected with the countertrade character of the business.

7. Advantages and disadvantages of countertrade

7.1. From the East European viewpoint

The foreign exchange saving and improvement in balance of payments are continually being cited as major advantages of countertrade. But there are other, less obvious, attractions.

For the U.S.S.R., cooperation agreements offer the possibility of undertaking large-scale projects through capital imports. Long-term foreign credits are repaid by goods rather than currency and sufficient products remain to satisfy national needs more adequately. With the easier availability of long-term financial assistance, a rolling-over of financial risks is sometimes achieved. Such is the case of a Russian-Japanese cooperation agreement for the exploration and development of oil and gas deposits. The financing is only repayable by deliveries when the exploration is successful.

Smaller countries which are developing their own manufacturing industry also see similar advantages in cooperation. They cite better provision for domestic needs and improvement in export supply through repayment in products which satisfy Western quality requirements, as well as an accelerated import of technology. These advantages are sometimes called into question, however, by East European and Third World nations, especially as far as the import of the latest technology and adjustment to technological advance are concerned. Critics are of the opinion that the West tends to rid itself of lapsing means of production and markets to Eastern Europe and the developing countries, while itself making inroads into new technologies and markets.

A further advantage of countertrade operations is their easy incorporation into a planned economy. This is especially true for long-term counterdelivery agreements. Countertrade transactions are readily agreed to by East European countries as a buffer for goods which cannot be disposed of, but which are already planned for export, though low quality East European goods, brought onto Western markets at throw-away prices, may damage the reputation of such goods. Only in the rarest cases have the compensation and buy-back commitments of Western firms subsequently led to voluntary repeat orders. A few trading companies have used existing supplier connections for countertrade, where buy-back goods are linked with, and set off against, counterpurchases. In such cases, however, the question arises of whether a direct sale on the free market at a price reduced by the trading company's subsidy would not improve the product's image and build up a lasting distribution network in the West.

Another advantage of countertrade is the handing over of marketing and distribution problems to the Western purchaser. The scarcity of repeat orders by Western purchasers shows, however, that the sale prospects of some countertraded products are not improved by using already existing Western distribution channels. If the Western purchaser of the buy-back goods does not succeed in recovering his distribution costs, he will distribute these goods only until expiry of his contractual commitment, trying to get rid of them as quickly as possible in order not to cause long-term damage to his own market.

7.2. From the Western viewpoint

For the Western exporter, payment for his goods in foreign currency is the rule. However, in business with a few developing countries and above all with the socialist nations of Eastern Europe, he must sometimes forego this normal form of payment and put up with repayment in goods. Since money is incurred in his production costs, he must exchange the buy-back goods for money. This involves the risk of a loss, which he does not run when paid in foreign currency. Countertrade must, therefore, be considered disadvantageous.

Nevertheless, countertrade deals possess some advantages for the Western exporter. They allow him access to markets where foreign currency is lacking. The often increased currency and transfer risk in trade with nations short of foreign exchange does not apply, and instead of the danger of having to roll over a credit, the supplier receives an assumed transfer of goods. A counterpurchase can sometimes also lead to further, unconditional transactions being concluded. If the Western exporter succeeds in having his deliveries absorbed into the East European country's economic plan, then foreign currency will as a rule be reserved for him. Similarly, repeat orders for attachments and replacement parts are often made free of conditions.

Certain Western companies have, through compensation obligations, discovered new sources of supplies, and what are originally compensation deals can lead quite happily to genuine cooperation. The supply argument can become appreciable in the field of raw materials, where a spread of supplier risk is desired. This access to a source of raw materials is important and has already resulted in many industrial cooperation projects.

The supposed advantages of this form of business for the West should nevertheless not obscure the fact that it is very unlike the Western market system. It is complicated and long-drawn out. Often, despite lengthy negotiations, transactions cannot be concluded because at the last stage of negotiations it emerges that counterpurchase commitments cannot be fulfilled. This increases Western companies' disinclination towards compensation obligations, especially since word about bad experiences with conditional transactions gets around more quickly than about good ones.

CHAPTER TWO
Bills of exchange

Nikolas P. Soskin

1. Definition of a bill of exchange

There is no unified international law covering the definition of a bill of exchange. The different national systems of the law of negotiable instruments are to a large extent based either on the U.K. Bills of Exchange Act 1882 or on the European system, which is founded on the Uniform Law on Bills of Exchange and Promissory Notes as drafted at the Geneva Conventions on Bills of Exchange of 1932. In 1973 the United Nations Commission on International Trade published the Draft Uniform Law on International Bills of Exchange, with the aim of providing an optional alternative specifically for international trade transactions.

1.1. In the U.K.

The U.K. Bills of Exchange Act 1882 defines a bill of exchange as:

> "An unconditional order in writing addressed by one person to another, signed by the person giving it requiring the person to whom it is addressed to pay on demand or at a fixed or determinable future time a sum certain in money to or to the order of a specified person or to bearer."

Exhibit 201: The face of a bill

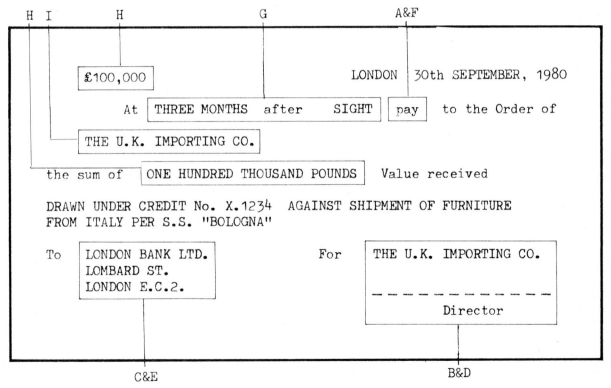

Explanation:

    a. an unconditional order in writing
    b. addressed by one person (the drawer)
    c. to another (the drawee)

d. signed by the person giving it (the drawer)
e. requiring the person to whom it is addressed (the drawee, who when he signs becomes the acceptor)
f. to pay
g. on demand, or at a fixed or determinable future time
h. a sum certain in money
i. to, or to the order of, a specified person, or to bearer (the payee).

1.2. International

The Uniform Law on Bills of Exchange and Promissory Notes as drafted by the Geneva Conventions on Bills of Exchange of 1932 stipulates that:

"A bill of exchange contains:

1. the term "bill of exchange" inserted in the body of the instrument and expressed in the language employed in drawing up the instrument;
2. an unconditional order to pay a determinate sum of money;
3. the name of the person who is to pay (drawee);
4. a statement of the time of payment;
5. a statement of the place where payment is to be made;
6. the name of the person to whom or to whose order payment is to be made;
7. a statement of the date and of the place where the bill is issued;
8. the signature of the person who issues the bill (drawer)."

Countries which are members of the Geneva Convention:

Belgium	France	Italy	Norway
Brazil	Greece	Japan	Austria
Denmark	Poland	Luxembourg	Switzerland
Germany	Portugal	Monaco	U.S.S.R.
Finland	Sweden	Netherlands	Hungary

Other countries have signed the Geneva Convention with certain reservations, and others have included similar wordings in their laws.

The Draft Uniform Law on International Bills of Exchange and International Promissory Notes as drawn up by the United Nations Commission on International Trade in 1973 stipulates that:

"An international bill of exchange is a written instrument which:

(a) contains, in the text thereof, the words 'Pay against this International Bill of Exchange, drawn subject to the Convention of . . .' (or words of similar import); and
(b) contains an unconditional order whereby one person (the drawer) directs another person (the drawee) to pay a definite sum of money to a specified person (the payee) or to his order; and
(c) is payable on demand or at a definite time; and
(d) is signed by the drawer; and
(e) shows that it is drawn in a country other than the country of the drawee or of the payee or of the place where payment is to be made."

The principal difference between the U.K. Act and the Geneva Law is that the Geneva Law requires the words "Bill of Exchange" to be included in the text and a statement of the date and of the place where the bill is issued. The Draft Law of the United Nations Commission is aimed at providing rules for a special negotiable instrument for optional use in international transactions.

2. The parties involved: definitions

2.1. The drawer

The seller or exporter and the person who draws the bill.

2.2. The drawee

The person to whom the bill is addressed. This is normally either the buyer or the importer, or a bank which will guarantee payment on the buyer's behalf.

2.3. The acceptor

The drawee becomes the acceptor as soon as he has signed his name across the bill, thereby signifying his assent to the transaction, and his willingness to pay the bill at maturity.

2.4. The endorser

A payee or any other person who signs his name on the back of the bill. A bill is drawn in favour of a particular party. Should that party sell or discount the bill, he will endorse it on the reverse in favour of the purchaser, or in blank in which case it becomes a bearer instrument. However, anyone who adds his signature to a bill also becomes liable for its payment at maturity, in the event that the principal parties to the bill fail to meet payment. The negotiating of bills *without recourse* is discussed in Chapter VIII, see especially Exhibit 801.

Very often, in the case of a trade bill, if the drawee is a small subsidiary of a larger concern, the drawer will request the endorsement of the drawee's parent company, thereby obtaining that company's guarantee that the bill will be met at maturity.

3. The purpose and advantage of the bill of exchange

3.1. The purpose

The bill of exchange is an instrument of credit: a document drawn up by the vendor thereby indicating his agreement to deferred payment, and accepted by the purchaser acknowledging the liability to pay at an agreed future date.

Bills may be drawn for any period, the most usual being 90 days, or three months, but many are drawn for anything from 30 days to six months. These *term* bills are negotiable instruments which may be bought and sold. *Sight* bills are bills drawn payable at sight, or on demand. As sight bills are paid immediately they are presented to the person on whom they are drawn, the question of discounting them does not arise. However, the underlying principles and procedure for a bill drawn at sight are very similar to those described as applicable to a term bill.

It should also be remembered that a substantial part of international trade is financed by means of sight bills, particularly at a time of sellers' markets. When markets are favouring buyers, the seller may find that he has to accord longer credit terms to the buyer, and this will lead to the drawing of term bills, or, as they are sometimes known in international trade, *usance* bills.

3.2. The documentary bill

When a bill is drawn to cover an actual movement of goods from the seller to the buyer, and the relative documents (bill of lading, insurance policy, etc.) are attached to the bill when it is drawn, the bill is known as a documentary bill.

The buyer of the goods may ask the seller to draw a term bill on him direct (trade bill), or he may open a credit in favour of the seller with a bank on whom the seller will draw his bill (bank bill). In either case, the bill both before and after it is accepted is negotiable. The seller of the goods can sell it for immediate cash to his local bankers or, after it is accepted, to a discount house. The seller is thus paid for his goods when they are despatched. The buyer, for his part, does not have to pay until the bill, having been duly accepted, matures, and this will usually be after the goods have reached their destination and/or have been re-sold.

If the bill is drawn on the buyer himself, he must meet it at maturity; if the bill is drawn on a banker under a credit opened on behalf of the buyer, he must put the banker in funds by the maturity date on which the banker has to pay the bill. During the lifetime of the bill the goods are being transported, or are in course of resale or use, and the period of the perfect bill is just enough to span the interval between shipment by the exporter and receipt of cash from the resale by the importer. The buyer may have contracted beforehand to sell the goods to a customer of his own, the proceeds of the sale providing the cash to meet the bill. In such a case the bill is aptly described as *self-liquidating*, but bills are in practice regarded as self-liquidating when it is in the normal course of the buyer's business to sell the underlying goods.

It is appropriate to point out to buyers of goods an important advantage in having bills drawn on and accepted by their bankers, instead of themselves. If there has been a delay in the arrival of the goods, or if for any other unforeseen reason the buyer is not in funds when a bill which he has accepted falls due for payment, he must nevertheless pay the bill, and it might be highly inconvenient, or in difficult times even impossible, for him to do so. The holder of the bill will have the right of immediate action against him. If, however, he has arranged for a bank to accept the bill for him, the bill will certainly be paid to the holder at its maturity.

When a bill is drawn to finance a movement or shipment of goods, the drawer should put on the face of the bill a few words describing the nature of the transaction. For example, "exports of machine tools to South Africa per S.S. Fortress", or "imports of x bales of wool from Australia per S.S. Golden Fleece". The insertion of such phrases is commonly called *clausing*. Clausing makes clear the nature of the transaction which is being financed. The banks, who buy bills, like to see evidence of the underlying transaction, and the clausing answers in advance questions which might otherwise be asked. It is a wise precaution, when dealing with instruments of credit, to make any questioning of the underlying transaction unnecessary.

Although the nature of the underlying transaction will be studied by an individual or organization asked to discount a bill, or to accept it as security for a loan, the respect enjoyed by a bill of exchange depends above all on the standing and credit of the acceptor and the drawer.

3.3. The finance bill

There is much discussion about the meaning of the term finance bill. No exact definition can be easily given. Bills drawn to finance the holding or processing of stocks of raw materials, or to enable the drawer to give credit to his customer by hire purchase or by simple credit terms, are frequently—but not invariably—described as finance bills.

Institutions which deal in bills do not always look on finance bills as being quite such attractive investments as bills covering the movement of goods, and the amount of finance paper that can be discounted in the market may be limited. Nonetheless, many of the finest names to be found on bills in the market have at times been on finance bills, drawn to supply working capital for a limited period until it could be favourably obtained from an alternative source. Many first-class bills have been drawn not *for value received*, but merely as a convenient means of taking a loan (see Chapter VIII, Exhibit 801).

Since a finance bill is not linked to a specific underlying transaction or movement of goods, its quality is even more dependent on the names of the drawer and acceptor. The less the evidence of an actual transaction underlying a bill, the stronger these names must be.

A bill is the property of the drawer until he sells or discounts it; once sold, it belongs to the buyer. And, the acceptor having played his part by signing across the bill his promise to pay, it is to the drawer or owner of the bill, or to his order, that the proceeds of discounting will be paid. The drawer or owner, therefore, has the right to decide with whom the bill shall be discounted, although practice varies.

Banks will usually tell the drawer or owner of a bill that he is free to discount it when, and with whom he wishes. They will also tell the drawer or owner that they are quite willing to act on his instructions to hand the bill for discount to a bank or discount house named by him, or, if he prefers, of their own choice.

4. Practical mechanics

4.1. The bill of exchange and the exporter

The bill of exchange offers the exporter several methods of financing a shipment of goods.

4.1.1. The irrevocable documentary letter of credit (see Chapter III)
For an exporter of finished goods from Germany to the U.S., whose customer requires credit during transit and for several weeks thereafter, the best procedure is to ask his customer to open an irrevocable documentary letter of credit with a German bank in his (the exporter's) favour. If the importer's U.S. bank has an office in Germany, it will request this office to issue to the exporter an irrevocable letter of credit. In this letter of credit, the German office of the U.S. bank undertakes to accept a bill drawn on them by the exporter, against surrender to it of the shipping documents relating to the goods.

When the bill drawn under this credit has been accepted by the German branch of the U.S. bank, the exporter can at once offer it to a bank or discount house which will discount it for him (i.e., buy it from him at a discount) at an agreed rate.

Whether the exporter bears the cost of discounting the bill, or whether he includes this charge separately in his invoice or in the price of his goods, will depend on his contract with the buyer. The buyer himself will normally be responsible for the accepting commission, and when the bill matures he has to put his bank in funds to meet the bill, i.e., he has to deposit the face value of the bill with the bank where the bill is payable.

Exhibit 202 is an example of a bill drawn under this method.

The procedure for financing such a transaction, should the U.S. customer's bank not have an office in Germany, is similar. The difference is that the customer's bank asks its German correspondents to advise the exporter that it, the importer's bank, has opened an irrevocable credit in the exporter's favour, available by drawing bills on the German correspondent. This means that the exporter relies on the strength of his customer's bank, but the German correspondent bank

Exhibit 202: An irrevocable documentary letter of credit

```
DM 300,000              FRANKFURT           OCTOBER 10, 1980

AGAINST THIS BILL OF EXCHANGE AT 60 DAYS after SIGHT pay to
OUR Order _____
THE SUM OF DEUTSCHE MARKS THREE HUNDRED THOUSAND Value received
DRAWN UNDER THE AMERICAN IMPORT BANK INC., ATLANTA, GEORGIA,
CREDIT No. 7694 COVERING EXPORT OF 30 MOTOR CARS TO THE U.S.
PER S.S. "GOETHE".


To:   AMERICAN IMPORT BANK INC.    For:   DEUTSCHE EXPORT A.G.
      FRANKFURT BRANCH
      FRANKFURT                     _ _ _ _ _ _ _ _ _ _ _ _ _ _
      WEST GERMANY                          (signature)
```

Note: As this bill is payable in Frankfurt, German law applies. Therefore the bill needs to meet the conditions mentioned in section 1.2 of this chapter.

has given him no undertaking to accept his bill when he presents it. However, the importer's bank will, if the exporter so stipulates in his contract, ask its German correspondent bank to confirm the credit to him, so binding itself to accept his bill. In this case, it is a confirmed irrevocable credit.

4.1.2. Acceptance credit
An alternative to the letter of credit is to obtain an acceptance credit from a bank.

4.1.2.1. *The credit*
A company of good standing, doing a valuable export trade, will find there are a number of banks which will be keen to help it with the finance. Such a company in the U.K. may decide to discuss the business with a London bank or accepting house.

Suppose, for example, that a company's annual exports total about £2 million, spread evenly over the year, so that it will have to find about £500,000 every three months. On this basis, the accepting house agrees to grant the company an acceptance facility of say 80%, or £400,000 outstanding at any one time, so that if it has free capital of its own of about £100,000 it will, with the bank's assistance, be able to find the whole amount. In other words, the accepting house agrees to accept bills up to a running maximum of £400,000 drawn on it by the company at three months sight. Such a credit may be granted *until further notice*, or, by arrangement, for a fixed period such as one year, during which any bills that mature and are paid off may be replaced by other bills, when it is known as a revolving credit.

When the bills have been accepted by the accepting house, the company may discount them with a bank or discount house and receive its money. At the end of the three months, having met the first £400,000 of bills, the company will probably have to produce evidence for the accepting house that a further £500,000 of export business is outstanding, against which it will be entitled to draw and discount a further £400,000 of bills.

4.1.2.2. *Security*
The accepting house may require security, such as hypothecation to them of the relative shipping documents, but in some cases, and for borrowers of high standing, they are prepared to grant a *clean* or *unsecured* credit, on the understanding that they are furnished with evidence of the shipments or transactions against which the bill is drawn.

Where security is required, this is a matter for negotiation between the accepting house and the borrower. In some cases, the accepting house would wish to keep under its control the bills of lading or other documents of title covering its client's exports. It would send these to its own agent in the country to which the goods are consigned, for release to the importer against payment, or by other agreed arrangement.

The exporter may be accustomed to drawing trade bills on his overseas customers. If so, the accepting house may grant him the credit facility for which he is asking against the collection of these bills, duly hypothecated (i.e., made over) to them by way of security. All these and other essential details will be negotiated with the accepting house at the time of opening the credit.

Exhibit 203 is an example of a bill drawn under method 4.1.2.

Exhibit 203: A bill drawn under English Law

```
£ 45,000              LONDON          JULY 15, 1980

AT 90 DAYS after SIGHT pay to the Order of _____
THE U.K. EXPORTING CO.LTD. _____

THE SUM OF   FORTY FIVE THOUSAND POUNDS   Value received
DRAWN UNDER CREDIT No. B.3027   AGAINST SHIPMENT OF MOTOR BICYCLES
TO NORWAY PER S.S. "NEPTUNE".

To:  THE MERCHANT BANK LTD          For:  THE U.K. EXPORTING CO.LTD.

     LONDON E.C.3.                        _ _ _ _ _ _ _ _ _ _ _ _ _
                                          Director
```

Note: As this bill is issued and payable in the U.K., it is governed by the law as described under section 1.1.

While these are the principal bill methods in general use, an exporter will find a bank very flexible in its approach to his particular problems. Provided that the parties to the transaction are of good standing, and the business is genuine export business, the finance will be forthcoming in the manner, and on the terms, appropriate to the case.

In many countries, it is possible to insure overseas business against the risk of non-payment, etc., through an export credit guarantee department (ECGD) of the Ministry of Trade (see Chapter V, Exhibit 503). This gives an added sense of security to all parties to the credit, though no mention of this precaution will normally appear on the bills themselves, which are dealt with on their own merits.

4.1.3. The negotiated bill negotiated under credit or authority to negotiate

Trade with a customer whose bank has a branch in the country of the exporter may be financed by means of bills to be negotiated under a credit.

The importer, instead of opening an acceptance credit, or a credit providing for sight bills in the exporter's favour, arranges for his bank's branch in that country to issue to the exporter a credit, in which the bank undertakes to *negotiate* bills drawn up by him on the importer. The exporter draws bills on the importer and presents them, with documents attached, to the local branch of the importer's bank, which buys them from him for cash, and sends them out to its head office. There, the bank hands the documents to the importer, the drawee, against payment, or at their discretion against acceptance if the bill is drawn at usance (i.e., for a period).

4.1.4. The foreign domicile bill

A customer asks his overseas supplier to draw bills on him direct. If the supplier cannot persuade the customer to open a credit in his favour with a local bank, he may agree to do this, even if the customer has not arranged for a bank to negotiate the bills (see section 4.1.3) under authority from his own bank. The supplier or exporter draws the bills on his overseas customer and takes them, with documents attached, to his own bankers who will do one of three things for him. Either (a) they will buy the bills from him; or (b) they will make him an advance, against the security of the bills; or (c) they will simply handle the bills for collection through their overseas correspondents, but will neither buy them nor make an advance against them. The three courses of action by the bankers are:

4.1.4.1. *The bank buys the bill*

If the bank agrees to buy these bills from the exporter (or to make him an advance against them—see 4.1.4.2), it is largely on the strength of his good name that it does so, and it is to him as the drawer of the bills that *the bank will have recourse* for payment if for any reason the overseas client fails to pay on the due date. (See Chapter VIII for a discussion of purchase without recourse.)

The price which the bank will pay the exporter for a bill will vary with current money rates. If the bill is drawn in foreign currency, the bank, provided it is at that time a buyer of that particular currency, will pay him at its current buying rate for drafts on the country of the drawee. In either case, in fixing the price at which it will buy the bill, the bank will include a provision for its own handling charges and for those of its overseas correspondents, who will present the bill to the drawee for acceptance and later for payment by him at maturity. Meanwhile, the exporter has had the advantage of being paid cash for his shipment.

4.1.4.2. *The bank makes an advance*
The bank makes an advance, against the security of the bills. When the exporter takes the bills, with documents attached, to his bank, the bank, by previous agreement, makes him a cash advance, at current advance rates, of say 80% of the face value of the bills. The bank then forwards the bills to its overseas correspondents for presentation to the drawee for acceptance, and later for payment. When, in due course, the overseas customer pays the bills at maturity, the exporter's bank credits him with the proceeds, and his advance is paid off. His bank will debit him for its handling charges, and for those of its overseas correspondents, and will pay to him the balance remaining from the margin of 20% of the face value of the bills.

4.1.4.3. *The bank collects*
The bank may only be prepared to handle the bills for collection. The bank may not be willing either to buy these foreign domicile bills, or to make an advance against them. Its willingness to do so depends largely on the exporter's own credit standing, but to some extent also on its assessment of the standing of the drawee, and of the economic, political, and foreign exchange factors ruling in the country to which the goods are consigned.

If the bank is not willing to buy the bills, or to make an advance against them, it will simply handle them in accordance with The International Chamber of Commerce Uniform Rules for the Collection of Commercial Paper, sending them out to its overseas correspondents for presentation to the drawee for acceptance, and again at maturity for payment, thus collecting the proceeds for the exporter's account. For these services, the bank will make a handling charge which may include the charges of its overseas banking correspondents.

Exhibit 204 is an example of a bill drawn under methods 4.1.3 and 4.1.4.

Exhibit 204: A bill drawn under Napoleonic law

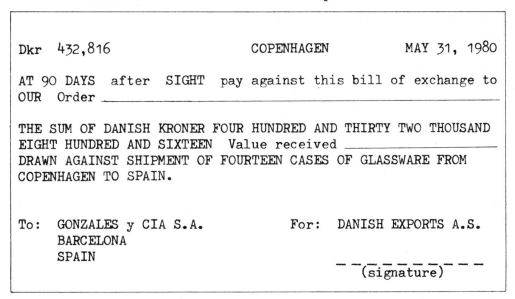

Note: This bill is drawn in accordance with Napoleonic law; Spain has also signed the Geneva Convention—see section 1.2.1.

4.2. The bill of exchange and the importer

When examined from the viewpoint of the importer, there are also a number of forms of the bill of exchange.

4.2.1. The irrevocable documentary letter of credit (in favour of the exporter)

Example: A French importer of timber from Sweden is required by his supplier to make payment against shipment, which means he will be out of his money for the period the goods are in transit, and probably for longer. He therefore asks his bank to open an irrevocable documentary letter of credit in favour of the Swedish seller. If it agrees to act for him in this way, the bank will issue through its agents in Sweden a letter of credit in favour of the exporter. In this letter, the bank will undertake to accept a term bill of exchange drawn on it by the exporter, provided the bill is accompanied by all the correct shipping documents relating to the goods.

The exporter draws the bill on the bank (see Exhibit 205) and hands it, with documents attached, to his local bank, which buys the bill from him for cash. His bank then forwards the bill and the

Exhibit 205: In favour of the exporter

```
Skr  278,694              STOCKHOLM              DECEMBER 16, 1980

AT 90 DAYS  after  SIGHT  pay against this bill of exchange to the
Order of SWEDISH TIMBER A.S. _____
THE SUM OF SWEDISH KRONER TWO HUNDRED AND SEVENTY EIGHT THOUSAND
SIX HUNDRED AND NINETY FOUR _____ Value received
DRAWN UNDER CREDIT No. H.1547 AGAINST SHIPMENT OF TIMBER TO
FRANCE PER S.S. "Goteborg".

To:  BANQUE FRANÇAISE S.A.      For:  SWEDISH TIMBER S.A.
     STOCKHOLM
     SWEDEN
                                      _ _ _ _ _ _ _ _ _ _ _ _
                                          (signature)
```

Note: The bill is payable in Sweden, so Swedish law applies (section 1.2.).

documents to its French correspondents for presentation to the importer's bank for acceptance, and the documents are surrendered to the importer's bank against its acceptance of the bill.

The importer's bank will release the documents to the importer against payment of the amount of the bill, or it may by special arrangement be prepared to release them to him in trust in advance of payment, so that he can obtain delivery of the goods. In any event, at or before maturity of the bill, he will have to put his bank in funds to meet it, but by that time, in most cases, he will have sold the goods and will have the funds available. (See also Chapter III.)

4.2.2. Acceptance credit (in favour of the importer)

Another option available to the importer is to obtain an acceptance credit. For example, an importer of furniture to the U.K. from Italy may go to a bank or accepting house and ask it to open an acceptance credit in his favour. This, on the basis of his good name and of the figures he shows them, it agrees to do. He arranges the details of the credit and these are put in writing in the form of an acceptance credit facility signed by the accepting house, who thereby agrees that it will accept bills drawn on it by him, subject to the stated conditions. He signs the appropriate form of agreement and undertaking.

When the importer is due to make payment to this Italian supplier, he will draw a bill at, say, three months sight on the accepting house, which he will send for acceptance and, at the same time, give instructions in a covering letter, that it be passed to a discount house for discount. He sends a copy of this letter to the discount house, with instructions to it to pay the proceeds of the discount to his own commercial bank. The money now being with his commercial bank, he is able to send a remittance to the Italian exporter in payment for the goods. Three months later, when the bill falls due, he will have to put the accepting house in funds to meet it.

Whether the accepting house will require security for granting the facility is a matter for negotiation. In normal times, and for borrowers of the highest standing, accepting houses are willing to offer *clean* facilities.

Alternatively, instead of the importer undertaking to remit the funds directly to the exporter, there may be an agreement that the exporter will draw up a bill on the importer, payable at sight. The exporter will probably negotiate this bill through his own bankers, who will forward it to London where it will be presented to the importer with documents attached, and he will have to pay it in cash. To obtain the funds, he will simultaneously draw a term bill of his own on the accepting house, under an acceptance credit which it has previously agreed to open in his favour, and he will discount the bill in London. This credit, too, may be on a clean basis, but it is more likely that the accepting house will require him to deposit the shipping documents with it under a letter of hypothecation. Later, if it considers the importer's standing sufficiently good, it may release the documents to him in trust, as mentioned under method 4.2.1.

An example of the bill which he would draw in either case appears in Exhibit 206.

Exhibit 206: In favour of the importer

```
£ 100,000                    LONDON              SEPTEMBER 30, 1980

AT 90 DAYS  after  SIGHT  pay  THIS FIRST BILL OF EXCHANGE
(SECOND OF SAME TENOR AND DATE BEING  to the order _____ _____
OF THE U.K. IMPORTING CO. _____
THE SUM OF  ONE HUNDRED THOUSAND POUNDS  Value received
DRAWN UNDER CREDIT No. X.1634 AGAINST SHIPMENT OF FURNITURE
FROM ITALY PER S.S. "BOLOGNA"

To:  LONDON BANK LTD.              For:  THE U.K. IMPORTING CO.
     LOMBARD ST.
     LONDON EC2                     _____
                                          (Director)
```

4.2.3. The negotiated (trade) bill

An importer may arrange with his overseas seller that the latter shall draw bills on him for his shipments of goods, in fulfilment of his orders. A Dutch importer, for example, buys spices from an Indonesian company which wants immediate payment for its shipments, but the importer does not wish to pay for the spices until they reach Amsterdam, or until some time later. The Dutch importer asks his bank to authorize its Jakarta office to negotiate bills drawn on him by the exporter in guilders at, say, 90 days sight, to cover the c.i.f. value of a shipment of spices. The Indonesian exporter draws a bill on him and presents it, with all the relative shipping documents attached, to the Jakarta branch of the importer's bank, who negotiates it, i.e., buys it, from the exporter at the bank's buying rate of exchange for 90 days sight drafts in Amsterdam. The bank pays the exporter in local currency, and forwards the bill and the documents to its head office in Amsterdam.

The Dutch bank presents the bill to the importer for his acceptance, and then holds it, with the documents, until he pays it. Meanwhile, the Indonesian company having been paid in Jakarta, the spices are on their way across the seas to Amsterdam, and the importer does not have to pay for them until the bill falls due. If, however, he wishes to obtain earlier delivery of the spices, he may pay the bill before maturity, and in that case he will be allowed a rebate on the bill amount.

If he does not wish to take delivery before maturity of the bill, the Dutch bank, on arrival of the steamer, will see that the spices are stored in an approved warehouse. The importer, as the acceptor of the bill, is entitled to name the warehouse he prefers and he will have to provide adequate insurance cover on which the bank will require a lien. All landing charges, warehouse and other charges will be payable by the importer.

The importer may, by reason of his good credit standing, be able to arrange d/a (documents against acceptance) terms. This means that the Dutch bank will deliver the shipping documents to him against his acceptance of the bill. The Dutch bank will hold the bill, accepted by the importer, in its own portfolio, and it may at will endorse the bill and sell it.

This is a very brief description of the financing of a single shipment of one commodity, chosen only as an example. The expert knowledge of the banks and accepting houses, as well as of the shippers, merchants, warehouse companies and others concerned will produce a great variety of solutions for the many different problems which arise in international trade.

Exhibit 207 is an example of a negotiated bill, covering the import of spices from Indonesia to the Netherlands.

Exhibit 207: Documents against acceptance

```
Dfl  180,000              JAKARTA              FEBRUARY 20, 1980

     AT THREE MONTHS SIGHT  pay against this bill of exchange to
the Order of THE INTERNATIONAL BANK _____
the sum of   ONE HUNDRED AND EIGHTY THOUSAND FLORINS Value received
DRAWN AGAINST SHIPMENT OF SPICES FROM INDONESIA TO THE NETHERLANDS
PER S.S. "BATIK".

To:  THE DUTCH SPICE CO.          For:  THE INDONESIA SPICE CO.
     AMSTERDAM

                                  _ _ _____ _ _ _ _ _
                                       (signature)
```

4.2.3.1. *Bank-endorsed bills*
If the Dutch bank decides not to hold the bill until maturity, but to sell it, it may endorse it, making it a bank-endorsed bill. Such bills will be more negotiable because they will bear the endorsement of the Dutch bank, and bills which carry the endorsement of a bank are of the same quality as those accepted by a bank, since *the endorsement is in effect a guarantee* that if for any reason the acceptor and the drawer both fail to meet the bill at maturity, the bank, as endorser, will do so.

4.3. The bill of exchange and the manufacturer

4.3.1. General remarks
One of the problems faced by a manufacturer is the need to finance purchases of raw materials required in his factory: i.e., to cover the period between his payment for them, and such a time as he receives payment for the finished product. The balance not covered by his own resources is normally provided by a bank advance. Similarly, it is possible to borrow a part of the money on bills of exchange to cover the period during which the raw materials are on their way to the factory, waiting in the warehouse, or passing through the processes of manufacture. For borrowers of high credit standing, banks or accepting houses are usually prepared to grant acceptance facilities for that purpose.

A manufacturer in such a position discusses his problem with a bank or accepting house, who would agree to grant him a credit. He then draws bills at, say, 90 days sight on the bank, which accepts them and either holds them in portfolio or discounts them, but pays the net proceeds to the manufacturer. On the maturity of the bills, the manufacturer will have to put the bank in funds to meet them. This may, by agreement, be done by his drawing and discounting a new set of bills and paying the proceeds to the bank to meet the bills falling due. In theory, the 90 days is the approximate interval between paying for the raw materials and receiving proceeds of sale of the made-up article; the assumption is that by maturity of one set of bills, the manufacturer will be ready to take up fresh raw materials, thus justifying the drawing of new bills.

This procedure can be repeated as long as the facility remains open. Subject to the limit of the credit, variations in the amount required are provided for by drawing a larger or smaller total of bills on renewal.

4.3.2. Finance bills
As discussed in sections 3.2. and 3.3., bills of this type are sometimes classified as *finance bills*, but much depends on the nature of the trade. A specimen bill is shown in Exhibit 208. Nowadays in the international market, professionals often refer to finance bills when a bill is issued for a loan, without any reference to a trade transaction (see Exhibit 801).

38

Exhibit 208: A finance bill

```
Swfr  400,000              GENEVA              MARCH 24, 1980

     AT THREE MONTHS  after  DATE  pay against this bill of exchange
to OUR Order the sum of  FOUR HUNDRED THOUSAND SWISS FRANCS  Value
received DRAWN UNDER CREDIT No. M.1733 AGAINST PURCHASES OF COCOA.


To:  BANQUE de GENEVA  SA          For:  SWISS CHOCOLATES SA
     GENEVA
                                      - -_-_-_-_-_-_-_- - -
                                          (signature)*
```

* Swiss companies are usually committed by the joint signature of two persons authorized to sign.

4.3.3. Trade bills

A company may be in a business in which it is customary for it, the seller of the goods, to draw bills of exchange direct on its customers, who are buying the goods from it. A bill so drawn is known as a *trade bill* (see Exhibit 209).

Exhibit 209: A trade bill

```
£ 30,478                   LONDON              APRIL 25, 1980

On JULY 25, 1980 _____ Pay to Our Order

the sum of  THIRTY THOUSAND FOUR HUNDRED AND SEVENTY EIGHT
POUNDS _____ _____ Value received
DRAWN AGAINST SALES OF PAINT.


To:  THE INDUSTRIAL CO.          For:  THE TRADING CO.
     MANCHESTER
                                      - -_-_-_-_-_-_-_- -
                                          (Director)*
```

* British companies are often committed by one signature of a director.

Trade bills are well recognized, though they are not as readily negotiable as bank bills, and they do not command the same rates. This is of little importance when a company does not need money, and is therefore content to hold the accepted trade bills until maturity. If, however, it wished to have the money at once, or at any time before the bills fell due, it could offer the bills for discount either to its own bankers or to a discount house. A company's normal outlet for trade bills is with its bankers, who have intimate knowledge of the company's business.

The rate which a bank or discount house will quote for a trade bill will depend on its assessment of a number of factors. A company will normally get a keen quotation for its trade bills if: both it and its customer enjoy good credit standing; if the trade against which the bills are drawn is considered suitable for finance by means of bills; and if there is not too great a volume of trade bills already in circulation, and especially trade bills carrying the company's name, that of its customer, or covering the same type of goods as those in which it is dealing. Trade bills which are pure finance bills (see section 3.3.) may not be well received.

There is an element of uncertainty in the ability to discount any large amount of trade bills, and this could be a serious disadvantage to a seller of goods who requires immediate cash. For this reason, many leading business concerns prefer to incur the small additional expense of opening acceptance credits with their bankers. They thus ensure that the bills they draw will always be saleable at a good rate.

A trader, drawing a substantial amount of trade bills on good customers in the normal course of his business, might find that a bank or accepting house would be willing to grant him an acceptance credit secured by the deposit of some of his trade bills. The bank or accepting house would need to be satisfied with the credit standing both of the trader and of the customer on whom he was drawing his bills, and the amount of the trade bills which he put up as security would have to exceed the amount of his own drawings against these bills by a margin agreed between him and the bank or accepting house.

A credit of this kind would not greatly differ from that outlined in section 4.1.2.

4.4. The bill of exchange and the international trader

A trader dealing with the purchase, shipment and sale of goods and commodities in various parts of the world may deal not only with imports and exports of his own country, but also in shipments which never enter that country. He may need to be able to borrow money rapidly and easily when, as often happens, the money he is due to receive from one customer does not coincide with the money he is having to pay another. Banks and accepting houses are normally prepared to issue letters of credit to, or on behalf of, such international traders.

When a trader is acting as a buyer, he may obtain bill finance just as an importer does, even though the goods he is buying may be going directly to some foreign country. He may arrange credits in the manner outlined in section 4.2.1. In such a case, the exporter will be the drawer of the bills. Alternatively, he may arrange credit facilities for himself with a bank or accepting house along the lines described in section 4.2.2.

When a trader is acting as a seller or exporter, it will usually be the buyer or importer who will arrange for a credit, preferably an irrevocable credit, to be opened in his favour through a bank or accepting house, in which case the trader will draw the bill and sell it for cash to a bank or discount house (see section 4.1.1). Alternatively he may arrange credit facilities for himself with a bank or accepting house along the lines discussed in section 4.1.2.

A trader may thus, in the course of his varied business, have occasion to draw bills under a number of different credits. He will find it useful to have direct dealings with a London discount house, particularly for transactions denominated in pounds sterling, to have a regular outlet for his bills, and a source of information and advice on all matters concerning the bill market.

5. Costs and calculations

Several factors determine the cost of bill finance.

5.1. Interest

The underlying rate of interest will be based on the cost of funds for a similar period in the local money market of the currency in which the bills are drawn.

5.2. Acceptance costs

Where a bank's acceptance is included on the bills, the bank will make a charge. This is likely to be between 0·5% and 1·5% per annum, depending on market conditions and the quality of the other names on the bill.

5.3. Margin

The *loading* over market rates, (i.e., the additional margin charged by the discounter) will depend on the quality of the names on the bill and may also depend on the nature of the underlying transaction.

5.4. Remarks

A manufacturer, financing purchases of raw materials, will negotiate these costs himself. An importer who arranges for an exporter abroad to draw on his (the importer's) bank will have to pay the acceptance commission, but the cost of selling the bill will usually fall on the seller, who may or may not include all or part of the cost in his invoice. Frequently, though, these costs are borne by the buyer, in which case either the seller will receive, on presenting his bill, the face value thereof plus the cost of local bill stamps, if any, or, if he sells or discounts the bill himself, the costs incurred will be reimbursed to him.

5.5 Formulas

5.5.1. Discount calculations
The following formula is used for calculating the discount in a bill of exchange transaction:

$$\text{Discount} = \text{Principal} \times \frac{\text{Rate}}{100} \times \frac{\text{Days}}{360^*}$$

Therefore, the discount on a bill of US\$1 million for 91 days at 8·5% would be:

$$\text{Discount} = \$1,000,000 \times \frac{8 \cdot 5}{100} \times \frac{91}{360}$$
$$= \$21,486$$

Therefore: Proceeds = \$978,514

5.5.2. Yield calculation
The true cost, or yield, however, is always higher than the discount rate (see Chapter VIII, Exhibit 804). This is because the discount charge is deducted immediately, which effectively is equivalent to paying the interest in advance. The difference is small for short periods and when interest rates are low, but becomes more appreciable when the period is longer and/or interest rates are higher.

The method of calculating the true cost is as follows:

$$\frac{\text{Rate} \times \text{Amount}}{\text{Proceeds}} = \text{Cost}$$

$$\frac{8 \cdot 5 \times 1,000,000}{978,514} = 8 \cdot 69\%$$

Note: This formula is good for calculations up to three months; otherwise, quarterly interest adjustments are necessary.

---

* Exact days over 360 because U.S. dollars are involved. In the U.K., such transactions are calculated on a 365-day year basis if in sterling (see Chapter VIII, Exhibit 805).

CHAPTER THREE
Documentary collection and letters of credit

Paul O'Hanlon

1. Introduction

In the days when barter was the exchange mechanism, when goods and property were portable, or leadable in the case of livestock, and traded on the spot, the concept of credit did not exist, and it was unnecessary for buyers and sellers to employ documentation evidencing and accompanying transactions.

In the modern economy, the complexity of goods, and even staples which are increasingly differentiated to suit particular tasks, the regulations surrounding their production and distribution, and the universal extension of credit enabling their immediate consumption, have led to a different exchange system. In modern trade, goods are represented by documents, which are exchanged for cash or some kind of promise to pay. Unlike the days of primitive barter, it is not always possible for the buyer in the modern international trade economy to know for certain what he is buying, and the seller does not always know for certain whether he will be paid in full on time.

In primitive barter, the objectives of buyers and sellers were the same: to exchange one kind of good on the spot for another. The only problems, solved later by specie money, were comparability of value and convenience. Modern buyers and sellers, separated geographically and living in a world of financial uncertainty, have less convergent objectives.

The buyers objectives are:
    i. to receive goods of the correct quality and quantity, on time at the right place; and
    ii. to pay as late as possible.

The seller's objectives are:
    i. to receive payment of the correct amount of money in the right currency; and
    ii. to be paid as soon as possible.

There are four major alternatives available to the trade partners in resolving the conflicts in their objectives:
    i. pre-payment by the buyer;
    ii. open account terms;
    iii. a bank collection; and
    iv. a bank letter of credit.

Prepayment obviously suits the seller's objectives but not the buyer's. The purchase order and payment will go out together, and at a later date the goods will be shipped by the seller. All the onus of trust is on the buyer, and he will need to have considerable confidence in the seller, based on either the seller's reputation or, much more likely, past experience. Prepayment, therefore, will usually not satisfy a new buyer's objectives.

Open account is the usual basis of sale for domestic trade. All that happens is that the seller ships the goods with an invoice, which gives the buyer time to pay. Here the onus of trust is on the seller, so that the new seller will probably find such terms unsatisfactory.

This chapter examines two methods of payment, the first a compromise in trust which on balance favours the buyer and the second which favours the seller. Both, however, have safeguards for the other party not present in open account or prepayment.

It is possible for export sellers to avoid the difficulty of reconciling their objectives with import buyers themselves, by using export or confirming houses as agents. For anything other than small export volumes, this is inefficient and expensive, and raises its own problems.

2. Definition of a bank collection

A bank collection is a method of settlement of payment by a buyer in one country to a seller in another country through bank channels at low cost. It is called a collection because the seller uses the bank system to collect payment from the buyer; the bank acting for the seller is called the remitting bank, since it remits documents to the buyer's country, and the remitting bank's correspondent or agent in the buyer's country is called the collecting bank. The collecting bank need not necessarily have a banking relationship with the buyer. There are two kinds of collection, and in both, documents are moved by banks from seller to buyer.

2.1. Clean collection

A clean collection consists exclusively of documents for payment of money, such as bills of exchange, promissory notes or cheques. The seller sends the payment instrument without any other trade documents such as invoices or bills of lading, to the seller, through banks channels.

2.2. Documentary collection

A documentary collection consists, like a clean collection, of a payment instrument but also has commercial or transport documents included for completing the transaction. Usually, these documents confer, fully or partially, title to the goods on the holder, and typically they would be bills of lading. In a clean collection, banks do not control title to the goods whereas in a documentary collection banks do have control. The documentary collection is, therefore, safer for the seller than the clean collection, which is only slightly removed from open account.

2.2.1. Documents included in a documentary collection

The usual payment instrument in a collection is the bill of exchange. In the case of a sight bill, acceptance and payment occur at the same time, which is when the documents are presented by the collecting bank. Term bills requiring payment at a future date are a method for the seller to allow credit or time to pay to the buyer.

There are two ways in which the remitting bank can send a term bill to the collecting bank. The first is for acceptance by the buyer and return to the remitting bank for eventual return to the seller. This is called *acceptance and return*. When the seller returns the accepted bill, close to maturity, back to the buyer through the banking system, the collection is a clean collection, and this is how most clean collections arise.

By far and away the great majority of collections are not on acceptance and return, but completed by the simpler route of the collecting bank retaining accepted bills until payment. Usual trade documents included in the collection are transport documents, such as bills of lading or warehouse receipts, giving title to stored goods.

Bills of lading (usually prepared in sets of two or more originals) are a combined receipt from the shipping company for the goods, a contract between the seller and shipping company as a common carrier specifying the latter's obligations, and thirdly and most importantly, a negotiable document of title. Negotiability, in this context, is the quality of being transferable by endorsement free from prior claims. This quality is essential in ensuring simplicity in commcercial transactions and permitting straightforward financing of international trade, as it enables bills of lading and other such negotiable instruments to be used as security for finance.

Warehouse receipts are given by warehousers in exchange for the goods after unloading. In certain cases these receipts are negotiable but such cases are limited mainly to primary commodities stored by Western European and North American warehouses.

2.3. Purpose of collections

Since the valuable documents of title to the goods being traded are held by banks during a collection, the seller has a greater degree of security than with open account. Using the banking system as an intermediary, the seller can specify that the buyer will not get title until he has paid cash or accepted a bill drawn on him. The buyer can inspect documents before payment or acceptance and so long as the documents are satisfactory, he partially satisfies his objectives of assurance in quality and quantity.

Collections are, therefore, intended as a compromise mechanism somewhere between open account and pre-payment, facilitated by the action of the banking system as a reliable intermediary.

2.4. Practical mechanics

Exhibit 301 shows the flows of documents and payment in an open account transaction, and Exhibit 302, those in a straightforward documentary collection against payment. If the two exhibits are compared, it will be seen that in the collection the buyer is still trusting the seller along the purchase order limb, but the seller is no longer trusting the buyer along the payment limb.

44

Exhibit 301: Open account transaction

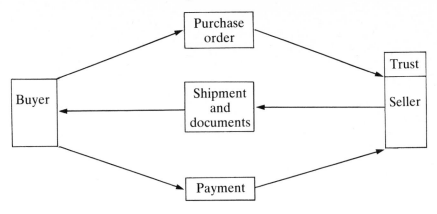

Exhibit 302: Documentary collection

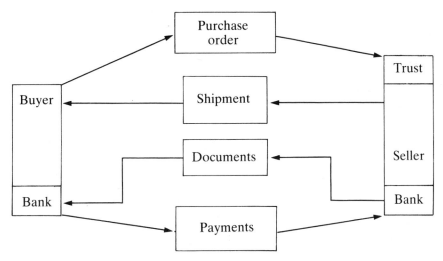

Notes: 1. Bank acts as a collection intermediary, keeping documents from the buyer until payment or acceptance of draft.
2. Bank neither provides guarantee of payment nor enforces collection.
3. Title to goods passes to buyer only upon payment or upon acceptance of draft.

The buyer still has to trust the seller to perform quickly in processing the purchase order and also not to produce fraudulent or completely spurious documents. This is because the intermediary role of the banking system does not extend to providing guarantees of documents or enforcement of responsibilities on either the buyer or seller's part under the sale contract.

Collection procedure is simple throughout (see Exhibits 303a and b). What happens is that, shortly after shipment by the seller, the remitting bank will receive from the seller the documents, including a bill of exchange if one is being used, together with instructions for payment (either cash or against a sight or time bill). The remitting bank sends all these to the collecting bank. Practice amongst collecting banks for presentation of the documents to the buyer varies considerably. Some banks will require the buyer to come to the bank's office to inspect, others release the documents with or without receipt. Practice also varies amongst branches of banks depending on local business procedures in different countries.

2.5. Obligations of the banks

The International Chamber of Commerce (ICC) publishes a wide range of documents for the assistance of importers and exporters, which taken together comprise an informal code or set of guidelines used by both commercial corporations and banks. These documents do not have the force of law, but describe current commercial practice. ICC Publication No. 322 of 1978 describes uniform rules for collections generally adhered to by all major international banks, and these are reproduced in Appendix I.

45

Exhibit 303a: Collection procedure

```
              CITIBANK NA
              WORLD CORPORATION GROUP
              COLLECTION OPERATION
              PO BOX 2003 GRAND CENTRAL STATION
              NEW YORK NY 10017
              (212 558 5770)


   AIRMAIL 10 COLLECTING BANK                    DATE 08/09/77
   DEUTCHE BANK AG
   MUNICH, GERMANY


   REF: OUR COLLECTION NO. 165288W
        IN AMOUNT OF    200,000.00 TO BE PAID AT SIGHT
        DRAWER
        DRAWEE B.BUYER


   GENTLEMEN:
        THIS ITEM IS SENT FOR COLLECTION AND REMITTANCE IN NEW YORK
   FUNDS AFTER FINAL PAYMENT. ADVICES OF PAYMENT, ACCEPTANCE AND
   DISHONOR SHOULD BE SENT BY AIRMAIL UNLESS OTHERWISE SPECIFIED BELOW.
   IF DRAWN IN YOUR CURRENCY, PLEASE CREDIT OUR ACCOUNT AFTER FINAL
   PAYMENT, ONLY UNDER ADVISE TO US.

        IF DOLLAR EXCHANGE IS NOT IMMEDIATELY AVAILABLE AT MATURITY
   (OR ON PRESENTATION IF DRAWN AT SIGHT) AND IT IS NECESSARY TO
   PROVISIONALLY ACCEPT LOCAL CURRENCY PENDING AVAILABILITY OF DOLLAR
   EXCHANGE, IT MUST BE DISTINCTLY UNDERSTOOD THAT THE DRAWEE SHALL
   REMAIN LIABLE FOR ALL EXCHANGE DIFFERENCES. AT THE TIME OF DEPOSIT
   OF LOCAL CURRENCY, OBTAIN FROM DRAWEES THEIR WRITTEN UNDERTAKING TO
   BE RESPONSIBLE FOR ANY EXCHANGE DIFFERENCES. THE DRAFT MUST NOT BE
   SURRENDERED TO DRAWEES UNTIL FINAL PAYMENT FOR FACE AMOUNT IN
   U.S. DOLLAR EXCHANGE.


      ┌──────────────────────────────────────────────────────────┐
      │ COLLECTION INSTRUCTIONS:                                   │
      │      DELIVER DOCUMENTS AGAINST PAYMENT.                    │
      │      ADVISE NON-PAYMENT BY CABLE.                          │
      │      REMIT PROCEEDS BY CABLE AT DRAWER'S EXPENSE.          │
      │      DO NOT PROTEST.                                       │
      │      COLLECTING BANK CHARGES ARE AT DRAWEE'S EXPENSE.      │
      │      IN CASE OF NEED REFER TO KURT SCHMIDT, AGENT, 14 BACHSTRASSE│
      │      MUNICH, WHO MAY ASSIST IN OBTAINING PAYMENT OF DRAFT, BUT IS│
      │      NOT TO ALTER ITS TERMS IN ANY WAY.                    │
      └──────────────────────────────────────────────────────────┘


        THIS COLLECTION IS SUBJECT TO  UNIFORM RULES FOR THE COLLECTION
   OF COMMERCIAL PAPER, INTERNATIONAL CHAMBER OF COMMERCE BROCHURE
   NO.322 PLEASE USE OUR REFERENCE NUMBER 165288W IN ALL CORRESPONDENCE.
   THANK YOU.


   HR                                    WCG COLLECTION OPERATIONS
                                              COLLECTION LETTER
```

Exhibit 303b: Customer acknowledgement

```
                    CITIBANK NA
                    WORLD CORPORATION GROUP
                    COLLECTION OPERATION
                    P O BOX 2003 GRAND CENTRAL STATION
                    NEW YORK NY 10017
                    (212 558 5770)

                                              DATE 08/09/77
A. SELLER                     EXP CODE 884   OUR REF. 165288W
1000 BROAD STREET
NEW YORK, NEW YORK 10005




         REF: YOUR COLLECTION ITEM LBIC 1/500  OF 06/24/77
              IN AMOUNT OF   200,000.00 AT SIGHT


         DRAWER

         DRAWEE B. BUYER




GENTLEMEN:
     WE HAVE ENTERED THIS ITEM FOR COLLECTION, WITH THE FOLLOWING
INSTRUCTION
```

```
    DELIVER DOCUMENTS AGAINST PAYMENT.
    ADVISE NON-PAYMENT BY CABLE.
    REMIT PROCEEDS BY CABLE AT DRAWER'S EXPENSE.
    DO NOT PROTEST.
    COLLECTING BANK CHARGES ARE AT DRAWEE'S EXPENSE.
    IN CASE OF NEED REFER TO KURT SCHMIDT, AGENT, 14 BACHSTRASSE
    MUNICH, WHO MAY ASSIST IN OBTAINING PAYMENT OF DRAFT , BUT
    IS NOT TO ALTER ITS TERMS IN ANY WAY.
```

```
     PAYMENT OR NON-PAYMENT WILL BE ADVISED AFTER PRESENTATION TO THE
DRAWEE OR OTHER PAYOR.

     OUR HANDLING OF THIS COLLECTION IS SUBJECT TO UNIFORM RULES FOR
THE COLLECTION OF COMMERCIAL PAPER, INTERNATIONAL CHAMBER OF
COMMERCE BROCHURE NO. 254 . PLEASE USE OUR REFERENCE NUMBER 165288W
IN ALL CORRESPONDENCE. THANK YOU.

                              WCG COLLECTION OPERATIONS

                              ACKNOWLEDGEMENT ONLY
HR
+
NNNNJ
```

Obligations of the collecting and remitting bank in accordance with these rules may be summarized as follows:

    i. To follow exactly the instructions of the seller or of his bank.

    ii. At all times to control and ensure the safety of documents in the collection while in the bank's possession.

    iii. To act promptly both in executing instructions and in advising the seller or his bank of all developments.

    iv. Banks are not responsible for the actions of their agents, or in general for anything not directly attributable to their own negligence or that of their own employees. In particular, banks are not responsible for the validity or efficacy of any documents.

2.6. Problem/danger areas

Whilst the collection process adds a measure of commercial safety to the seller's dealings, problems may arise with delays caused by international postage or slowness on the part of the banks being used, or on the part of the buyer in paying.

Sometimes the collecting bank has the buyer as a general customer and may not be inclined to exert pressure to obtain quick payment or return of the documents, although a good bank will always exert pressure for prompt payment. Claims for interest where there is unreasonable delay may not be an entirely satisfactory remedy, as recoverable amounts may be small and difficult to collect without expense.

Slowness in postal transmission is mainly a problem on short voyages, where the vessel may well arrive before the documents of title to the goods. Not only can this create problems in unloading, but it can occasion warehousing charges when the goods are unloaded. Additionally, there may be difficulties in the collection itself if the title documents specified are bills of lading, and these have now been replaced by warehouse receipts or other documents.

Problems with documents, or in the collection, are most speedily dealt with by the seller nominating an agent in the buyer's country. Such an agent effectively replaces the seller in the collection, and is called the *case of need*. Because he has title to the goods, he can arrange storage or decide, if necessary, on legal action.

In a clean collection, if the bill is unpaid at presentation or on maturity, i.e., the bill is dishonoured after it has been accepted, there is an established legal procedure called noting or protest. This procedure is designed to establish sufficient evidence of the dishonour for a subsequent legal action.

Noting is a cheaper process than protesting, and consists of initialling of the bill by a notary public (a specialist lawyer) who under international law has credibility everywhere. Protesting involves the notary making out a formal certificate. Generally speaking, protesting is to be preferred to noting, as the law of most foreign countries requires it and it is therefore necessary on bills drawn under an export sale.

2.7. Costs

Collections are cheap, and a bank's commission rate is usually *ad valorem* and less than $\frac{1}{5}$ of 1% with a ceiling of £100 or so. The buyer and seller reach agreement on which one of them bears charges, but in general it is the buyer who pays.

2.8. Recent developments in collections: direct collection

Many banks now offer a service called direct collection, designed to speed up the movement of documents between themselves acting as remitting bank, and their customer as seller. The seller is given a supply of special bank stationery (see Exhibit 304 on p. 50) which is completed and sent directly to the collecting bank together with the documents. Time is saved because the remitting bank does not have to duplicate the information on the collection letter.

2.9. Advantages and disadvantages

Advantages for seller

    i. Collections are simple and usually cheap.

    ii. Control of the valuable title documents is retained.

    iii. In some cases, a collection may facilitate financing the sale.

Disadvantages for seller

    i. If the goods are refused by the buyer, unquantifiable demurrage, storage, insurance and agents' costs may well be incurred.

    ii. If the shipping vessel docks late, or there is

iv. Communications with the foreign country of the buyer are usually simplified.

a delay in a government import license, the seller will not be paid until funds are received by the remitting bank.

iii. The ICC Code is not legally enforceable.

Advantages for buyer	Disadvantages for buyer

Advantages for buyer

i. Collections usually favour the buyer rather than the seller, since the buyer basically has time to inspect the goods (or the documents of title to them) before paying. This is particularly so with a clean collection, which is effectively the same as open account.

ii. Payment is deferred until the goods arrive, or later under a term bill.

Disadvantages for buyer

i. The use of a bill of exchange makes the buyer legally liable for his default in payment after acceptance, regardless of the underlying contract for sale of the goods.

ii. If the bill is unpaid in error, or protested in error by the seller, the buyer's trade reputation may be seriously damaged.

3. Definition of a letter of credit

A letter of credit is a written undertaking by a bank, the *issuing bank*, to the seller, *the beneficiary* in accordance with the instructions of the buyer, *the applicant*, to effect payment up to a prescribed amount within a prescribed time period against prescribed documents, provided these are correct and in order, i.e., they conform with the instructions of the applicant.

The documents include those required for the commercial purpose of effecting the sale, insurance and transport (usually bills of lading). Payment is made either against presentation of the documents on their own, or against the documents together with a bill (usually called a *draft*) drawn against the bank where the letter of credit is available. The draft may be a sight draft, or a time draft payable a specified number of days after a specific date, commonly the bill of lading date.

There are usually at least two banks involved in a letter of credit: the issuing bank is the buyer's bank, the second bank, called the *advising bank*, is a bank in the seller's country and is usually the seller's bank. The advising bank undertakes transmission of the credit, and authenticates the validity of the issuing bank's execution, but undertakes no commitment to pay the seller.

In a case where the issuing bank is too small for the seller to trust it to pay, or where the seller feels that there is a political risk in dealing with banks in a certain country, the beneficiary will ask the advising bank to *confirm* the credit. The effect of this is for the advising (and now confirming) bank to substitute itself for the issuing bank in meeting obligations to the beneficiary to make payment.

A third bank comes into the picture if the currency of settlement of the transaction is not that of the country of the issuing bank. It would be unsatisfactory for an issuing bank in London to undertake to pay a credit in Malay dollars on a specific date, as that bank might not have Malay dollars available on that date, and to purchase them might be unnecessarily expensive against sterling. Therefore, a bank, called the *paying bank* is nominated in the country of the currency. The paying bank is either a branch or correspondent of the issuing bank, holding the latter's account in the currency, so that after payment the paying bank may obtain re-imbursement.

Merely acting as paying bank imposes no obligation on the bank to pay. Indeed, it is more prudent for the paying bank to send documents to the issuing bank for checking before payment. If this should inconvenience the beneficiary, his solution is to require the paying bank to act as confirming bank.

3.1. Purpose of a letter of credit

A letter of credit guarantees payment to the seller on the simple condition that he presents the correct documents, and does so independently of the underlying contract of sale or the financial condition of the buyer at the time of presentation. All the financial risk is passed to the issuing bank, and this security for the seller is the fundamental purpose of a letter of credit. The necessity for the seller to trust the buyer is entirely obviated—the seller is sure of payment and the buyer, for his part, is sure of receiving the correct documents.

3.2. Types of letter of credit

The letter of credit is a versatile and adaptable instrument. All letters of credit stem from two basic varieties, revocable and irrevocable.

Exhibit 304: Direct collection form

| London Direct Collection — Original | **CITIBANK⊕** |

Citibank N.A.
P.O. Box 78
336 Strand
London WC2R 1HB

Date   JUNE 24,   (CURRENT YEAR)

Subject to "Uniform Rules for Collection"
as provided in the International Chamber
of Commerce brochure No 322

Mail to

DEUTSCHE BANK,
2, LINDENSTRASSE,
MUNICH,
GERMANY

Mailed by

A. SELLER,
1000 BROAD STREET,
NEW YORK   NY 10005,
U.S.A.

Drawers ref no.

We enclose the following draft and documents for collection and disposal of proceeds as instructed below. This collection is to be handled by you as if received direct from Citibank N.A. London, who will confirm by follow copy.

Citibank N.A. Reference	Amount	Drawee and address	Date of Draft	Tenor
NBG /DC	$200,000.00	B. BUYER, 2, LINDENSTRASSE, MUNICH	6/24/ CURRENT YEAR	SIGHT

Documents	Draft	Inv	Con. Inv.	CVO	Ins	B/L	PPR	Miscellaneous Documents	Vessel
Attached									
Duplicates to follow									

Please follow instructions marked X

X	Deliver documents against		If necessary warehouse and insure
X	Payment/acceptance may be deferred pending arrival of shipment		Do not insure
	Protest non-payment	X	Advise acceptance promptly by airmail/cable
	Protest non-acceptance		Advise dishonour promptly by airmail/cable
X	Do not protest non-payment		Collect interest at % p.a. from date of draft to approx. date of receipt of proceeds in London
X	Do not protest non-acceptance		Waive charges if refused

Collect Citibank N.A. charge of 1% min £5 max £20	Plus all other charges
Accept local currency deposit and written exchange undertaking	

In case of need refer to:

	Who will endeavour to obtain honour of draft as drawn KURT SCHMIDT, 14 BACH STRASSE, MUNICH
X	Whose instructions regarding disposal of goods and/or documents may be followed unconditionally

Payment Instructions

Place adhesive label here

Special Instructions

This collection is to be handled as if received by you from
Citibank N.A. P.O. Box 78, 336 Strand, London WC2R 1HB
to whom please acknowledge receipt and send all
communications quoting Citibank N.A. (London) DC Number

SPECIMEN ONLY

Sender's signature

A. SELLER CORP

Incorporated with limited liability under the National Bank Act of the United States of America
A Subsidiary of Citicorp New York USA

50

3.2.1. Revocable letters of credit

A revocable letter of credit can be amended or cancelled at any time without prior notice to the beneficiary. It provides the seller with no greater security than a documentary collection or order to pay, and is therefore generally unsatisfactory, since the seller is in the same position of trust as he is without the credit.

3.2.2. Irrevocable letters of credit

An irrevocable credit cannot be amended or cancelled without the beneficiary's consent. It is the only true kind of letter of credit. For the remainder of this chapter, all discussion of letters of credit will assume irrevocability.

Letters of credit are either *straight* or *negotiation* credits.

3.3. Straight and negotiation credits

The beneficiary may well not be close to the paying bank. In order for him to save time by presenting documents to his local bank, he will ask for the credit to be opened as a negotiation credit in which the issuing bank agrees to pay not just the beneficiary, but also any bona fide holders of drafts presented with the documents.

A negotiation credit enables either a specifically nominated bank (or any bank, if the words "freely negotiable by any bank" are used in the credit) to check the documents and, if they are in order, to pay them less interest for the time it will take to obtain re-imbursement from the issuing bank. Sellers should require negotiation credits where the currency of the credit is not their own currency, or where the seller's local bank offers preferential rates or service.

Generally, a negotiating bank pays with recourse to the beneficiary if anything goes wrong, but the legal position is by no means settled. This is a very important point for the beneficiary, as under every other kind of letter of credit, there is no recourse to him. All beneficiaries under negotiation credits should settle with the negotiating bank at payment, whether recourse to the beneficiary is reserved or not.

Straight and negotiation credits distinguish methods of settlement. Such settlement can be either at sight or by acceptance.

3.3.1. Sight credits

Sight credits are payable against drafts drawn on the paying bank at sight, i.e., payable immediately the documents are checked and found to be in order.

3.3.2. Acceptance credits

These are payable by acceptance of the paying bank of a term bill or draft drawn on it, payable at a specified date in the future. The paying bank must be specifically nominated as accepting bank under the credit.

The value of an acceptance credit is that the seller can extend time to pay to the buyer, who will not have to pay the face amount until maturity, and at the same time obtain a negotiable document, the bank acceptance, readily discountable for cash.

3.4. Less-usual forms of credit

There are four types of less-usual credit, adaptable to specific situations:

3.4.1. Revolving credits

A revolving credit is for a specific amount which stays the same without amendment, despite drawings under the credit. Such credits revolve either in time or value.

A credit revolving in time is available for a specific amount every week or month or year until expiry, regardless of whether any amount was drawn in the preceding time period. A credit revolving in time can be cumulative or non-cumulative, cumulative meaning that unused portions are carried forward for availability in the next period.

Revolving credits are useful where a seller has a long-term contract to supply a fixed quantity and value of merchandise over a specific time period.

3.4.2. Red clause credits

Red clause credits contain an authorization by the issuing bank to the advising or confirming bank to make advances to the beneficiary before presentation of documents. The description red clause arises from the colour of the ink that is used to draw attention to the credit's special condition.

The purpose of these credits is to provide pre-shipment finance to the seller, who might not be otherwise capable of raising the finance to produce the merchandise desired by the buyer. It is a method of financing between the buyer and seller; in the event of the seller not shipping the merchandise, the advising or confirming bank recovers the advances plus interest from the issuing bank, which in turn recovers from the applicant.

Red clause credits were once very common, particularly in the Australian wool trade with London. Woolbrokers in England used them as a way of financing Australian farmers' working capital needed to mature sheep for shearing. There were also blue-clause credits (only the ink was different) for New Zealand. Nowadays these credits are rare.

3.4.3. Transferable credits

A transferable credit enables the original beneficiary to transfer to one or more second beneficiaries. The transfer must be made by means of an advice given by a named bank, effecting the transfer to the second beneficiary in exactly the same wording as the original credit, with only three possible changes:

    i. the transferee's name and address is substituted for the beneficiary's;

    ii. the amount of credit may be reduced to allow for the first beneficiary's profit;

    iii. the expiry date may be brought forward to allow for movement of documents from the bank effecting the transfer to the issuing bank.

Transferable credits are generally used by middlemen desiring to keep their identity secret from the seller, so as to protect their trade connections from becoming known. Normally, they work well and are not as complicated as they might seem at first sight, particularly if partial transfers are permissible. However, to ensure his profit under a partial transfer the first beneficiary must make certain that he presents on time his invoice for the full amount of the original credit to the bank effecting the transfer. If he fails to do so, the bank will present the second beneficiary's invoice direct to the issuing bank, and obviously this invoice will not include the first beneficiary's profit.

A transferable credit may be transferred once only.

3.4.4. Back-to-back credits

The idea of a back-to-back credit sounds simple, but in practice such credits are difficult to structure satisfactorily from the point of view of the issuing bank. The principle of a back-to-back credit is that the seller, as beneficiary of the first credit, offers it as security to the advising bank for it to open a second credit in favour of the seller's own supplier.

A back-to-back would be useful in the same circumstances as a transferable credit, and particularly useful to a more remote beneficiary than the second beneficiary who, under the provision that a transferable credit is only transferable once, cannot himself transfer a credit on. The back-to-back would enable him to use the transferred credit as security for a credit in his supplier's favour.

Many banks are reluctant to open back-to-back credits without other security, because they are required to pay the beneficiary regardless of whether the applicant is paid himself. There are two difficulties:

    i. The back-to-back must match the wording of the first credit exactly, with only the amount and shipping dates changed to reflect the applicant's profit and earlier shipment.

    ii. The applicant might agree to amendments to the first credit detrimental to the interests of the issuing bank of the back-to-back without informing it.

One way out of this is for the issuing bank of the back-to-back to become the confirming bank of the first credit, but this may be difficult where the issuing bank is weak or objects to its credits being confirmed. Generally speaking, banks confine issue of back-to-backs to situations where they know there is an alternative source of repayment than the first credit, usually the applicant's general financial resources.

3.5. Practical mechanics

The general procedure in a letter of credit usually follows the sequence below:

    i. The buyer and seller agree terms of sale, including payment by letter of credit.

    ii. The buyer completes an instruction to the issuing bank to issue the credit (Exhibit 305). The buyer will have needed to obtain a credit line from the issuing bank specifying the total amount of credits that the bank will issue on his behalf, and he will need availability under this line.

    iii. The issuing bank instructs the advising or confirming bank, including specification of documents.

    iv. The advising bank informs the beneficiary.

TO: **CITIBANK, N.A.**

P.O. Box 78, 336 Strand, London WC2R 1HB.

DOCUMENTARY CREDIT IRREVOCABLE		CREDIT NUMBER	
	OF ISSUING BANK	OF ADVISING BANK	
———ADVISING BANK———		———APPLICANT———	
———BENEFICIARY———		———AMOUNT———	
		———EXPIRY———	
	DATE AT THE COUNTER OF:		

Available by the beneficiary's draft(s) drawn at:
☐ Sight ☐ _____days Sight ☐ _____days Date (Drafts to be dated same date as Bill of Lading)
☐ _____Other
drawn on   ☐ Citibank, N.A. London for_____% invoice cost.
☐ _____ for_____% invoice cost.
accompanied by the following documents which are indicated by "X", duly in order:
☐ Commercial Invoice in_____copies.
☐ Marine and War Risk Insurance Policy or Certificate, in negotiable form, in the currency of the credit including_____
☐ Full set clean on Board original Ocean Bills of Lading or Container
    Bills of Lading or Bills of Lading bearing container endorsement,
    issued to order of:_____
    marked notify _____
    Marked: Freight   ☐ Collect   ☐ Paid
☐ Airway Bill consigned to_____
☐ Other documents _____
☐ Insurance covered by applicant:
    COVERING:

Terms: ☐ FOB_____ ☐ C&F_____ ☐ CIF_____ ☐ C&I_____
              (Location)   (Location)   (Location)   (Location)
Imported under: ☐ Open General Licence   ☐ Import Licence No_____
Each draft or presentation of documents must indicate the credit number of the issuing bank and
the credit number of the advising bank (if indicated)

Despatch/Shipment/Taking in Charge Latest _____ From _____To _____	Partial Shipments ☐ Permitted ☐ Prohibited	Transhipments ☐ Permitted ☐ Prohibited

Drafts and documents must be presented to negotiating or paying bank within_____days after the date
of issuance of the Bills of Lading or other Shipping documents but within expiry.

1248 5/77

53

v. The beneficiary, if he accepts the advice and is happy with it, arranges shipment.

vi. The seller obtains the bills of lading from the shipping company, origin certificates and whatever else is required and delivers them to the issuing, paying, accepting or negotiating bank, whichever is the appropriate one for the settlement.

vii. The bank checks the documents and, if they are in accordance with the instructions from the issuing bank, or the applicant if the issuing bank is the paying bank, effects payment as appropriate, the paying or negotiating bank re-imbursing itself as appropriate.

viii. If the paying bank is not the issuing bank, it sends the documents to the issuing bank, which checks them and, if they are correct, releases them to the buyer upon payment of the amount of the credit or on such other terms, including a loan to the buyer, as may have been previously agreed.

ix. The buyer uses the documents to obtain possession of the goods.

For the simple case of a straight credit, the whole of this procedure is summarized in Exhibit 306, and the typical form of such a credit is shown in Exhibit 307.

Exhibit 306: Procedure used in a letter of credit

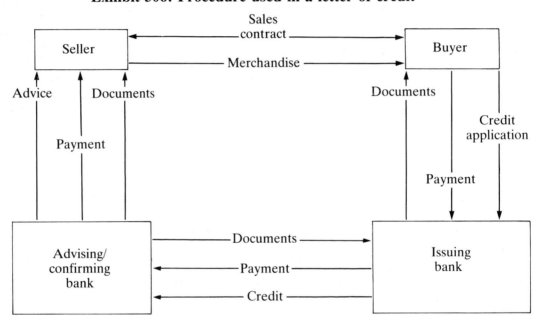

3.6. Documents required in a letter of credit

The bank letter of credit imposes no greater requirement than the buyer would impose on the seller under any other trade terms save that negotiable transport documents must be included if the issuing bank is to obtain security over the documents (which is normally required). This is a key point in the banking system's availment of credits. Banks may well be willing to issue payment guarantees without security for some of their customers, but certainly not for as many as they will issue letters of credit. The reason is that *in extremis* the issuing bank can sell the merchandise to repay itself because the negotiable transport documents give it title. There may be a loss but not as much as without the merchandise.

Usual transport documents are the following:

3.6.1. Bill of lading

Details on the bill of lading should include:

i. description of the merchandise consistent with the credit;

ii. identifying marks or numbers on the merchandise;

iii. vessel's name;

iv. evidence of loading usually by the imposition of the words "on board";

v. loading and discharge ports;

vi. names of shipper (the seller) and consignee (the buyer, his agent or sometimes "to order");

vii. whether freight is pre-paid or not;

Exhibit 307: Typical form of a letter of credit

```
                    DEUTSCHE BANK

                    Munich, Germany

                                        JULY 26, (CURRENT YEAR)

A. SELLER CORP
1000 BROAD STREET
NEW YORK, NEW YORK 10015

IRREVOCABLE STRAIGHT CREDIT NO. 315

GENTLEMEN;

    AT THE REQUEST B. BUYER CORP., 2 LINDENSTRASSE, MUNICH, GERMANY,
    AND FOR THE ACCOUNT OF SAME, WE HEREBY OPEN IN YOUR FAVOR OUR
    IRREVOCABLE CREDIT NO. AS INDICATED ABOVE, FOR A SUM OR SUMS NOT
    EXCEEDING A TOTAL OF U.S. $200,000. - (TWO HUNDRED THOUSAND UNITED
    STATES DOLLARS) AVAILABLE BY YOUR DRAFT(S) AT SIGHT ON US, TO BE
    ACCOMPANIED BY:

        1.
        2.      REQUIRED DOCUMENTATION
        3.

    EACH DRAFT DRAWN RELATIVE HERETO MUST BE MARKED, "DRAWN UNDER
    CREDIT NO. 315".

    DOCUMENTS MUST BE PRESENTED AT OUR OFFICE WITHIN 10 DAYS OF BILL
    OF LADING DATE.

    THIS CREDIT IS SUBJECT TO THE UNIFORM CUSTOMS AND PRACTICE FOR
    DOCUMENT CREDITS (1974 REVISION) INTERNATIONAL CHAMBER OF COMMERCE
    PUBLICATION NO. 290.
```

> WE HEREBY AGREE TO HONOR EACH DRAFT DRAWN UNDER AND IN COMPLIANCE
> WITH THE TERMS OF THIS CREDIT, IF DULY PRESENTED (TOGETHER WITH
> THE DOCUMENTS AS SPECIFIED) AT THIS OFFICE ON OR BEFORE OCTOBER 15,
> (CURRENT YEAR).

```
                                        VERY TRULY YOURS,



                                        AUTHORIZED SIGNATURE
```

vii. the number and date of bills. The date is perhaps the most important requirement. Firstly, it shows whether the goods are shipped within a required time for shipment under the credit; secondly it enables determination of presentation within the validity of the credit or, if no date is specified, 21 days of the date of the bills; thirdly, it permits determination of the acceptability of the accompanying insurance document.

The law affecting bills of lading is fairly complicated but, in essence, these are common sense documents. Any marks or comments on bills should be treated with care. For example, if the credit calls for merchandise to be stowed, and the bills are marked that goods are loaded on deck, they are not acceptable and indeed the insurance cover may not be effective either.

A bill of lading is shown in Exhibit 308. The name of the consignee is sometimes not specified but shown as "to order" to allow the issuing bank to obtain title, as otherwise the buyer (presuming he is the consignee) alone would be entitled to obtain possession. This does not affect the implied lien of the issuing bank over the goods, but enables it to obtain immediate possession of the merchandise.

Exhibit 308: Bill of lading

SHIPPER:	CONSIGNEE:
H. K. EXPORTER CORPORATION 1000 BROAD STREET NEW YORK, NEW YORK 10005	ORDER OF THE SHIPPER

NOTIFY PARTY:

L. B. IMPORTER COMPANY
RIO DE JANEIRO, BRAZIL

VESSEL: S/S QUOVIS	PORT OF LOADING: NEW YORK	PORT OF DISCHARGE RIO DE JANEIRO

MARKS AND NUMBER	NO. OF PKGS.	PARTICULARS FURNISHED BY SHIPPER DESCRIPTION OF MERCHANDISE	GROSS WEIGHT
LBIC 1/500 LOADED ON BOARD JULY 14, (CURRENT YEAR) CARRIER LINE INC. AGENT _____	500 CTNS.	WIDGETS FREIGHT PREPAID	25,000 LBS.

FREIGHT CHARGES PAYABLE AT NEW YORK BY SHIPPER

DETAILS OF FREIGHT CHARGES		SHORT FORM BILL OF LADING IN
PREPAID	COLLECT	WITNESS WHEREOF, THE CARRIER MASTER OR AGENT OF SAID VESSEL HAS SIGNED AND THE SHIPPER HAS RECEIVED THIS ONE ORIGINAL BILL OF LADING DATED AT NEW YORK CARRIER LINE INC.
TOTAL		BY_____ JULY 13, (CURRENT YEAR) B/L. NO. 1

3.6.2. Combined transport document

Where several modes of transport are to be employed, say, ocean-going vessel, inland waterways barge and trucks for container loads, either a *through* bill of lading or combined transport document is used. The word *transhipment* is more generally used to describe use of more than one mode of transport of the same kind, but can refer to multiple modes.

Whilst there is probably no greater significant risk of loss or damage of container loads in multiple modes of transport, it is desirable to have one document only, as railway bills, airway bills, truckers' bills and such like are not in themselves strictly negotiable.

3.6.3. Insurance certificate

Such a certificate is shown in Exhibit 309. Essentially, it only needs to be consistent with the other

Exhibit 309: Insurance certificate

NAME OF INSURANCE COMPANY

SPECIAL MARINE POLICY   ORIGINAL

PLACE AND DATE, NEW YORK, JULY 13 (CURRENT YEAR)

INSURED: H. K. EXPORTER CORPORATION NEW YORK, N.Y.

SUM INSURED: $1,000,000.00 (ONE MILLION AND 00/100 DOLLARS)

SHIPPED BY VESSEL: S/S QUOVIS B/L NO.1 DATED JULY 13, (CURRENT YEAR)
                   OF CARRIER LINE INC.

FROM: NEW YORK   TO: RIO DE JANEIRO

LOSS, IF ANY, PAYABLE TO THE ORDER OF: H. K. EXPORTER CORPORATION

MARKS AND NUMBERS	NO. OF PKGS.	NO. OF UNITS	DESCRIPTION OF GOODS
LBIC 1/500	500 CTNS.	1000	WIDGETS

TERMS AND CONDITIONS

VARIOUS TERMS AND CONDITIONS INCLUDING MARINE AND WAR RISKS.

NOT TRANSFERABLE UNLESS
COUNTERSIGNED BY AN
AUTHORIZED REPRESENTATIVE
COUNTERSIGNED:

IN WITNESS WHEREOF
THIS COMPANY HAS
EXECUTED AND ATTESTED
THESE PRESENTS.

_____   _____

documents called for in the credit and cover the required risk. However, in the absence of specific requirement the certificate must:

    i. be issued by an insurer;

    ii. provide cover from date of shipment;

    iii. be for at least the c.i.f. value of the merchandise.

The policy should also be endorsed so that the issuing bank becomes the beneficiary.

Various other documents are needed for specific cargoes, and it is the responsibility of the buyer and seller to ensure that these are adequate for the export of the merchandise. A widely used document is a certificate of origin (Exhibit 310), stating where the goods originate; unless the issuer is specifically stated, or qualifying words are used in the credit, the beneficiary can prepare this himself.

Most transactions also call for a series of invoices prepared by the beneficiary and a quality or inspection certificate prepared by professional inspectors.

3.7. Problem areas

As with most documentary transactions, discrepancies occur from time to time which are generally simple to correct, and which arise more from oversight than fundamental problems in the credit system. Most commonly, discrepancies arise with bills of lading either through clauses written on the bill stating defective condition of the merchandise, by which the bills are said to be *unclean*, or through presentation of the wrong kind of bill, usually a charter party bill.

If bills of lading are marked "freight prepaid" and the shipper is the owner of the vessel, the applicant and the issuing bank are safe in assuming that the applicant has title to the goods and the issuing bank has an indefeasible lien. However, if the shipper is a charterer, the owner of the vessel has a prevailing claim against the deadweight for unpaid charter fees, and indeed the carriage of certain merchandise may amount to a fundamental breach of the charter.

If the credit request by the buyer permits charter party bills of lading, the issuing bank will usually ask to see a summary of the charter party which will be required to be in acceptable form, i.e., that loading and discharge parts are permissible under the charter, that the merchandise is not prohibited, and that the charter, if it is a time charter, will not expire during the voyage.

Exhibit 310: Certificate of origin

Consignor: [1] Noxell Corporation (UK) Ltd., Flanshaw Way, Wakefield WF2 9NA West Yorkshire England	A/ 115112
	Consignor's ref.: [4]
Consignee: [2] Modern Pharmaceutical Co., P.O. Box 1586 Dubai United Arab Emirates	CERTIFICATE OF ORIGIN The undersigned authority certifies that the goods shown below originated in: [5] UNITED KINGDOM
Consigned by: [3] Vessel : Margorie Y From : South Shields	 ARAB-BRITISH CHAMBER OF COMMERCE

Marks and Numbers:	Quantity and Kind of Packages:	Description of Goods:	Weight (gross & net): [6]
	NOXELL – COVER GIRL Cosmetics		
	120 Shippers	Nail Polish Remover	
ModernPharm/ 125/78/UK/Dubai	6 Shippers	Eye Make Up Remover	319.38Kgs 266.80K
	Manufactured by: Vanda Beauty Counsellors, Gladdon Place Skelmersdale, Lancs.		

CERTIFIED BY

19 MAY 1978

Arab-British Chamber of Commerce
AUTHORISED SIGNATURE

KIRKLEES AND WAKEFIELD
CHAMBER OF COMMERCE AND INDUSTRY

ARAB-BRITISH CHAMBER OF COMMERCE

Place and Date of Issue	Issuing Authority

881

For some cargoes, especially crude petroleum, control of the vessel may be a crucial point in the issuing bank's willingness to open the credit. Cargoes of oil frequently exceed US$50 million in value, and the risk of diversion of the vessel after a credit is opened to more profitable buyers is not insignificant where unscrupulous owners who are also sellers of oil are tempted by rising oil prices. Banks are also concerned with the difficult question of liability for pollution damage which may occur with large oil cargoes. The charter party should make clear whose is the primary responsibility in such risk, and whose for secondary risk such as inspection of cargo holds, the condition of which may affect the quality of the merchandise. Generally speaking, deterioration of volatile materials (which would include even animal fats) is a risk which should be clearly stated between owner and charterer.

All bills of lading tendered under credits must be *order* bills and not straight bills, unless specifically stated otherwise. An order bill directs the carrier to deliver the goods to the order of a designated party, and is a proper negotiable document of title granted to the addressee (sometimes a notify party is also shown on the bill but such a party has no title in the bill). A straight bill, which is always so described in its heading, states a specific consignee without use of the words "to the order", or "order of". It is not a title document and is, therefore, not good security for the issuing bank. Normally, straight bills are used only where the buyer has made payment in advance, and they seldom arise under documentary credits.

There is a more far-reaching problem with credits extending beyond the technical issues which arise from discrepancies, which is best described as the ambiguous role of the banks. Just as the ICC have produced a uniform Code for Collections, so they have for credits, and it is called the Uniform Customs and Practice for Documentary Credits, 1974 Revision (see Appendix II). Although this does not have the force of law, it does have the practically universal support of major banks in prescribing their obligations. The key article is article 8, which states that: "In documentary credit operations all parties concerned deal in documents and not in goods".

On the face of it, therefore, the issuing and the paying bank have no responsibility for innocent or fraudulently misrepresentative documentation—the risk is the applicant's. This responsibility is controversial, and of considerable importance to an issuing bank faced with misrepresentative documents which it must pay, and also an applicant unwilling or perhaps unable to pay the issuing bank. Innocent misrepresentation (that is not fraudulent) on documents usually arises through incompetence or negligence. For example, an inspection certificate called for under the credit may have been negligently made out, with resulting loss to the buyer.

If a leading or properly qualified inspection firm is used, such problems are less likely to arise. However, the uniform code excludes the use of phrases such as "first class" or "qualified" on documents, so that banks are not concerned with even the minimal restraint on incompetence which such wording would allow. Only the identity, and not the capacity, of issuers of documents is of concern to banks, and even this is only partially true of origin certificates, unless specifically described in detail in the credit application.

Whether or not this is reasonable depends on the applicant's understanding of the role of issuing banks—they do not offer counsel on the commercial risks of the transaction for the buyer, nor do they monitor the implementation of the underlying contract between buyer and seller through the credit. Banks merely facilitate payment.

The ambiguity in this definition of role arises in one of the cases where the bank is entitled not to pay. There are only three grounds on which the bank may refuse to pay: failure of the beneficiary to meet the conditions precedent which there may be under the credit; a common mistake between buyer and seller leading to issue of the credit; and lastly, fraud by the seller.

It is fraud by the seller as grounds for refusal to pay that creates the ambiguity, since detection of fraud, or even reaction to suggestion of fraud, requires the bank to go beyond the documents. In the straightforward case of the paying bank being aware of fraud before documents are presented by the seller, the refusal to pay is clearly not only morally laudable but entirely sensible: the seller keeps his fraud and the buyer keeps his money.

Complications only really arise where there are other parties involved who have given consideration for the proceeds of the credits, or where there are other banks which, after negotiation or payment, are requesting re-imbursement from the opening bank on documents or on a transaction now found to be fraudulent. In such cases, should issuing banks do any more than just look at the documents on their face value and ignore the underlying transaction? Or should the risk of fraud, surely remote in most credits, make them enquire deeper?

Since 1976, the celebrated case of Singer and Friedlander ("Singer") on behalf of itself and 10 other banks, against Creditanstalt-Bankverein ("Creditanstalt") has been pursued in Vienna on (*inter alia*) the issue of fraud as a defence to payment by the issuing bank. The facts of the case are somewhat complicated but, in outline, what happened was that Creditanstalt opened letters of credit for the purchase of pharmaceuticals by two Austrian companies from a Dutch company, which subsequently transferred the credits to a consortium of banks led by Singer. The pharmaceuticals were, in fact, to be on-sold to a Yugoslavian trading company, which Creditanstalt subsequently claimed was acting as agent for the Dutch seller, so that the sale was merely a pretence designed to obtain value for the pharmaceuticals which in reality, so Creditanstalt also claimed, were rubbish. Singer, having given consideration for the transfer of the Creditanstalt credits by the Dutch company, presented the documents to Creditanstalt for payment, which it refused on certain technical grounds, and because of the alleged fraud in the transaction and in the goods.

The case is as yet undecided and the leading European legal authorities are divided, as are many banks, as to which side they support. The case really arises because there is a loss, and the disputants are attempting to ensure it does not fall on them. Most banks agree that it is right not to pay against fraudulent documents to prevent any loss arising, but enquiry into fraudulent transactions or goods is an onus which the banking system seems unable to bear, particularly at the low rates now charged for credits and within the time frame allowed by commercial pressures for transactions to proceed. However, the ambiguity remains and probably will, even after the Singer–Creditanstalt decision. The lesson for applicants, who in the great majority of cases will bear the loss on frauds is, as with all buyers, to beware their sellers.

Some protection for buyers may be had from a cross-credit or performance bond opened by the seller in their favour. Usually, these are limited to 10% only of the amount of the credit, and are difficult to obtain in sellers' markets which are normally those in which credits are opened by buyers anyway.

3.8. Costs

Although more expensive than collections because the issuing bank does take a risk on the applicant and charges for it, credits are a relatively cheap way for buyers to facilitate international transactions. Rates vary, depending on the credit standing of the applicant, the tenor of the credit, the amount of the credit and the merchandise, but a normal scale would be $\frac{1}{4}$% *ad valorem* commission for opening, plus $\frac{1}{8}$% per month for a credit permitting time drafts. Very large credits with sight drafts are frequently charged at considerably less than this, however.

In addition to opening charges, banks other than the issuing bank involved in the credit have charges, and tariffs vary widely depending on the country in which the bank is located. Negotiating banks also charge for interest for the time between negotiation and their re-imbursement. On a currency negotiation credit, an overall cost of $\frac{1}{2}$% or more might be typical.

Part of the cost, normally charges other than opening commission, may be met by the beneficiary, but against this he can set certainty of payment and also the time value of money paid earlier than later. Generally, credits are paid within 14 days from start to finish, even on long sea voyages, as bills of lading may be sent ahead of the vessel by air.

3.9. Recent developments in letters of credit

Letters of credit without the requirement for presentation of transport or commercial documents are called *clean* credits, and are analogous to, although not legally identical with, guarantees. These credits are extremely flexible and may be used in an almost unlimited variety of situations, from construction bonding to the finance of margin requirements on futures markets, where some kind of financial surety is required of the applicant.

Two kinds of clean credit which are relatives of the documentary letter of credit and which are making an increasingly common appearance are of particular interest. The first is the standby letter of credit, in which the issuing bank undertakes to pay if the applicant does not. Documents normally called for are evidence of the underlying transaction (such as non-negotiable copies of bills of lading), and the beneficiary's certificate of non-payment by the applicant. Such credits are useful in the purchase of crude oil, where it is particularly difficult to present negotiable documents speedily.

Sometimes the standby credit is coupled with a credit in favour of the applicant, used in lieu of negotiable documents as security for the issuing bank, which represents a particularly tricky instance of the back-to-back credit discussed earlier. The issuing bank will probably have to rely more on its knowledge of the parties and the transaction, than on the goods in such transactions.

The second is the indemnity for missing documents given to shipping companies, so that they will release merchandise to the applicant. This is a document of long standing in itself, but increasingly shipping companies are requesting such indemnities to have long expiry periods or no expiry date, and to be for a considerable multiple of the c.i.f. value of the cargo. Their reason for doing this is to protect themselves against unanticipated incidental damages, if at any time in the future the real owner of the cargo should appear.

Clearly, banks must know their applicants well before issuing such indemnities, but such large contingent risks, unlimited in time, are undesirable from both the banks' and the applicant's point of view, and it may be that the ease with which such indemnities have been issued will diminish.

The great boom in letters of credit was after World War II when there was much financial uncertainty. Since then, the decline of the letter of credit on the grounds of cost and, in some arguments, on the grounds that credits foster excessive trust in documents, has been continuously forecast. In fact, this has not happened, save possibly in the area where credits would be of most use because of the amounts of money involved, i.e., in the financing of the crude oil trade. For a number of reasons, but chiefly that major oil routes (for example, across the Mediterranean) are short and vessels arrive before documents, whilst demurrage is highly expensive or that vessels sail to save time before documents are ready, it is difficult to compose classical documentary letters of credit in the finance of oil. Instead, a guarantee for payment similar to a standby credit is frequently used.

3.10. Advantages and disadvantages of letters of credit

Advantages for seller
i. Letters of credit generally provide immediate finance, either by payment or bank acceptance.
ii. There is an effective guarantee of payment against the proper documents, regardless of the buyer's capacity to make payment. The bank cannot refuse payment for proper documents.
iii. Simple and minimal communication is necessary between seller and buyer, once the credit is established.

Disadvantages for seller
i. Really none, except that even a letter of credit is not as good as payment in advance.

Advantages for buyer
i. Deferred credit terms are simpler and easier to get, as the seller can be offered a bank rather than trade acceptance.
ii. Erroneous protest for non-payment is not possible.
iii. Buying is always easier with a letter of credit as incentive to the seller to sell.

Disadvantages for buyer
i. The buyer is sure of getting the documents he wants, but not necessarily the goods. Where there is a difference between the two, he must rely on the contract of sale for recovery of any loss, having already paid the issuing bank. Letters of credit are less favourable to buyers than collections.
ii. Letters of credit are more expensive and more work than collections.

Appendix I: Uniform rules for collections

(*Effective 1 January, 1979*)
International Chamber of Commerce Publication No. 322

GENERAL PROVISIONS AND DEFINITIONS
(*a*) These provisions and definitions and the following articles apply to all collections as defined in (*b*) below and are binding upon all parties thereto unless otherwise expressly agreed or unless contrary to the provisions of a national, state or local law and/or regulation which cannot be departed from.
(*b*) For the purpose of such provisions, definitions and articles:
1. (i) 'Collection' means the handling by banks, on instructions received, of documents as defined in (ii) below, in order to
    (a) obtain acceptance and/or, as the case may be, payment, or
    (b) deliver commercial documents against acceptance and/or, as the case may be, against payment, or
    (c) deliver documents on other terms and conditions.

    (ii) 'Documents' means financial documents and/or commercial documents

        (a) 'financial documents' means bills of exchange, promissory notes, cheques, payment receipts or other similar instruments used for obtaining the payment of money;

        (b) 'commercial documents' means invoices, shipping documents, documents of title or other similar documents, or any other documents whatsoever, not being financial documents.

    (iii) 'Clean collection' means collection of financial documents not accompanied by commercial documents.

    (iv) 'Documentary collection' means collection of

        (a) financial documents accompanied by commercial documents;

        (b) commercial documents not accompanied by financial documents.

2. The 'parties thereto' are:

    (i) the 'principal' who is the customer entrusting the operation of collection to his bank;

    (ii) the 'remitting bank' which is the bank to which the principal has entrusted the operation of collection;

    (iii) the 'collecting bank' which is any bank, other than the remitting bank, involved in processing the collection order;

    (iv) the 'presenting bank' which is the collecting bank making presentation to the drawee.

3. The 'drawee' is the one to whom presentation is to be made according to the collection order.

(c) All documents sent for collection must be accompanied by a collection order giving complete and precise instructions. Banks are only permitted to act upon the instructions given in such collection order, and in accordance with these rules.

If any bank cannot, for any reason, comply with the instructions given in the collection order received by it, it must immediately advise the party from whom it received the collection order.

Article 1
Banks will act in good faith and exercise reasonable care.

Article 2
Banks must verify that the documents received appear to be as listed in the collection order and must immediately advise the party from whom the collection order was received of any documents missing.

Banks have no further obligation to examine the documents.

Article 3
For the purpose of giving effect to the instructions of the principal, the remitting bank will utilize as the collecting bank:

    (i) the collecting bank nominated by the principal, or, in the absence of such nomination,

    (ii) any bank, of its own or another bank's choice, in the country of payment or acceptance, as the case may be.

The documents and the collection order may be sent to the collecting bank directly or through another bank as intermediary.

Banks utilizing the services of other banks for the purpose of giving effect to the instructions of the principal do so for the account of and at the risk of the latter.

The principal shall be bound by and liable to indemnify the banks against all obligations and responsibilities imposed by foreign laws or usages.

Article 4
Banks concerned with a collection assume no liability or responsibility for the consequences arising out of delay and/or loss in transit of any messages, letters or documents, or for delay, mutilation or other errors arising in the transmission of cables, telegrams, telex, or communication by electronic systems, or for errors in translation or interpretation of technical terms.

Article 5
Banks concerned with a collection assume no liability or responsibility for consequences arising out of the interruption of their business by Acts of God, riots, civil commotions, insurrections, wars, or any other causes beyond their control or by any strikes or lockouts.

Article 6
Goods should not be dispatched direct to the address of a bank or consigned to a bank without prior agreement on the part of that bank.

In the event of goods being dispatched direct to the address of a bank or consigned to a bank for delivery to a drawee against payment or acceptance or upon other terms without prior agreement on the part of that bank, the bank has no obligation to take delivery of the goods, which remain at the risk and responsibility of the party dispatching the goods.

Article 7
Documents are to be presented to the drawee in the form in which they are received, except that remitting and collecting banks are authorized to affix any necessary stamps, at the expense of the principal unless otherwise instructed, and to make any necessary endorsements or place any rubber stamps or other identifying marks or symbols customary to or required for the collection operation.

Article 8
Collection orders should bear the complete address of the drawee or of the domicile at which presentation is to be made. If the address is incomplete or incorrect, the collecting bank may, without obligation and responsibility on its part, endeavour to ascertain the proper address.

Article 9
In the case of documents payable at sight the presenting bank must make presentation for payment without delay.
   In the case of documents payable at a tenor other than sight the presenting bank must, where acceptance is called for, make presentation for acceptance without delay, and where payment is called for, make presentation for payment not later than the appropriate maturity date.

Article 10
In respect of a documentary collection including a bill of exchange payable-at-a-future date, the collection order should state whether the commercial documents are to be released to the drawee against acceptance (D–A) or against payment (D–P).

PAYMENT

Article 11
In the case of documents payable in the currency of the country of payment (local currency), the presenting bank must, unless otherwise instructed in the collection order, only release the documents to the drawee against payment in local currency which is immediately available for disposal in the manner specified in the collection order.

Article 12
In the case of documents payable in a currency other than that of the counry of payment (foreign currency) the presenting bank must, unless otherwise instructed in the collection order, only release the documents to the drawee against payment in the relative foreign currency which can immediately be remitted in accordance with the instructions given in the collection order.

Article 13
In respect of clean collections partial payments may be accepted if and to the extent to which and on the conditions on which partial payments are authorized by the law in force in the place of payment. The documents will only be released to the drawee when full payment thereof has been received.
   In respect of documentary collections partial payments will only be accepted if specifically authorized in the collection order. However, unless otherwise instructed, the presenting bank will only release the documents to the drawee after full payment has been received.
   In all cases partial payments will only be accepted subject to compliance with the provisions of either Article 11 or Article 12 as appropriate.
   Partial payment, if accepted, will be dealt with in accordance with the provisions of Article 14.

Article 14
Amounts collected (less charges and/or disbursements and/or expenses where applicable) must be made available without delay to the bank from which the collection order was received in accordance with the instructions contained in the collection order.

ACCEPTANCE

Article 15
The presenting bank is responsible for seeing that the form of the acceptance of a bill of exchange appears to be complete and correct, but is not responsible for the genuineness of any signature or for the authority of any signatory to sign the acceptance.

PROMISSORY NOTES, RECEIPTS AND OTHER SIMILAR INSTRUMENTS

Article 16
The presenting bank is not responsible for the genuineness of any signature or for the authority of any signatory to sign a promissory note, receipt, or other similar instrument.

Article 17

The collection order should give specific instructions regarding protest (or other legal process in lieu thereof), in the event of non-acceptance or non-payment.

In the absence of such specific instructions the banks concerned with the collection have no obligation to have the documents protested (or subjected to other legal process in lieu thereof) for non-payment or non-acceptance.

Any charges and/or expenses incurred by banks in connection with such protest or other legal process will be for the account of the principal.

CASE-OF-NEED (PRINCIPAL'S REPRESENTATIVE) AND PROTECTION OF GOODS

Article 18

If the principal nominates a representative to act as case-of-need in the event of non-acceptance and/or non-payment the collection order should clearly and fully indicate the powers of such case-of-need.

In the absence of such indication banks will not accept any instructions from the case-of-need.

Article 19

Banks have no obligation to take any action in respect of the goods to which a documentary collection relates.

Nevertheless in the case that banks take action for the protection of the goods, whether instructed or not, they assume no liability or responsibility with regard to the fate and/or condition of the goods and/or for any acts and/or omissions on the part of any third parties entrusted with the custody and/or protection of the goods. However, the collecting bank must immediately advise the bank from which the collection order was received of any such action taken.

Any charges and/or expenses incurred by banks in connection with any action for the protection of the goods will be for the account of the principal.

ADVICE OF FATE, etc.

Article 20

Collecting banks are to advise fate in accordance with the following rules:

    (i) Form of advice—All advices or information from the collecting bank to the bank from which the collection order was received, must bear appropriate detail including, in all cases, the latter bank's reference number of the collection order.

    (ii) Method of advice—In the absence of specific instructions the collecting bank must send all advices to the bank from which the collection order was received by quickest mail but, if the collecting bank considers the matter to be urgent, quicker methods such as cable, telegram, telex, or communication by electronic systems, etc. may be used at the expense of the principal.

    (iii) (a) Advice of payment—The collecting bank must send without delay advice of payment to the bank from which the collection order was received, detailing the amount or amounts collected, charges and/or disbursements and/or expenses deducted, where appropriate, and method of disposal of the funds.

(b) Advice of acceptance—The collecting bank must send without delay advice of acceptance to the bank from which the collection order was received.

(c) Advice of non-payment or non-acceptance—The collecting bank must send without delay advice of non-payment or advice of non-acceptance to the bank from which the collection order was received.

The presenting bank should endeavour to ascertain the reasons for such non-payment or non-acceptance and advise accordingly the bank from which the collection order was received.

On receipt of such advice the remitting bank must, within a reasonable time, give appropriate instructions as to the further handling of the documents. If such instructions are not received by the presenting bank within 90 days from its advice of non-payment or non-acceptance, the documents may be returned to the bank from which the collection order was received.

INTEREST, CHARGES AND EXPENSES

Article 21

If the collection order includes an instruction to collect interest which is not embodied in the accompanying financial document(s), if any, and the drawee refuses to pay such interest, the presenting bank may deliver the document(s) against payment or acceptance as the case may be without collecting such interest, unless the collection order expressly states that such interest may not be waived. Where such interest is to be collected the collection order must bear an indication of the rate of interest and the period covered. When payment of interest has been refused the presenting bank must inform the bank from which the collection order was received accordingly.

If the documents include a financial document containing an unconditional and definitive interest clause the interest amount is deemed to form part of the amount of the documents to be collected. Accordingly, the interest amount is payable in addition to the principal amount shown in the financial document and may not be waived unless the collection order so authorizes.

Article 22
If the collection order includes an instruction that collection charges and/or expenses are to be for account of the drawee and the drawee refuses to pay them, the presenting bank may deliver the document(s) against payment or acceptance as the case may be without collecting charges and/or expenses unless the collection order expressly states that such charges and/or expenses may not be waived. When payment of collection charges and/or expenses has been refused the presenting bank must inform the bank from which the collection order was received accordingly. Whenever collection charges and/or expenses are so waived they will be for the account of the principal, and may be deducted from the proceeds.

Should a collection order specifically prohibit the waiving of collection charges and/or expenses then neither the remitting nor collecting nor presenting bank shall be responsible for any costs or delays resulting from this prohibition.

Article 23
In all cases where in the express terms of a collection order, or under these Rules, disbursements and/or expenses and/or collection charges are to be borne by the principal, the collecting bank(s) shall be entitled promptly to recover outlays in respect of disbursements and expenses and charges from the bank from which the collection order was received and the remitting bank shall have the right promptly to recover from the principal any amount so paid out by it, together with its own disbursements, expenses and charges, regardless of the fate of the collection.

Appendix II: Uniform customs and practice for documentary credits

Source: United States Council of the International Chamber of Commerce Publication No. 290

Foreword to the 1974 revision

For many years the ICC Banking Commission has contributed to the facilitation of international trade through the formulation of sets of rules governing documentary credits. The last (1962) revision of the *Uniform Customs and Practice for Documentary Credits,* published as ICC Brochure 222, was used by the banks and banking associations of virtually every country and territory in the world.

Considerable changes have since taken place in international trading and transport techniques. Terms of purchase and sale have swung from the traditional FOB and CIF towards "Delivered to Buyer's Premises", and the through, multi-modal movement of unitized cargo is increasingly competing with the traditional single-mode carriage of break-bulk cargo. Consequential changes have become necessary in documentary credit practice.

Therefore we have taken a careful and critical look at the 1962 rules, amending them as appropriate to fit the 1970s and prepare for the 1980s. The changes made particularly concern the documentary aspects of multi-modal transport and unitized cargoes, the easier production and processing of documents in "short form", and the problem of "stale" documents.

Revision has been greatly assisted by the cooperation of the United Nations Commission on International Trade Law (UNCITRAL). Banks in the Socialist countries have also contributed through an ad hoc Working Party.

In conclusion I would like to give our wholehearted thanks to the Chairman of the Banking Commission, Bernard Wheble and the Commission members for their untiring efforts to achieve agreement on this most important text, and to the many ICC members who have given their executives time to work on the new revision.

Carl-Henrik Winqvist
Secretary General of the ICC

General provisions and definitions

    a. These provisions and definitions and the following articles apply to all documentary credits and are binding upon all parties thereto unless otherwise expressly agreed.

    b. For the purposes of such provisions, definitions and articles the expressions "documentary credit(s)" and "credit(s)" used therein mean any arrangement, however named or described, whereby a bank (the issuing bank), acting at the request and in accordance with the instructions of a customer (the applicant for the credit),
    i. is to make payment to or to the order of a third party (the beneficiary), or is to pay, accept or negotiate bills of exchange (drafts) drawn by the beneficiary, or
    ii. authorizes such payments to be made or such drafts to be paid, accepted or negotiated by another bank,
    against stipulated documents, provided that the terms and conditions of the credit are complied with.

    c. Credits, by their nature, are separate transactions from the sales or other contracts on which they may be based and banks are in no way concerned with or bound by such contracts.

d. Credit instructions and the credits themselves must be complete and precise.
In order to guard against confusion and misunderstanding, issuing banks should discourage any attempt by the applicant for the credit to include excessive detail.

e. The bank first entitled to exercise the option available under Article 32b. shall be the bank authorized to pay, accept or negotiate under a credit. The decision of such bank shall bind all parties concerned.
A bank is authorized to pay or accept under a credit by being specifically nominated in the credit.
A bank is authorized to negotiate under a credit either
i. by being specifically nominated in the credit, or
ii. by the credit being freely negotiable by any bank.

f. A beneficiary can in no case avail himself of the contractual relationships existing between banks or between the applicant for the credit and the issuing bank.

A. Form and notification of credits

Article 1

a. Credits may be either
i. revocable, or
ii. irrevocable.

b. All credits, therefore, should clearly indicate whether they are revocable or irrevocable.

c. In the absence of such indication the credit shall be deemed to be revocable.

Article 2

A revocable credit may be amended or cancelled at any moment without prior notice to the beneficiary. However, the issuing bank is bound to reimburse a branch or other bank to which such a credit has been transmitted and made available for payment, acceptance or negotiation, for any payment, acceptance or negotiation complying with the terms and conditions of the credit and any amendments received up to the time of payment, acceptance or negotiation made by such branch of other bank prior to receipt by it of notice of amendment or of cancellation.

Article 3

a. An irrevocable credit constitutes a definite undertaking of the issuing bank, provided that the terms and conditions of the credit are complied with:
i. to pay, or that payment will be made, if the credit provides for payment, whether against a draft or not;
ii. to accept drafts if the credit provides for acceptance by the issuing bank or to be responsible for their acceptance and payment at maturity if the credit provides for the acceptance of drafts drawn on the applicant for the credit or any other drawee specified in the credit;
iii. to purchase/negotiate, without recourse to drawers and/or bona fide holders, drafts drawn by the beneficiary, at sight or at a tenor, on the applicant for the credit or on any other drawee specified in the credit, or to provide for purchase/negotiation by another bank, if the credit provides for purchase/negotiation.

b. An irrevocable credit may be advised to a beneficiary through another bank (the advising bank) without engagement on the part of that bank, but when an issuing bank authorizes or requests another bank to confirm its irrevocable credit and the latter does so, such confirmation constitutes a definite undertaking of the confirming bank in addition to the undertaking of the issuing bank, provided that the terms and conditions of the credit are complied with:
i. to pay, if the credit is payable at its own counters, whether against a draft or not, or that payment will be made if the credit provides for payment elsewhere;
ii. to accept drafts if the credit provides for acceptance by the confirming bank, at its own counters, or to be responsible for their acceptance and payment at maturity if the credit provides for the acceptance of drafts drawn on the applicant for the credit or any other drawee specified in the credit;
iii. to purchase/negotiate, without recourse to drawers and/or bona fide holders, drafts drawn by the beneficiary, at sight or at a tenor, on the issuing bank, or on the applicant for the credit or on any other drawee specified in the credit, if the credit provides for purchasers negotiation.

c. Such undertakings can neither be amended nor cancelled without the agreement of all parties thereto. Partial acceptance of amendments is not effective without the agreement of all parties thereto.

Article 4

a. When an issuing bank instructs a bank by cable, telegram or telex to advise a credit, and intends the mail confirmation to be the operative credit instrument, the cable, telegram or telex must state that the credit will only be effective on receipt of such mail confirmation. In this event, the issuing bank must send the operative credit instrument (mail confirmation) and any subsequent amendments to the credit to the benficiary through the advising bank.

b. The issuing bank will be responsible for any consequences arising from its failure to follow the procedure set out in the preceding paragraph.

c. Unless a cable, telegram or telex states "details to follow" (or words of similar effect), or states that the mail confirmation is to be the operative credit instrument, the cable, telegram or telex will be deemed to be the operative credit instrument and the issuing bank need not send the mail confirmation to the advising bank.

Article 5

When a bank is instructed by cable, telegram or telex to issue, confirm or advise a credit similar in terms to one previously established and which has been the subject of amendments, it shall be understood that the details of the credit being issued, confirmed or advised will be transmitted to the beneficiary excluding the amendments, unless the instructions specify clearly any amendments which are to apply.

Article 6

If incomplete or unclear instructions are received to issue, confirm or advise a credit, the bank requested to act on such instructions may give preliminary notification of the credit to the beneficiary for information only and without responsibility; in this event the credit will be issued, confirmed or advised only when the necessary information has been received.

B. Liabilities and responsibilities

Article 7

Banks must examine all documents with reasonable care to ascertain that they appear on their face to be in accordance with the terms and conditions of the credit. Documents which appear on their face to be inconsistent with one another will be considered as not appearing on their face to be in accordance with the terms and conditions of the credit.

Article 8

a. In documentary credit operations all parties concerned deal in documents and not in goods.
b. Payment, acceptance or negotiation against documents which appear on their face to be in accordance with the terms and conditions of a credit by a bank authorized to do so binds the party giving the authorization to take up the documents and reimburse the bank which has effected the payment, acceptance or negotiation.
c. If, upon receipt of the documents, the issuing bank considers that they appear on their face not to be in accordance with the terms and conditions of the credit, that bank must determine, on the basis of the documents alone, whether to claim that payment, acceptance or negotiation was not effected in accordance with the terms and conditions of the credit.
d. The issuing bank shall have a reasonable time to examine the documents and to determine as above whether to make such a claim.
e. If such claim is to be made, notice to that effect, stating the reasons therefor, must, without delay, be given by cable or other expeditious means to the bank from which the documents have been received (the remitting bank) and such notice must state that the documents are being held at the disposal of such bank or are being returned thereto.
f. If the issuing bank fails to hold the documents at the disposal of the remitting bank, or fails to return the documents to such bank, the issuing bank shall be precluded from claiming that the relative payment, acceptance or negotiation was not effected in accordance with the terms and conditions of the credit.
g. If the remitting bank draws the attention of the issuing bank to any irregularities in the documents or advises such bank that it has paid, accepted or negotiated under reserve or against a guarantee in respect of such irregularities, the issuing bank shall not thereby be relieved from any of its obligations under this article. Such guarantee or reserve concerns only the relations between the remitting bank and the beneficiary.

Article 9

Banks assume no liability or responsibility for the form, sufficiency, accuracy, genuineness, falsification or legal effect of any documents, or for the general and/or particular conditions stipulated in the documents or superimposed thereon; nor do they assume any liability or responsibility for the description, quantity, weight, quality, condition, packing, delivery, value or existence of the goods represented thereby, or for the good faith or acts and/or omissions, solvency, performance or standing of the consignor, the carriers or the insurers of the goods or any other person whomsoever.

Article 10

Banks assume no liability or responsibility for the consequences arising out of delay and/or loss in transit of any messages, letters or documents, or for delay, mutilation or other errors arising in the transmission of cables, telegrams or telex. Banks assume no liability or responsibility for errors in translation or interpretation of technical terms, and reserve the right to transmit credit terms without translating them.

Article 11

Banks assume no liability or responsibility for consequences arising out of the interruption of their business by Acts of God, riots, civil commotions, insurrections, wars or any other causes beyond their control or by any strikes or lockouts. Unless specifically authorized, banks will not effect payment, acceptance or negotiation after expiration under credits expiring during such interruption of business.

Article 12

a. Banks utilizing the services of another bank for the purpose of giving effect to the instructions of the applicant for the credit do so for the account and at the risk of the latter.
b. Banks assume no liability or responsibility should the instructions they transmit not be carried out, even if they have themselves taken the initiative in the choice of such other bank.

c. The applicant for the credit shall be bound by and liable to indemnify the banks against all obligations and responsibilities imposed by foreign laws and usages.

Article 13
A paying or negotiating bank which has been authorized to claim reimbursement from a third bank nominated by the issuing bank and which has effected such payment or negotiation shall not be required to confirm to the third bank that it has done so in accordance with the terms and conditions of the credit.

C. Documents

Article 14
    a. All instructions to issue, confirm or advise a credit must state precisely the documents against which payment, acceptance or negotiation is to be made.
    b. Terms such as "first class", "well known", "qualified" and the like shall not be used to describe the issuers of any documents called for under credits and if they are incorporated in the credit terms banks will accept documents as tendered.

C.1.Documents evidencing shipment or dispatch or taking in charge (shipping documents).

Article 15
Except as stated in Article 20, the date of the Bill of Lading, or the date of any other document evidencing shipment or dispatch or taking in charge, or the date indicated in the reception stamp or by notation on any such document, will be taken in each case to be the date of shipment or dispatch or taking in charge of the goods.

Article 16
    a. If words clearly indicating payment or prepayment of freight, however named or described, appear by stamp or otherwise on documents evidencing shipment or dispatch or taking in charge they will be accepted as constituting evidence of payment of freight.
    b. If the words "freight pre-payable" or "freight to be prepaid" or words of similar effect appear by stamp or otherwise on such documents they will not be accepted as constituting evidence of the payment of freight.
    c. Unless otherwise specified in the credit or inconsistent with any of the documents presented under the credit, banks will accept documents stating that freight or transportation charges are payable on delivery.
    d. Banks will accept shipping documents bearing reference by stamp or otherwise to costs additional to the frieght charges, such as costs of, or disbursements incurred in connection with loading, unloading or similar operations, unless the conditions of the credit specifically prohibit such reference.

Article 17
Shipping documents which bear a clause on the face thereof such as "shipper's load and count" or "said by shipper to contain" or words of similar effect, will be accepted unless otherwise specified in the credit.

Article 18
    a. A clean shipping document is one which bears no superimposed clause or notation which expressly declares a defective condition of the goods and/or the packaging.
    b. Banks will refuse shipping documents bearing such clauses or notations unless the credit expressly states the clauses or notations which may be accepted.

C.1.1. Marine bills of lading.

Article 19
Unless specifically authorized in the credit, Bills of Lading of the following nature will be rejected:
i. Bills of Lading issued by forwarding agents.
ii. Bills of Lading which are issued under and are subject to the conditions of a Charter-Party.
iii. Bills of Lading covering shipment by sailing vessels.
However, subject to the above and unless otherwise specified in the credit, Bills of Lading of the following nature will be accepted:
i. "Through" Bills of Lading issued by shipping companies or their agents even though they cover several modes of transport.
ii. Short Form Bills of Lading (i.e. Bills of Lading issued by shipping companies or their agents which indicate some or all of the conditions of carriage by reference to a source or document other than the Bill of Lading).
iii. Bills of Lading issued by shipping companies or their agents covering unitized cargoes, such as those on pallets or in Containers.

Article 20
    a. Unless otherwise specified in the credit, Bills of Lading must show that the goods are loaded on board a named vessel or shipped on a named vessel.
    b. Loading on board a named vessel or shipment on a named vessel may be evidenced either by a Bill of Lading bearing wording indicating loading on board a named vessel or shipment on a named vessel, or by means of a notation to that effect on the Bill of Lading signed or initialled and dated by the carrier or his agent, and the date

of this notation shall be regarded as the date of loading on board the named vessel or shipment on the named vessel.

Article 21

    a. Unless transhipment is prohibited by the terms of the credit, Bills of Lading will be accepted which indicate that the goods will be transhipped en route, provided the entire voyage is covered by one and the same Bill of Lading.

    b. Bills of Lading incorporating printed clauses stating that the carriers have the right to tranship will be accepted notwithstanding the fact that the credit prohibits transhipment.

Article 22

    a. Banks will refuse a Bill of Lading stating that the goods are loaded on deck, unless specifically authorized in the credit.

    b. Banks will not refuse a Bill of Lading which contains a provision that the goods may be carried on deck, provided it does not specifically state that they are loaded on deck.

C.1.2 Combined transport documents.

Article 23

    a. If the credit calls for a combined transport document, i.e. one which provides for a combined transport by at least two different modes of transport, from a place at which the goods are taken in charge to a place designated for delivery, or if the credit provides for a combined transport, but in either case does not specify the form of document required and/or the issuer of such document, banks will accept such documents as tendered.

    b. If the combined transport includes transport by sea the document will be accepted although it does not indicate that the goods are on board a named vessel, and although it contains a provision that the goods, if packed in a Container, may be carried on deck, provided it does not specifically state that they are loaded on deck.

C.1.3 Other shipping documents, etc.

Article 24

Banks will consider a Railway or Inland Waterway Bill of Lading or Consignment Note, Counterfoil Waybill, Postal Receipt, Certificate of Mailing, Air Mail Receipt, Air Waybill, Air Consignment Note or Air Receipt, Trucking Company Bill of Lading or any other similar document as regular when such document bears the reception stamp of the carrier or his agent, or when it bears a signature purporting to be that of the carrier or his agent.

Article 25

Where a credit calls for an attestation or certification of weight in the case of transport other than by sea, banks will accept a weight stamp or declaration of weight superimposed by the carrier on the shipping document unless the credit calls for a separate or independent certificate of weight.

C.2. Insurance documents.

Article 26

    a. Insurance documents must be as specified in the credit, and must be issued and/or signed by insurance companies or their agents or by underwriters.

    b. Cover notes issued by brokers will not be accepted, unless specifically authorized in the credit

Article 27

Unless otherwise specified in the credit, or unless the insurance documents presented establish that the cover is effective at the latest from the date of shipment or dispatch or, in the case of combined transport, the date of taking the goods in charge, banks will refuse insurance documents presented which bear a date later than the date of shipment or dispatch or, in the case of combined transport, the date of taking the goods in charge, as evidenced by the shipping documents.

Article 28

    a. Unless otherwise specified in the credit, the insurance document must be expressed in the same currency as the credit.

    b. The minimum amount for which insurance must be effected is the CIF value of the goods concerned. However, when the CIF value of the goods cannot be determined from the documents on their face, banks will accept as such minimum amount the amount of the drawing under the credit or the amount of the relative commercial invoice, whichever is the greater.

Article 29

    a. Credits should expressly state the type of insurance required and, if any, the additional risks which are to be covered. Imprecise terms such as "usual risks" or "customary risks" should not be used; however, if such imprecise terms are used, banks will accept insurance documents as tendered.

    b. Failing specific instructions, banks will accept insurance cover as tendered.

Article 30

Where a credit stipulates "insurance against all risks", banks will accept an insurance document which contains any "all risks" notation or clause, and will assume no responsibility if any particular risk is not covered.

Article 31

Banks will accept an insurance document which indicates that the cover is subject to a franchise or an excess (deductible), unless it is specifically stated in the credit that the insurance must be issued irrespective of percentage.

C.3. Commercial invoices.
Article 32

    a. Unless otherwise specified in the credit, commercial invoices must be made out in the name of the applicant for the credit.
    b. Unless otherwise specified in the credit, banks may refuse commercial invoices issued for amounts in excess of the amount permitted by the credit.
    c. The description of the goods in the commercial invoice must correspond with the description in the credit. In all other documents the goods may be described in general terms not inconsistent with the description of the goods in the credit.

C.4. Other documents.

Article 33

When other documents are required, such as Warehouse Receipts, Delivery Orders, Consular Invoices, Certificates of Origin, of Weight, of Quality or of Analysis etc., and when no further definition is given, banks will accept such documents as tendered.

D. Miscellaneous provisions

Quantity and amount.

Article 34

    a. The words "about", "circa" or similar expressions used in connection with the amount of the credit or the quantity or the unit price of the goods are to be construed as allowing a difference not to exceed 10% more or 10% less.
    b. Unless a credit stipulates that the quantity of the goods specified must not be exceeded or reduced, a tolerance of 3% more or 3% less will be permissible, always provided that the total amount of the drawings does not exceed the amount of the credit. This tolerance does not apply when the credit specifies quantity in terms of a stated number of packing units or individual items.

Partial shipments.

Article 35

    a. Partial shipments are allowed, unless the credit specifically states otherwise.
    b. Shipments made on the same ship and for the same voyage, even if the Bills of Lading evidencing shipment "on board" bear different dates and/or indicate different ports of shipment, will not be regarded as partial shipments.

Article 36

If shipment by instalments within given periods is stipulated and any instalment is not shipped within the period allowed for that instalment, the credit ceases to be available for that or any subsequent instalments, unless otherwise specified in the credit.

Expiry date

Article 37

All credits, whether revocable or irrevocable, must stipulate an expiry date for presentation of documents for payment, acceptance or negotiation, notwithstanding the stipulation of a latest date for shipment.

Article 38

The words "to", "until", "till" and words of similar import applying to the stipulated expiry date for presentation of documents for payment, acceptance or negotiation, or to the stipulated latest date for shipment, will be understood to include the date mentioned.

Article 39

    a. When the stipulated expiry date falls on a day on which banks are closed for reasons other than those mentioned in Article 11, the expiry date will be extended until the first following business day.
    b. The latest date for shipment shall not be extended by reason of the extension of the expiry date in accordance with this Article. Where the credit stipulates a latest date for shipment, shipping documents dated later than such stipulated date will not be accepted. If no latest date for shipment is stipulated in the credit, shipping documents dated later than the expiry date stipulated in the credit or amendments thereto will not be accepted. Documents other than the shipping documents may, however, be dated up to and including the extended expiry date.

  c. Banks paying, accepting or negotiating on such extended expiry date must add to the documents their certification in the following wording: "Presented for payment (or acceptance or negotiation as the case may be) within the expiry date extended in accordance with Article 39 of the *Uniform Customs.*"

Shipment, loading or dispatch.

Article 40
  a. Unless the terms of the credit indicate otherwise, the words "departure", "dispatch", "loading" or "sailing" used in stipulating the latest date for shipment of the goods will be understood to be synonymous with "shipment".
  b. Expressions such as "prompt", "immediately", "as soon as possible" and the like should not be used. If they are used, banks will interpret them as a request for shipment within thirty days from the date on the advice of the credit to the beneficiary by the issuing bank or by an advising bank, as the case may be.
  c. The expression "on or about" and similar expressions will be interpreted as a request for shipment during the period from five days before to five days after the specified date, both end days included.

Presentation.

Article 41
Notwithstanding the requirement of Article 37 that every credit must stipulate an expiry date for presentation of documents, credits must also stipulate a specified period of time after the date of issuance of the Bills of Lading or other shipping documents during which presentation of documents for payment, acceptance or negotiation must be made. If no such period of time is stipulated in the credit, banks will refuse documents presented to them later than 21 days after the date of issuance of the Bills of Lading or other shipping documents.

Article 42
Banks are under no obligation to accept presentation of documents outside their banking hours.

Date terms.

Article 43
The terms "first half", "second half" of a month shall be contrued respectively as from the 1st to the 15th, and the 16th to the last day of each month, inclusive.

Article 44
The terms "beginning", "middle", or "end" of a month shall be construed respectively as from the 1st to the 10th, the 11th to the 20th, and the 21st to the last day of each month, inclusive.

Article 45
When a bank issuing a credit instructs that the credit be confirmed or advised as available "for one month", "for six months" or the like, but does not specify the date from which the time is to run, the confirming or advising bank will confirm or advise the credit as expiring at the end of such indicated period from the date of its confirmation or advice.

E. Transfer

Article 46
  a. A transferable credit is a credit under which the beneficiary has the right to give instructions to the bank called upon to effect payment or acceptance or to any bank entitled to effect negotiation to make the credit available in whole or in part to one or more third parties (second beneficiaries).
  b. The bank requested to effect the transfer, whether it has confirmed the credit or not, shall be under no obligation to effect such transfer except to the extent and in the manner expressly consented to by such bank, and until such bank's charges in respect of transfer are paid.
  c. Bank charges in respect of transfers are payable by the first beneficiary unless otherwise specified.
  d. A credit can be transferred only if it is expressly designated as "transferable" by the issuing bank. Terms such as "divisible", "fractionable", "assignable" and "transmissible" add nothing to the meaning of the term "transferable" and shall not be used.
  e. A transferable credit can be transferred once only. Fractions of a transferable credit (not exceeding in the aggregate the amount of the credit) can be transferred separately, provided partial shipments are not prohibited, and the aggregate of such transfers will be considered as constituting only one transfer of the credit. The credit can be transferred only on the terms and conditions specified in the original credit, with the exception of the amount of the credit, of any unit prices stated therein, and of the period of validity or period for shipment, any or all of which may be reduced or curtailed.
   Additionally, the name of the first beneficiary can be substituted for that of the applicant for the credit, but if the name of the applicant for the credit is specifically required by the original credit to appear in any document other than the invoice, such requirement must be fulfilled.
  f. The first beneficiary has the right to substitute his own invoices for those of the second beneficiary, for amounts not in excess of the original amount stipulated in the credit and for the original unit prices if stipulated in the credit, and upon such substitution of invoices the first beneficiary can draw under the credit for the difference, if any, between his invoices and the second beneficiary's invoices. When a credit has been transferred and the first

beneficiary is to supply his own invoices in exchange for the second beneficiary's invoices but fails to do so on first demand, the paying, accepting or negotiating bank has the right to deliver to the issuing bank the documents received under the credit, including the second beneficiary's invoices, without further responsibility to the first beneficiary.

g. The first beneficiary of a transferable credit can transfer the credit to a second beneficiary in the same country or in another country unless the "credit" specifically states otherwise. The first beneficiary shall have the right to request that payment or negotiation be effected to the second beneficiary at the place to which the credit has been transferred, up to and including the expiry date of the original credit, and without prejudice to the first beneficiary's right subsequently to substitute his own invoices for those of the second beneficiary and to claim any difference due to him.

Article 47

The fact that a credit is not stated to be transferable shall not affect the beneficiary's rights to assign the proceeds of such credit in accordance with the provisions of the applicable law.

CHAPTER FOUR
Financing trade in consumer goods

Charles J. Gmür

1. Introduction

The traditional cross-border trade in consumer goods is done as a cash sale, with bills of exchange, letters of credit or using over-draft financing. Whenever difficulties arise, the exporter will try to eliminate these by using government export credit guarantee schemes. Not only capital goods exports with extended credit terms, but also sales of consumer goods may be covered by government credit guarantee boards. The respective government export credit financing board (see Chapter V, Exhibit 503) or a commercial banker will provide the necessary details, which are being continually adjusted. Furthermore, there are two other forms of financing especially tailored for trade in consumer goods. Both apply also to inland trade. They are *accounts receivable financing* and *factoring*. Owing to their many similarities, these two financing methods are often considered the same. However, there are some essential differences which can be seen in Exhibit 401, and which are dealt with in the following section.

2. Definitions

2.1. Accounts receivable financing

In an accounts receivable financing, the bank provides credit to the seller of goods. The seller's claims against his customer serve as security for the bank. It is not sufficient for the bank to base its credit decision on information on the volume of turnover and debt position of the borrowing company. In an accounts receivable financing, the bank requires the contractual assignment of sufficient claims to secure the credit. Since returns, rebates and discounts often arise with sales of consumer goods, the lender will not, in most cases, grant a credit up to the full value of the assigned claims. In view of the additional risks with foreign business (ignorance of the customer's credit-worthiness, political and transfer risk, possible currency risk) only 65 to 70% of the assigned claims are usually advanced against credit; coverage of 140 to 150% is therefore demanded. In certain cases, greater cover must be called for.

In an accounts receivable financing the supplier's clients are not usually notified of the debt assignment. Accounts receivable financing thus rests broadly on the creditworthiness of the supplier, and is considered as a credit exclusively to him.

2.2. Factoring

Factoring does not represent a credit to the supplier of goods. The factor normally purchases his client's claims and assumes the commercial risk in them. It is primarily not the seller but the recipient of the goods who must be creditworthy. For this reason, cross-border factoring is usually carried out through a network of factoring companies in various countries who, with the help of their local knowledge, assess the economic risk of claims which their foreign partners wish to assume. As a rule, they take over the commercial risk from the *export factor* and, if necessary, the local collection. This service is known as *import factoring*.

It is usual, in factoring, for the debtors of the assigned claims to be made aware of the assignment, and to make their payments directly to the new owner of the claims, i.e., the factor. This is essential to the performance of the factor's collection and possible book-keeping functions, and frees the supplier from the supervision of incoming payments.

Factoring is a package of services which is known today by various terms, according to the combinations used. These include: the taking over of claims by assignment or purchase; the taking over of commercial risk; advance payment; collection; debtor book-keeping; and the compilation of statistics on debtor turnover, regional development, etc.

Genuine factoring or *old-line factoring* occurs when the factor takes over the commercial risk as well as collection, and usually also makes an advance payment on the claim. In pseudo-factoring or *recourse factoring*, the factor is involved more as a collection office. Insofar as he does not take over the commercial risk, he is in the strict sense not a purchaser of the claims, but merely the administrator. In Switzerland, recourse factoring is seldom practised, and is replaced by accounts receivable financing through banks.

Exhibit 401: Distinctions between accounts receivable financing and export factoring

Accounts receivable financing	Export factoring
1. Assignment of accounts receivable to the bank as security.	1. Sale of accounts receivable to the factoring company.
2. Advance payment of foreign accounts receivable up to 70%.	2. Purchase of 80% or more of the invoice value. The balance is paid later to the supplier after deduction of discounts or returns.
3. Often confidential.	3. Only confidential in exceptional cases.
4. The bank's debtor is the exporter.	4. The factoring company's debtor is the purchaser, i.e., the foreign importer.
5. Commercial risk remains with the exporter, as well as transfer and currency risks.	5. Usually purchase of accounts receivable with assumption of commercial risk by the factoring company (often in cooperation with a factoring company in the importer's country). Currency and transfer risks are usually not assumed by the factoring company.
6. Demands, collections, proceedings, etc., carried out by the exporter.	6. Demands, collections, proceedings, etc., carried out by the factoring company.
7. No services rendered by the bank, such as debtor accounting, sales statistics, VAT returns.	7. The factoring company usually supplies a range of services.
8. Often small turnover.	8. Usually large turnover.
9. Sole purpose: financing.	9. Purpose according to interest: financing, undertaking of commercial risk, collection services, statistics, etc. A suitable combination of these elements is possible.
10. Costs: current account interest together with usual commissions.	10. Costs: cost of finance plus a charge for the desired service.

3. Applications of accounts receivable financing and factoring

Accounts receivable financing and factoring are forms of finance tailored to the consumer goods industry. In this industry, where goods are usually of a short-lived nature, suppliers normally grant terms of not more than 30 to 120 days. This is also the usual time span for accounts receivable financing and advance payments in factoring.

Another characteristic of the consumer goods industry is the relatively fixed stock of customers who are supplied at short intervals. New transferable claims on already tried and tested customers, therefore, continually arise. Thus, the granting of credit can become to a certain extent automatic, and this facilitates the transaction. It is not necessary for the borrower and his bank, or factoring client and his factor to negotiate each credit anew; in unchanged circumstances, the supplier is assured of financing.

Accounts receivable financing serves exclusively as a means of financing, while factoring can also serve the broader requirements of a company. In the consumer goods industry, goods are turned over as a rule much faster than in the capital goods industry, with its longer construction periods and more complex products. The administrative cost of accounting and debtor supervision is correspondingly greater in the consumer goods industry. The broad range of services which factoring has to offer is tailored to the requirements of this branch of industry. Where no advance payment is agreed upon, the factor, as collector of the outstanding debts, pays out to the supplier on due date of the claim. Payment is also made after expiry of a certain period, even if the debtor has not yet paid. Within a certain fixed commercial risk limit, the factor thereby guarantees the solvency of the debtor and thus frees the supplier from commercial risk. Failures to pay, which originate in political or other circumstances independent of the buyer, remain uninsured. Factoring further serves to remove from the supplier the cost and trouble of collection involving demands, possible proceedings and in some cases also the keeping of debtor accounts. The aim of factoring is to relieve the supplier of administrative and financial tasks, so that the company can concentrate on selling products.

4. The execution of an accounts receivable financing

In an accounts receivable financing, the supplier assigns his outstanding book debts to the lender, as a rule his house bank, but possibly a finance company. This assignment is carried out for reasons of security and does not constitute a sale of the debts. To be valid it must be made in writing. Exhibit 402 shows an example of a contract of assignment.

Exhibit 402: Accounts receivable financing: contract of assignment

Assignment of Claims

1. The undersigned ....
hereby transfer(s) to Crédit Suisse his/their present and future claims (as shown attached) with all additional and preferential rights in any way connected therewith together with any past, current or future interest.

2. The assignment serves as security for all claims, present or future, which the bank holds against .... irrespective of their legal basis.

3. The undersigned declare(s) that he/they is/are the legal and rightful holder(s) of the claims and warrant(s) that they are valid and fully collectable.

4. The bank hereby acquires all the rights of the assignor. It has the right to but is not obliged to foreclose the claims, collect interest and capital at maturity, and to apply amounts received, after deducting its expenses, if any, to offset the claims. It is also entitled, at its discretion, to grant an extension to the third party. The undersigned will take every measure to protect and maintain the claims for the bank.

5. The undersigned will, on request from the bank, advise the third party of the assignment and instruct him to make all future payments direct to the bank. The bank is entitled itself to notify the third party of the assignment. Should any payments be made to the undersigned relating to the assigned claims, he/they will pass them on the bank without delay.

Place and Date ....

....

The bank will, as far as it is within its power and considered necessary, examine the legal form of the claims and the creditworthiness of the debtor. With claims on small foreign customers, this would be involved and costly, given that an examination is at all possible. Since such unconfirmed claims constitute a very illiquid, i.e., hardly negotiable security, the bank will, above all, carry out a check on the borrower's creditworthiness.

An accounts receivable credit, particularly when secured by foreign claims, demands the same strict requirements on the creditworthiness of the supplier as an unsecured credit. The bank will form an impression by studying the balance sheets and profit and loss accounts, as well as by private discussions with the company's personnel. Furthermore, it will later request that all annual accounts be submitted regularly, and will monitor the general indebtedness of the company. Accounts receivable financing, as a form of export finance, is a credit based on confidence, and is seen by many banks merely as a predominantly makeshift solution.

If the bank's investigations prove positive and a credit limit is granted to the client, then he can draw funds up to this amount against assigned claims at the agreed coverage ratio. The actual size of the credit will not always correspond to the amount of the limit, since the value of the eligible claims varies, particularly if trade is irregular and payments are retarded. Either insufficient claims are available to make assignments up to the limit, or incoming payments reduce the financing requirement of the borrower. Two examples are shown in Exhibits 403 and 404.

Exhibit 403: Accounts receivable credit: insufficient claims

Credit requirements of an assignment according to cyclical sales variations and with incoming payments regularly delayed by three periods.

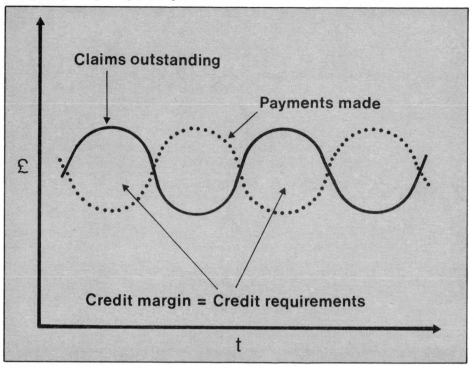

Exhibit 404: Accounts receivable credit: reduced borrower financing requirement

Company with growing turnover and incoming payments regularly delayed by three periods.

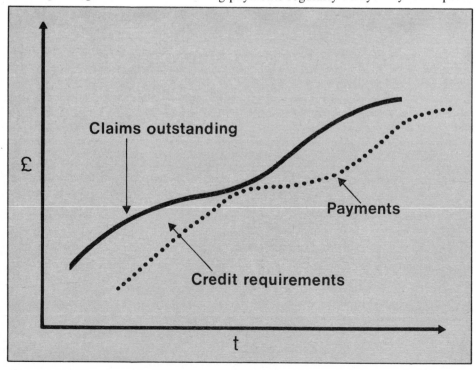

If the borrower wishes to use his credit limit fully, he will assign all new claims to the bank as they arise, and automatically obtain a loan against them. In order to guarantee that the revolving credit functions automatically, all of the buyer's payments will take place through the lending bank. This precaution serves as additional security to the bank to avoid considering already paid bills as eligible claims and advancing against them. The bank, which performs no collecting function in an accounts receivable financing, has no other possibility of reviewing existing claims (see Exhibits 405 and 406).

Exhibit 405: Accounts receivable financing

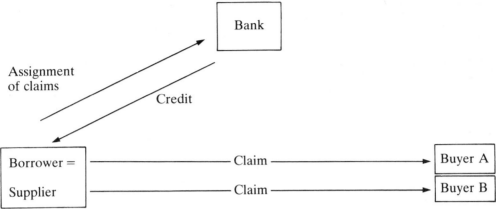

Exhibit 406: Method of payment

Reduction of the assigned claims outstanding and of the credit through payment by the debtor to the bank.

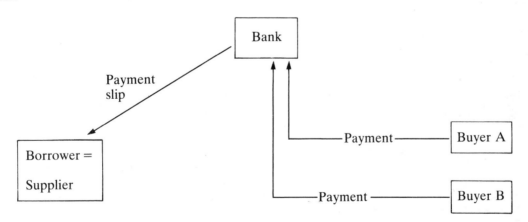

Since individual accounts are frequently not settled, the bank must check the age of assigned claims. It is customary that, in the case of retarded accounts, the borrower will be called upon to increase his cover. The bank will run an exact list of debtors to control the cover position; should the bank's borrower be threatened with bankruptcy, the bank must not delay in notifying the debtors of the assignment of the claim, and advising them of their direct payment obligation to the bank (see Exhibit 407). With notified claims, a payment discharges the debt only when it is made to the new creditor, the assignee. (In Switzerland, however, the notification has to be acknowledged by the debtor.) With unnotified claims, the payment is made in full settlement to the account of the supplier (assignor).

The assignor will continue to carry the assigned claims as assets in his books. More correctly, mention should be made of the assignment by a note on the assets or liabilities side. This is not, however, legally prescribed in all countries. In the case of bankruptcy of the assignor, the bank will secure its claims arising from the accounts receivable financing by showing the assignment to the

Exhibit 407: Notification: accounts receivable financing

We wish to inform you that ....
has assigned to us with all rights the following claim on you

Amount   Date of Invoice   Maturity

....

In your own interest we would like to draw your attention to the
fact that you can only legally make payments arising from the assigned
claim directly to our bank.

We kindly ask you to sign and return to us the enclosed confirmation.
If you should wish to contest the assigned claim in part or in whole
or lodge a counterclaim, please advise us of this at your earliest
convenience.

Yours faithfully,

....

Enclosures: Acknowledgment of the notification.
             Envelope addressed to notifying party (our bank).

bankruptcy office. This applies especially in Switzerland, where as a rule no assignment can be inferred from the asset postings in the balance sheet.

The costs to the borrower of an account receivable financing are usually a function of the degree of use of the credit limit. He does not pay for the arranged maximum credit, but only for credit which is used. Most banks charge a credit commission on the maximum or average balances used over a period of time.

5. Factoring

Factoring developed in the U.S., mainly in connection with the textile industry. Today, suppliers in various branches of the consumer goods industry there, and in other industrial countries, turn to their factor for financing and other services. In a non-binding application for factoring services (see Exhibit 408), the supplier will introduce himself, give the factor information about the size and structure of his turnover, and state the desired factoring services. This application should be accompanied by the latest accounts of the company, and a list of regular customers with names, addresses, bankers and average outstanding invoices. From this information, the factor will assess which services he can offer.

If the examination indicates that the debtors pay regularly and reliably, the factor will be prepared to take over a global assignment of all the claims, or groups of claims restricted to countries or industries. In the general factoring contract, he usually reserves the right, however, to decline individual debtors or currencies at a later date.

The supplier will complete a *notification and transfer of receivables* form for all existing claims, listed individually with name of debtor, invoice value and due date, with copies of invoices attached (see Exhibit 409). With this list of debtors the factor can, when dealing with foreign claims, obtain reinsurance from appropriate foreign factoring partners. The latter will set him individual debtor limits within which they are prepared to guarantee the solvency of the debtor. Covered in this way, the supplier's factoring company can, within the limits, take over the commercial risk in the claims and if demanded, make an advance payment. Should the foreign factor not guarantee individual claims, then the export factor will only arrange collection for his customer.

With the signatures of the supplier, his factor, and those of the foreign importing factor on the transfer of receivables form (see Exhibit 409), the accepted individual claims are sold to the factor and are no longer the supplier's property. They are also no longer booked as assets. Conversely, the supplier has a claim on the factor, payable either at maturity of the claim or before, according to the factoring contract, e.g., after presentation of delivery documents in line with an advance payment.

In *old line factoring*—the most extensive form of factoring—the commercial risk is covered by the factor up to an agreed amount. If an invoice is not paid by the debtor, the loss has to be taken by the factoring company. Funds paid out by the factor in advance or at maturity of the claim are thus at the disposal of the consumer goods company and increase liquidity.

Exhibit 408: Application for factoring (non-binding)

Applicant

Company .... Tel ....

Address .... Telex ....

Person to contact ....

Industry ....

Legal status .... Share capital ....

Date of formation .... Commercial register ....

Bankers ....

Details of turnover:

	Switzerland	Abroad (by country)
Total in previous year:	Fr	....
of which: Industrial	...............................%	...............................%
Wholesalers	...............................%	...............................%
Retailers	...............................%	...............................%
Dept. Stores	...............................%	...............................%
Administration	...............................%	...............................%
No. of invoices	....	....
Average debtor outstandings	....	....
Debtor losses in last three years	....	....
Conditions of payment	....	....

Services requested

Collection etc.

Commercial risk undertaking	yes/no	yes/no
Advance payment	yes/no	yes/no

Desired limit ....

Remarks ....

Date .... Signature ....

Please send together with the last two balance sheets and a list of customers (name, address, bankers, prospective maximum invoices outstanding per customer) to CS Factoring Ltd., P.O. Box, 8021 Zurich.

Exhibit 409: Notification and transfer of receivables

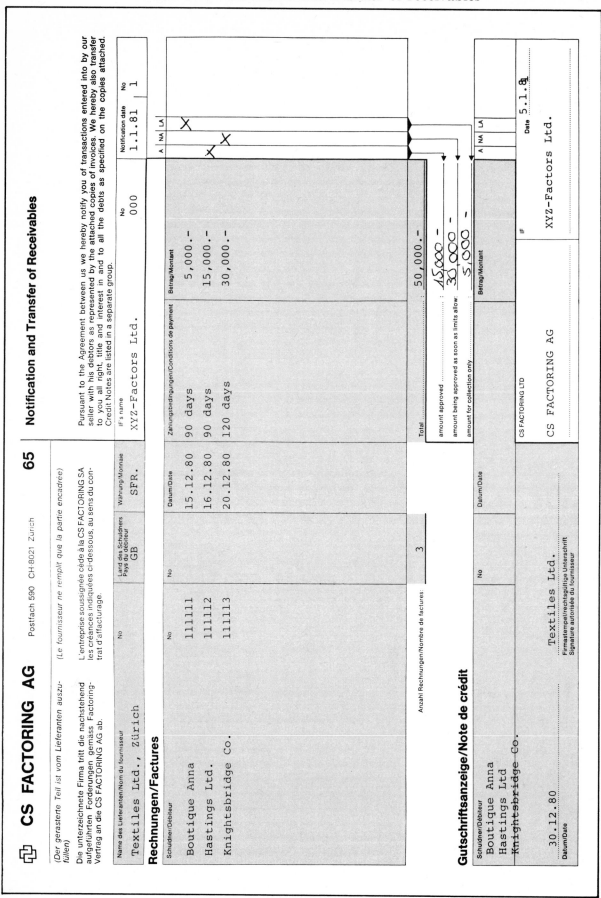

CS FACTORING AG
Postfach 590 CH-8021 Zürich **65**

Notification and Transfer of Receivables

(Der gerasterte Teil ist vom Lieferanten auszu-füllen)
(Le fournisseur ne remplit que la partie encadrée)

Die unterzeichnete Firma tritt die nachstehend aufgeführten Forderungen gemäss Factoring-Vertrag an die CS FACTORING AG ab.

L'entreprise soussignée cède à la CS FACTORING SA les créances indiquées ci-dessous, au sens du con-trat d'affacturage.

Pursuant to the Agreement between us we hereby notify you of transactions entered into by our seller with his debtors as represented by the attached copies of invoices. We hereby also transfer to you all right, title and interest in and to all the debts as specified on the copies attached. Credit Notes are listed in a separate group.

Name des Lieferanten/Nom du fournisseur		IF's name	No	Notification date	No
Textiles Ltd., Zürich		XYZ-Factors Ltd.	000	1.1.81	1

	Land des Schuldners Pays du débiteur	Währung/Monnaie				A	NA	LA
	GB	SFR.				X		

Rechnungen/Factures

Schuldner/Débiteur	No	Datum/Date	Zahlungsbedingungen/Conditions de payment	Betrag/Montant	A	NA	LA
Boutique Anna	111111	15.12.80	90 days	5,000.–		X	
Hastings Ltd.	111112	16.12.80	90 days	15,000.–			X
Knightsbridge Co.	111113	20.12.80	120 days	30,000.–			

Anzahl Rechnungen/Nombre de factures: **3**

		Total	50,000.–

amount approved 15,000.–
amount being approved as soon as limits allow. 30,000.–
amount for collection only 5,000.–

Gutschriftsanzeige/Note de crédit

Schuldner/Débiteur	No	Datum/Date		Betrag/Montant
Boutique Anna				
Hastings Ltd				
Knightsbridge Co.				

30.12.80	Textiles Ltd.		IF	XYZ-Factors Ltd.
Datum/Date	Firmastempel/rechtsgültige Unterschrift Signature autorisée du fournisseur			

CS FACTORING LTD

CS FACTORING AG

Date 5.1.81

The debt can only be taken over in so far as the claim is unprotested; the performance risk is not taken over. With protested claims, the factor suspends his commercial risk cover and returns the claims to the supplier to settle the dispute. If the problem is solved, then the factor assumes liability for payment backdated to the date guaranteed by him.

To enable the factor to carry out his collecting function, the debtor must be notified of the assignment. The supplier puts a special note on his invoices in the form of a stamp or sticker supplied by the factor. If a foreign factor takes over the collection in the country of the debtor, a corresponding note is made on the invoice. Exhibit 410 gives an example of this.

Exhibit 410: Note regarding assignment and payment

This account has been assigned to XYZ Factors Limited
and is to be paid to them at ABC Street, London, by
cheque or bankers draft in the currency of the invoice
in favour of:

CS Factoring AG, Zurich
....

XYZ Factors Limited alone is entitled to give a receipt
for payment and should be advised immediately of any
claims or disputes.

When a foreign factor is employed, to whom the debtor invoices are payable, the supplier has no direct contractual relationship with this import factor. The export factor has sole liability. It is, therefore, essential for the export factor to deal only with reliable and experienced import factors, since their guarantee to himself is only worth as much as their company. Internationally active factoring companies have formed themselves into groups for reasons of security and confidence. These groups usually encompass factoring companies in all industrial countries. When comparing different factoring companies, it is important for the supplier to know whether they serve his sales territories by reason of their membership of these groups.

As in all export business, there are various risks in factoring. The commercial risk cannot be excluded completely, but can be kept very small for the export factor by his checking the factoring partner in the debtor's country, and his guarantee performance. It is a different matter with the transfer and political risks of the debtor country. Protection against these risks cannot be guaranteed by the import factor. The export factor does not usually take on these risks, either, but the exporter can be insured against them through government export schemes or private insurance companies in many countries.

The commercial risk involves the export factor taking up to 100% of the commercial limit allowed him. Other credit insurances seldom cover this risk to such an extent. Since their costs climb progressively with the degree of cover, they are usually more expensive than factoring for a corresponding risk insurance. Additionally, with maturity factoring, the factors become liable for the debt payment at a specific time after maturity (usually 120 days) without demanding from the assignor proof of non-payment by the debtor, as credit insurers do before every payout. In some circumstances, it can take years before such evidence can be produced to the insurance company.

The supplier receives his payment still faster in a cash sale of claims to the factor. The percentage size of the factor's payout, which usually amounts to between 70 and 95%, depends on the size of allowances such as discounts, price reductions, etc; the balance is placed on a creditor account. Since the supplier must refund this money to the factor, insofar as it exceeds the debtor's liability, an excessive payout would entail unnecessary additional expenses.

Alongside the percentage limit, the factor will fix a limit for the supplier, up to which he will pay out against the aggregate of invoices presented and assigned him. The size of this limit relates to the turnover and balance sheet ratios of the supplier. A purchase of invoices which exceeds the balance sheet worth of the supplier is only possible when the debtor gives an unconditional promise to pay, and is considered good for the amount owing. Payout takes place within the fixed limits according to the supplier's requirements, and charges are made, as with accounts receivable financing, in line with usual bank overdraft rates on the amounts used.

The remaining costs of factoring depend on the services supplied by the factor. He will fix a factoring charge, corresponding to his average effective costs for administering the claims, i.e., book-keeping, supervision, monitoring and collection, as well as possibly a commercial risk premium. Depending on the volume of turnover, number of invoices, payments and receipts in the year, as well as the number and soundness of the customers, the factoring client will have to pay between 1 and 2% of the invoice value in charges.

6. The benefits of factoring and accounts receivable financing

The main duty of all company management is to maintain financial balance. Maintaining liquidity is an essential problem of every organization and must rank high in company policy. Expanding organizations are especially prone to fall into financial straits. Increased turnover usually requires an increased means of financing liquid assets. With investments, not only does demand for long-term financing increase, but usually more short-term capital also becomes necessary.

When a new or previously small company expands its sales, its ability to attract funds in the form of conventional credit does not always increase accordingly. If expansion occurs during a period of high inflation, supplier's prices may rise while debtors insist upon longer payment terms and thus endanger the liquidity of the company. In such cases, accounts receivable financing and factoring prove to be ideal aids.

The case of a U.S. toy producer has become a famous instance of this. During the hulahoop craze, the monthly sales of this firm increased from $25,000 to $1 million in less than 60 days. After studying the available accounts, no traditional lender would increase its involvement in line with the firm's requirements. The avalanche of incoming orders created many administrative problems to add to the problems of financing. A contract with a factoring company supplied the solution and allowed a healthy expansion. Despite the death of the hulahoop craze, the firm achieved a turnover of $27 million in 1978.

Such extreme cases are not needed to illustrate the benefits of accounts receivable financing and factoring. By receiving sufficient financing, many companies gain the advantages of paying their suppliers at a discount, and negotiating better prices with their suppliers, thanks to increased orders. On the distribution side, the possibility of granting payment terms to customers ensures better market prospects.

Where the assignment of claims is not to be made known to the customers, and the financing requirement is not too high, the supplier will choose accounts receivable financing. Should he want to exploit his financing possibilities to the maximum through assignment of claims, then he will decide on advance payments in factoring.

Factoring is also the ideal solution if he wishes to relieve his organization of debtor book-keeping and demands and collections. Collections alone from debtors resident abroad can involve considerable expenditure, and this makes a factoring contract worthwhile. The debtor's paying often improves when a local collector appointed by the export factor insists on punctual payment. For the supplier, it means that capital is tied up in outstanding debts for shorter periods of time, and interest costs are lower. Finally, the insurance of commercial risks provides an additional argument for factoring.

Accounts receivable financing and factoring offer a solution for medium-sized companies suffering from continuous reduction of capital and reserves and looking for new methods of financing. They are not a global means to entrepreneurial success, especially not for badly managed companies with sub-standard products. Only a good product finds buyers, and only good company management can guarantee that higher profits will be achieved as a result of increasing turnover. Accounts receivable financing and factoring both demand a good product, trustworthy management and a good clientele. Then, they become an excellent aid for the consumer goods industry.

CHAPTER FIVE
Financing trade in capital goods

Robert H. Miller

1. Introduction

Export financing of capital or investment goods differs from that of consumer goods (see Chapter IV) principally in the credit periods involved. Although it is conceivable that capital goods are sold on cash or near cash terms, for the purposes of the following discussion it will be assumed that credit periods encountered in such financings are either medium term (up to five years) or long term (five to 10 years). Credit periods in excess of 10 years are also possible in the field of large projects, but usually only with government participation or guarantees from first-class multinational companies.

2. Considerations

In today's highly competitive world of international trade in capital goods, consideration of price, technical specification and delivery are not always the deciding factors of an export sales contract. Confronted by two basically equivalent products from different countries, the prospective buyer can be expected to make his choice in favour of the exporter who is in a position to offer the most attractive repayment terms. This is because, by their very nature, capital goods are products which will produce income for the buyer throughout their useful lifetime. As their cost would often involve an appreciable capital outlay for the buyer, were he to pay for the goods in cash or near cash terms, it is in the purchaser's interest to be in a position to use the cash-flow generated by the object to repay the seller over the longest period possible. On the other hand, the risks of deferred payment are potential problem areas for the exporter, not only because of the appreciable sums of money which are invested in the production of capital goods, but also because the buyer, and after shipment, the goods themselves, are situated in another country. Domestic sales of capital goods are usually also financed by the seller, possibly by his bank, or either by the buyer or his bank. We shall not examine this question further, but merely conclude that domestic sales are somewhat simpler and less risky than international trade. The period over which repayments by the importer are planned, means that the exporter who finances his export sale by himself can have vast amounts of money tied up for periods of up to five years and beyond. The need, both from the exporter's and the importer's point of view, for competitive forms of export finance, cannot be disputed.

Capital goods exports can, of course, be paid for by cash or financed by the buyer by means of buyer credits (see Chapter VI). In this chapter, we will concern ourselves mainly with the financing for the exporter.

3. Forms of export finance

Such forms of export finance can be grouped in three categories.

    i. First, those forms of export finance where the exporter bears all of the risk himself:
        — foreign currency credits;
        — secured bank overdrafts;
        — the discount of trade receivables in either the exporter's own currency or in foreign currencies.
    ii. Second, those which require a risk participation by the exporter:
        — state controlled export guarantee schemes; and
        — credit insurance.
    iii. Third, those forms of export finance which permit the exporter to pass on all the risks of exporting to the financing institution or bank, among them:
        — confirming house facilities;
        — buyer credits;
        — export leasing;
        — forfaiting.

Exhibit 501: World trade, 1965–79 (value of total exports in U.S.$ billion)

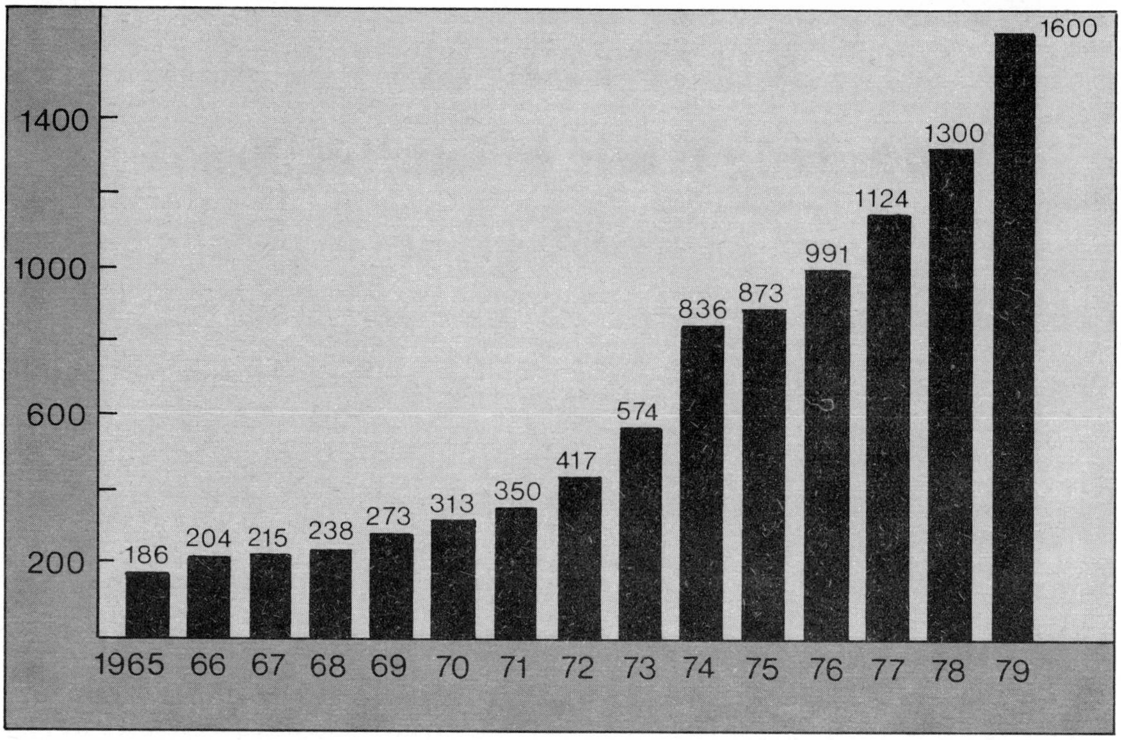

Source: GATT annual reports.

Each of these three categories will be examined in turn below. First, it is necessary to consider the risks inherent in any export sale, where the seller extends credit to the buyer.

4. Risks

4.1. Production risk

From the moment an exporter accepts an order, and more important, commits part of his production to the fulfilment of that order, sometimes for months or even years, he runs the risk of breach of contract prior to completion, owing either to a cancellation by the prospective buyer, or to non-performance by a sub-contractor who produces a component of the product. The exporter will then be confronted with the problem of disposing of the cancelled item. In cases where the product is standard, such as with cranes, trucks or certain earth-moving equipment, a cancelled order should not present a major difficulty. However, with important orders of a more custom-built nature, such as with machinery designed to do a specific job, (e.g., computers), cancellation may result in a potential capital loss of appreciable size for the exporter. We shall see later that the exporter can insure against this risk, but will have to bear a percentage of any loss resulting from the resale of the object.

4.2. Commercial or delcredere risk

We have seen that capital goods require, by their very nature, credit periods which are qualified as medium or long term. The buyer's ability to pay over such periods must, therefore, be a prime consideration in an exporter's decision to extend credit. This decision is often made more difficult by differing accounting principles in various countries which often render almost meaningless an examination of the buyer's accounts/balance sheet. This risk may be compounded by the passage of time where circumstances, unforeseen at the outset, can fundamentally alter the creditworthiness of the buyer. An exporter, when in doubt, should request the buyer to provide a local bank guarantee—a common requirement of state credit insurers and banks providing export finance. Certain government credit insurers, such as the Swiss ERG will not cover the commercial risk for private buyers, rendering the provision of a bank guarantee all the more essential. Country risk is made up of both the political and transfer risks.

84

4.3. Political risk

Having resolved the problem of the commercial risk and assured himself of the buyer's willingness and ability to pay, an exporter must consider the political situation of the country to which he plans to export. He must determine whether there may be any reason for payment being withheld for political reasons. The assessment of the political risk has become, over the past few years, more and more difficult owing to a polarization of East–West relations over the industrialized world's total dependence on energy from oil. Long-term projections have proved to be hazardous.

4.4. Transfer risk

An exporter must face the risk of the central bank in the importer's country being unwilling, or unable, to make freely convertible foreign exchange available for the importer to service his debt. Payment in an unconvertible local currency is of no use to the exporter; payment in a currency other than the agreed currency of invoice can create problems for the exporter who may be financing the transaction, for example, on an overdraft basis in his domestic currency.

4.5. Currency risk

Whenever the exporter invoices his buyer in a currency not that of his own country, he runs the risk of the currency of invoice depreciating against the domestic currency. When he converts the repayment instalments, they may be worth much less to him than he expected when signing the sales contract.

The various possibilities available for the financing of trade in capital goods, bearing in mind in each case an apportionment of the risks involved between exporter, financing institution or government export credit guarantee department, are discussed below.

5. Financing with full recourse to the exporter

Situations may arise where the exporter is unwilling or unable to obtain cover from a government export-credit facility or from private-sector credit insurance. At the same time, the avenues of fully non-recourse financing might be closed to him. The decision, then, to use a form of finance which allows the financing institution full recourse against him may result from two considerations. Either the exporter feels confident that there is virtually no risk of non-payment (such as when a multi-national company exports to one of its foreign subsidiaries), or cover for that particular country is not available. The following are some of the possibilities open to him, but in each case the financing institutions retain full recourse against the exporter.

5.1. Secured bank overdraft

This form of finance is not really suited for the financing of export sales with long credit periods, since theoretically bank overdrafts are repayable on demand. However, when overdraft financing is used, banks will often require security for lending, and the exporter will have to assign to the bank either all his rights under a particular export transaction; or, in the case of credit given by the exporter to the importer against the importer's bills of exchange, be it promissory notes or accepted drafts, he will have to assign those documents. If the exporter has a government export-credit policy, this can sometimes be assigned to the financing institutions (see also Chapter IV).

5.2. Discount and negotiation of trade bills and drafts

Unlike forfaiting (see Chapter VIII), where the exporter can sell his trade bills to a financing institution without recourse to himself, bill discounting and negotiating facilities are with recourse to the exporter. In the case of discount, the bank purchases for cash from the exporter the notes or bills of the importer. When bills are negotiated, advances are made against the notes or bills to a percentage of their face value. In both cases, the bank retains the right of recourse against the exporter, in the event that the bills be dishonoured at maturity. Although such discounting and negotiating facilities are usually short term, they also apply to medium-term maturities.

There are two financing techniques, both arranged by banks with full recourse to the exporter, which serve to cover the currency risk for the exporter. The first of these does not represent a provision of finance, but rather a method of avoiding the risk.

5.3. Forward foreign exchange sale

Whenever the exporter invoices in a currency other than his own, he runs the risk of a devaluation in the currency of credit against the domestic currency, with a resulting shortfall in the amount expected in repayment after conversion. To avoid this, the exporter can usually arrange with his bank to sell his foreign currency receipts forward against his own currency.

If it is possible to determine the exact maturity of a future repayment from the buyer, his bank will be able to fix a rate, either higher or lower than the spot rate, at which it will purchase his foreign currency receipts at maturity. If the exact maturity date is not known, the exporter can take out an option contract entitling him to sell the foreign currency receipt at the agreed rate, but within a fixed period of time. It is also possible to roll over an outright forward contract.

From the bank's point of view, in either case, the risk lies in the exporter's ability to deliver the foreign currency in fulfilment of the contract within the agreed time frame. Should the expected repayment not materialize at the agreed maturity, the exporter will have to purchase foreign currency in the market for delivery to the bank with whom he has concluded the forward contract.

Although there is not a forward market for all currencies, most major currencies can be covered by forward sale for periods of up to five years. The cost of forward cover is determined by the interest rate differential between the exporter's domestic currency and the currency of invoice. The latter can be either at a premium or at a discount in relation to the exporter's own.

5.4. Foreign currency credits

Another means of avoiding the currency risk is for the exporter to finance the credit which he is effectively giving his buyer through a foreign currency loan. He will thus be able to match the instalments owed to the financing bank with the repayments expected from the foreign buyer. The interest rate differential between the rate at which he can obtain the credit and the rate at which he could obtain an equivalent credit in domestic currency represents an opportunity cost. In some countries where exchange control exists, such credits need to have the approval of the authorities. Very often, in such cases, authorization can be obtained for exporters to maintain balances in foreign currency receipts. which will be set off against outgoings in the same currency, so enabling the exporter to pay foreign suppliers without having to go through the foreign exchange markets.

6. Risk participation by the exporter

6.1. Government export credit guarantee schemes

It is not the intention of this section to examine in detail the different national export credit guarantee programmes. There are, however, common factors which can be discussed.

Under government export credit guarantee schemes, credit is usually provided by commercial financial institutions of the exporter's country up to a large percentage of the total purchase price of the exported goods. Access to such financing, which in many countries is at subsidized rates of interest, is through guarantees of the government export credit guarantee department of the country of export. Such guarantees normally cover 95% of the political risk, and 85–95% of the commercial risk.

The similarities between the various government export credit guarantee schemes of the countries of Western Europe reflect the worldwide desire to standardize export credit support with a view to limiting the degree of interest rate subsidy, the maximum length of credit and the minimum down-payment requirements. However, there are countries which do not give interest rate subsidies, as in the case of Germany and Switzerland. In such countries, the level of interest rates applied to export credits may be lower than in those countries where there is a subsidy. Exhibit 502 sets out these international consensus guidelines.

In most countries, the mechanism for providing support is split between:
— an official guaranteeing institution providing cover for a large percentage of the commercial, political and transfer risks;
— the financing institutions, either commercial banks or official institutions, which extend credit at subsidized rates of interest. The commercial banks can then go back to the guaranteeing institution to make up the interest rate differential between their cost of funding at market rates and the rate at which credit was extended. Such subsidized finance is usually only available for transactions covered by the official guarantee.

Exhibit 503 (on p. 88) sets out the parameters of government export credit in the countries of Western Europe. Government-supported finance can take the form of both buyer and supplier credit. For large contracts with long construction periods, the exporter can often arrange cover for a

Exhibit 502: International consensus guidelines on interest rates

	Min. down-payment	Min. interest rates for credit up to five years	Min. interest rates for credit over five years	Max. credit period
	%	%	%	%
Low-income countries	15	$7\frac{1}{2}$	$7\frac{3}{4}$	10
Middle-income countries	15	8	$8\frac{1}{2}$	$8\frac{1}{2}$
High-income countries	15	$8\frac{1}{2}$	$8\frac{3}{4}$	8

percentage of an increase in his production costs. Most government support schemes also provide for the issue of performance bonds and for foreign currency cover.

6.1.1. Advantages
The advantages for the exporter of obtaining finance for capital goods exports through a government export credit guarantee facility may be summarized as follows:
— The guarantee of payment should the buyer become insolvent or should payment be withheld for political or transfer considerations.
— Finance at interest rates which are below prevailing market rates and which are fixed for the duration.
— The possibility of raising finance for periods in excess of that which financing institutions would normally be prepared to offer, in the absence of a guarantee.
— The availability of cover for difficult markets.
— Assurance of finance, where basic cover is available.
— Ancillary services such as performance bonds, etc. (see Chapter X).

6.1.2. Disadvantages
On the other hand, the potential disadvantages of such financing are:
— The risk retention aspect, a percentage of which is borne by the exporter, may vary according to the particular national export guarantee scheme.
— Claims are paid only after a certain period (usually six months) after a default, during which time the exporter may be incurring heavy interest costs.
— The fact that in the event of default, the exporter may be required to involve himself directly in the recovery of the amounts outstanding.
— The procedure for arranging cover is often cumbersome and time-consuming, involving much form-filling and documentation.
Exporters can arrange for government export credit guarantee cover either directly with the local office of their government agency, or with the help of credit insurance brokers.

6.2. Private sector credit insurance

Private sector credit insurance for export transactions is provided throughout the world by a number of specialized institutions who, however, underwrite only the risk of buyer insolvency or protracted default. This means that the exporter must bear any loss resulting from political or transfer considerations. Furthermore, in the event of a claim under the insurance policy, the exporter is usually expected to carry a certain percentage of the initial loss himself. This percentage varies from country to country according to local practices. Compensation is usually paid only when the insolvency of the buyer has been officially established in a court of law. Because no cover is offered for the political risk, exporters rarely use private sector credit insurance to cover their exports to the more exotic countries.

The advantages to the exporter are mainly those of flexibility. Unlike most government export credit guarantee facilities, where the exporter must insure his whole export turnover on a comprehensive basis and take out specific cover where necessary, private sector credit insurance allows the exporter to be selective, and insure either isolated contracts or his whole export turnover. The disadvantages lie in the risks which private sector cover insurance does not cover. However, the effects of those risks are minimized by the comparative better quality of country risk associated with cover of this nature.

Exhibit 503: Comparison of European export credit guarantee facilities

Country	Max. term in years	Interest rates (%)	Guarantor	Insurance cover†	Fees (%) Commitment	Fees (%) Management
Austria	8	$7\frac{1}{4}$–$7\frac{7}{8}$	Oesterreichische Kontrollbank AG	C 100% P 100%	0·4 p.a.	0·5 flat
Belgium	10	$7\frac{1}{2}$–$8\frac{3}{4}$	Office National du Ducroire (OND)	C 90–95% P 95%	0·2 p.a.	1 flat
France	10	$7\frac{1}{2}$–$8\frac{3}{4}$	Compagnie Française d'Assurance pour le Commerce Extérieur (COFACE)	C 95% buyer P 95% buyer C 85% supplier P 90% supplier	0·3 p.a. min.	0·3 flat min.
Germany	no max. term	as defined in the AKA credit lines*	Hermes Credit Insurance	C 95% buyer P 95% buyer C 85% supplier P 90% supplier	0·5 p.a.	0·5 flat
Great Britain	10	$7\frac{1}{2}$–$8\frac{3}{4}$	Export Credit Guarantee Department (ECGD)			0.75 flat
Italy	10	$7\frac{1}{2}$–$8\frac{3}{4}$ Eurocur. 8·6–9.35 Lire	Sezione Speciale per l'Assicurazione del Credito all'Esportazione (SACE)	C 100% buyer P 100% buyer C 90% supplier P 90% supplier	0·5 p.a.	variable
The Netherlands	10	$10\frac{1}{2}$–$11\frac{1}{2}$	Nederlandsche Credietverzekering Maatschappij NV (NCM)	C 90% P 90%	1·0 p.a.	0·5 flat
Norway	10	$7\frac{1}{2}$–$8\frac{3}{4}$	Garanti-Instituttet for Eksporkreditt	C 90% P 90%		1.3 flat
Spain	5	$7\frac{1}{2}$–$8\frac{3}{4}$	Compania Espanola de Seguros de Credito a la Exportacion (CESCE)	C 90% P 95%		—
Sweden	10	$7\frac{3}{4}$–9 Eurocur. $8\frac{1}{4}$–$9\frac{1}{2}$ Swkr	Exportkreditnämden	C 90% P 95%	0·1 p.a.	0·5 flat
Switzerland	10	$6\frac{3}{4}$–$7\frac{1}{4}$ for Swfr up to 5 yrs.	If buyer public entity: Geschäftsstelle für die Exportrisikogarantie (ERG) (If buyer privately owned: P 0%, C is private insurance company.)	C 90% P 90%	handling 0.75 p.a.	—

* "A" line $9\frac{3}{4}$% p.a. fixed rate for up to 10 years.
"B" line 9% p.a. fixed rate for up to 2 years.
"C" line $9\frac{3}{4}$% p.a. fixed rate for up to 10 years.
† C = commercial risks.
P = political risks.

88

7. Export finance without risk for the exporter

There are a number of ways in which banks or financing institutions take over from the exporter the commercial or delcredere risk, as well as the political, transfer and currency risks. These forms of export finance also remove the need for the exporter to himself administer the credit, something he would have to do were he to finance his export sales in another manner. All the following export finance techniques have the advantage of allowing the exporter to negotiate a straightforward credit sale and convert it into a (for him) risk-free cash sale.

7.1. Confirming house facilities

Confirming house facilities, particularly those in London, represent an easy way for the exporter to obtain non-recourse financing. Basically, confirming houses act as agents for foreign buyers, and either:
— *confirm*, as principals, orders placed with the exporter, thereby undertaking to pay him without recourse on evidence of shipment; or
— *merchant* the product for their own account, i.e., purchase the goods from the exporter and sell them abroad.

For the exporter, the result is the same in both cases, since the confirming house takes over the risks of the credit sale and pays the exporter cash. The confirming house, in turn, can insure itself with a government export credit guarantee which will allow it to qualify for subsidized funding, the benefit of which will be passed on to the importer. Thus, the importer benefits from the highly competitive financing costs and from a source of credit which the exporter was perhaps unable, or unwilling, to offer. Confirming house facilities also cover consumer goods sales.

7.2. Buyer credit

Buyer credits quite often run into large amounts. The importer will either ask for credit to be extended by a bank in the exporting country, or the exporter arranges for a bank in his country to extend credit to the prospective buyer for the purchase of the exported goods. Such credits are often covered by government export credit guarantee programmes.

Terms between the bank, the state export credit insurer and the foreign buyer are often negotiated through the exporter. Credits between the exporter's bank and the importer's bank can also be arranged. (See also Chapter VI.)

7.3. Export leasing

The exporter may sell his product to a leasing company for cash. The leasing company will then lease the product to a foreign lessee. As there are numerous legal and practical pitfalls in export leasing, especially concerning the leasing companies' rights of repossession of the leased object in the country of the lessee, unconditional bank guarantees covering the outstanding lease rentals are sometimes requested. Such leases are often of the full payout type. (See also Chapter VII.)

7.4. Forfaiting

Forfaiting (see Chapter VIII) is the sale without recourse by an exporter of trade receivables relating to a capital goods export. Such receivables, which usually take the form of promissory notes or bills of exchange, are medium term in character. The sale is effected by discounting the obligations at a fixed rate. Unconditional and irrevocable bank guarantees, or avals from a bank in the importer's country, are normally required for the financing institution to contain the commercial risk. *Project finance* often takes the form of forfaiting.

8. Cooperation financing

During the past few years, companies throughout the world have signed cooperation agreements (see Chapter I). Purchases of machines and production units have to be financed over the lifetime of a large project, and such financing can be based on a charge on returns from sales of the final product of such projects. Both the importer and the exporter may be liable, in cooperation finance, for the repayment of capital lent by a bank.

CHAPTER SIX
The importer: buyer credits from the Euromarkets

Thomas Teichman

1. Definition and scope

This chapter deals with buyer credits, where the importer (buyer) also acts as *direct borrower* of funds to cover his foreign purchase. Export credit insurance and linked credit at subsidized rates from government export credit agencies such as ECGD in the U.K., Eximbank of the U.S., and ERG in Switzerland are not covered in this section. Provision of finance comes from the *Euromarkets*, the pool of funds outside domestic monetary markets. The provider of credit is normally a bank not involved in the underlying commercial transaction as party to any commercial contract. The exporter or seller has no role in the credit operation apart from acting as, in some cases, an initiator, to find finance for his sale. The buyer acts as a direct borrower from the lending bank or group of lending banks.

2. The source: the pool of funds

Since the early 1960s an important source of finance, the Euromarket, has built up, which is highly flexible, has been consistently liquid and, over the years, has always been available to finance many types of projects and sales of capital goods. In particular, it is an extremely adaptable form of financing for the provision of buyers credits for importers.

Throughout petrodollar and foreign exchange crises the pool of funds has been available at all times. It is estimated that at the end of 1979 total funds in circulation in the Eurocurrency markets were approximately the equivalent of U.S.\$1,100 billion.

3. Size of the market

To illustrate the magnitude and importance of the Eurocurrency lending market, Exhibit 601 shows the estimated total size of the market in medium-term Eurocurrency credits, 1977–80 (first quarter). At least one quarter of the volume of medium-term Eurocurrency credits relate to the financing of sales of capital goods on a buyer credit basis, the remainder being financial credits. This important source of funds provides an ideal method of financing all types of trade and, particularly, large buyer credits where substantial funds are required.

4. Where is the market?

The principal financial centre through which larger Eurocurrency buyer credit transactions have been made over the years has been London. This is partly due to London's fine communication links with the rest of the world, the existence of a well-developed financial infrastructure, and experienced personnel, particularly in the field of international trade financing. However, Eurocurrency buyer credits have been provided (and larger ones syndicated) in other financial centres such as New York, Zurich, Paris, Bahrain and Panama, particularly when the seller or buyer of goods was located in one of those particular areas.

5. What is a buyer credit?

The essential features of a buyer credit are:

5.1. The relationship between the exporter and the importer

The relationship between the exporter and the importer is of a *commercial* nature only, i.e., a commercial contract covering the actual sale of goods.

Exhibit 601: Estimated medium-term Eurocurrency credits, 1977–80

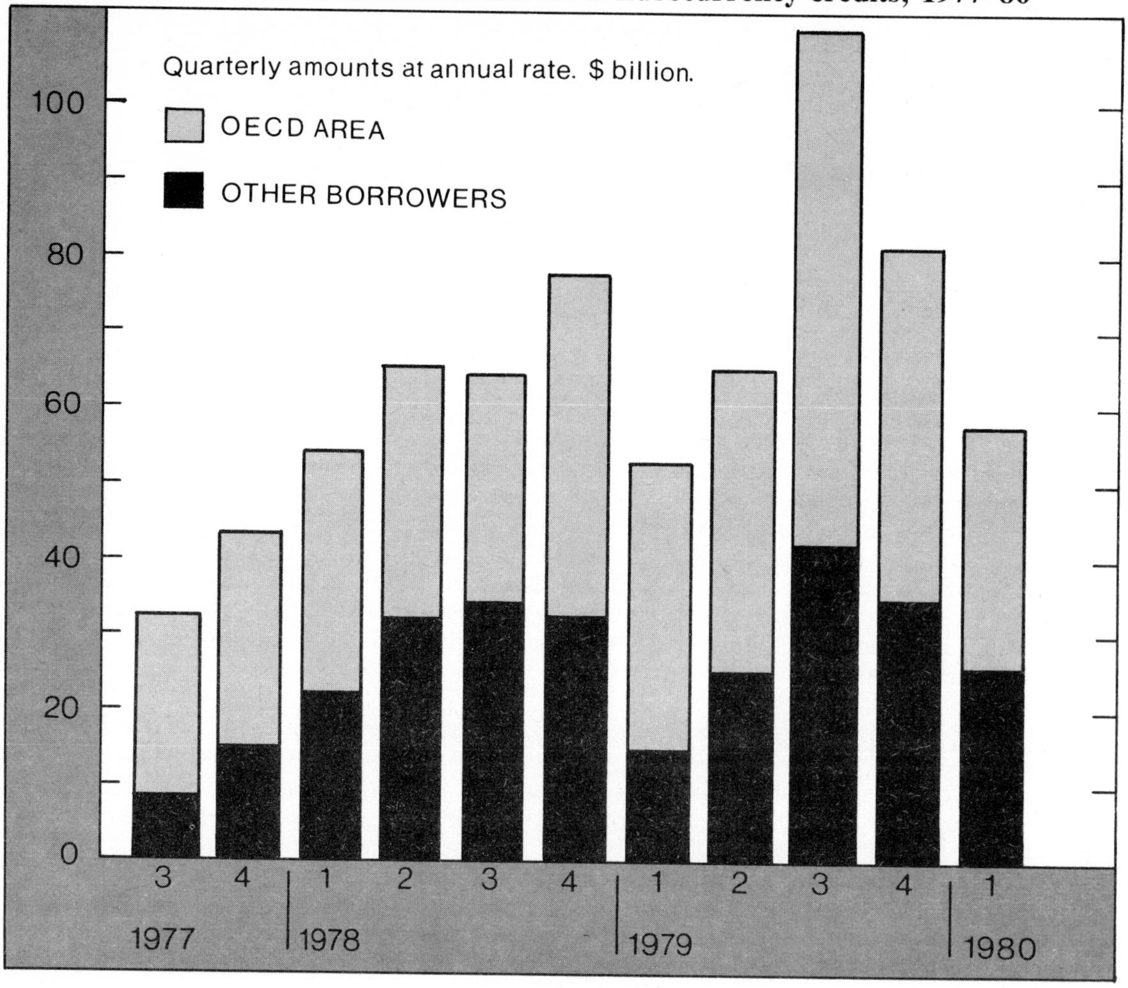

Quarterly amounts at annual rate. $ billion.

□ OECD AREA

■ OTHER BORROWERS

Source: OECD.

5.2. The relationship between the financier and the buyer

The entire *credit* relationship is between the financier (the lending bank) and the buyer of the goods, the importer. The exporter is generally in a non-recourse situation, and once he has shipped his goods the credit relationship is no longer of financial concern to him. If the importer fails to eventually pay, the exporter has received his cash on delivery of his goods from the lenders and is no longer at financial risk. It is up to the banks and the importer to establish their credit relationship *parallel* to the commercial contract.

6. Type of transaction covered by a buyer credit

6.1. Size of transaction

Buyer credits are generally suited to larger financings of capital goods imports as opposed to raw materials, semi-finished or consumer goods. Ideally, buyer credit arrangements cover sales of capital goods with a minimum value of about U.S.$ 1 million or its equivalent in another currency. Smaller transactions are better suited to financing by supplier credits on the basis of promissory notes or bills of exchange which can then either be discounted (see Chapter II) or forfaited (see Chapter VIII), or held by the exporter until maturity for collection (see Chapter II, 4.1.4.3).

Buyer credits can be for very substantial amounts; the main limiting factor to the maximum amount is the creditworthiness of the importer, or the guaranteeing party—in the event that the importer does not have sufficient credit standing on his own to justify the provision of a loan.

The larger buyer credits which have been arranged in recent years have included dam projects, the provision of aluminium or steel smelters or complete steel works in countries as diverse as Brazil, Dubai and Yugoslavia, and the sale of jumbo aircraft and nuclear power plants, where the total amount of the buyer credit can run to U.S.$ 300 million or more, and where the bank syndication system is used.

The amounts of a buyer credit do not have to be round U.S.$ 5 million tranches, but can be for the exact amount of the import contract. Larger syndicated credits are generally, however, for round amounts for the sake of convenience. Buyer credits are often for a larger amount than the actual specific price of the imported equipment, to cover *downpayments*, i.e., the first 5–10% normally payable at contract signature. They can also include a certain portion of funds for *local costs*, say, 10 to 25% of the principal value of the commercial contract, since major projects usually entail substantial local costs. A steel works, for example, requires construction of roads, power plants and similar civil works which can be financed by adding a sufficient amount to the value of the commercial contract, thereby making the whole transaction covering the import, local costs, downpayments and long-term finance, a package deal.

6.2. Syndications

Small buyer credits of, say, U.S.$ 1–5 million, can be provided by a single bank. But much larger amounts of, say, U.S.$ 20 million or more, where even major banks like to limit the extent of their risk to any particular buyer, and in any particular transaction, can be syndicated among a group of banks, but still on a buyer credit basis.

6.3. Currencies

An attractive feature of the buyer credit, which is a result of flexibility of the Euromarket from which it is financed, is that the cedit can be in a number of currencies; it does not necessarily have to be in the currency of the commercial contract, although this is normal. It is, however, open to the importer to, say, purchase his equipment from the United States in U.S. dollars and then to finance the operation in Deutschemarks, French francs or even in a mixture of three to four currencies in a larger buyer credit, to spread his currency risk. It is even possible to arrange buyer credits in parallel with a Eurobond issue in a different currency (see Chapter IX), to cover a portion of the import price.

6.4. Term or maturity

The general term of a buyer credit is not less than three to four years (to finance a crane, textile machinery or similar), and the maximum maturity can be anything up to 16 years (a nuclear power plant, metropolitan subway system or similar) from the time of signature to the time of final repayment, although the norm in the Euromarket would be six to eight years from the time of signature to the time of final repayment of the last instalment of the loan.

7. How is a buyer credit arranged?

7.1. The best source

The best source of funds for a buyer credit, assuming government-subsidized export credits are not available—these are usually the preferred and cheaper form of buyer credit—is generally the exporter's house bank, or a bank which has a close link with the importer and is keen to conclude a credit arrangement with the importer. Thus, the natural first choice for an exporter arranging a buyer credit should be the banker to whom most of his government-backed export finance business would be referred, or with which he has a close all-round relationship. Alternatively importers may have their own special contacts which can be employed; or a blend of both the importer's and exporter's financial contacts can be used, especially if these banks have an intimate knowledge of local financial conditions in the buyer's country.

The types of banks to be approached on these types of operation are varied, but generally can be divided into the following categories:

7.1.1. *Specialist banks*, which play a purely advisory or arranging role. Usually, these would be the merchant banks, the U.K. Accepting Houses, some of which are particularly active in the field of arrangement of buyer credits, or a small number of U.S. investment banks specializing in export finance, usually through their European subsidiaries. These institutions rarely provide substantial amounts of their own funds in the credit.

7.1.2. *Major international banks*, be they North American, Swiss, German or British clearers, who have sufficient technical expertise and size to provide technical advice and substantial finance for a buyer credit operation from their own resources.

7.1.3. A *consortium bank* or smaller commercial bank or other financial institution with a specialized knowledge of, or representation in, the area where the borrower is located, possibly with high-quality local contacts.

7.2. Competitive offers

In the present buyer credit market, it is quite common for the importer or the exporter to approach a selection of banks in the above groups to see what terms they can offer for a buyer credit, particularly if the transaction is for a large amount, and will not only require expertise in trade finance and commercial documentation, but also the knowledge, ability and financial capacity to provide or to syndicate a larger transaction, viz., over U.S.$20–50 million.

7.3. The areas of competition between banks

The following points should be seen as key questions and variables requiring close study by exporters and importers arranging a buyer credit:

— Is a guarantee required or not? Can the bank offer credit without the need for local guarantees or a parent company comfort letter from the importing group?
— Can the lender provide all the funds in-house (preferred), or does he need to syndicate due to lack of financial capacity?
— Can the offer cover downpayments and local costs, as well as the costs of the capital goods?
— How long is the drawdown period?
— What is the margin or spread per annum ($\frac{1}{2}$%–2% p.a.), and commitment fee on the undrawn portion of the loan ($\frac{1}{4}$%–$\frac{3}{4}$% p.a.)?
— What is the final maturity (four to 12 years), and what is the grace period (six months to six years) from signing the buyer credit agreement?
— How large is the prepayment penalty ($\frac{1}{8}$%–1% flat)? (The word *flat* means once payable only, compared with the indication p.a., calculated annually or *pro rata temporis*.)
— What is the agency fee per annum (U.S.$ 5,000 to U.S.$ 50,000, depending on complexity)?
— Is there a limit to the managing bank's expenses? Is it appropriate?
— How complicated and burdensome is the loan documentation? (This varies from bank to bank. Obviously, the simpler the better.)
— What is the governing law and who are the lawyers the banks are proposing to use? Are they experienced in this area of the world? Are they too academic or do they take a practical approach?

7.4. Seeking offers

The information listed in Exhibit 602 is generally required by a bank asked to make a bid to finance a buyer credit.

Exhibit 602: Questionnaire for buyer credits

Amount and currency of export contract?

Amount of downpayments and local costs?

Source of the export goods?

Type of export goods?

Name and domicile of the importer?

Name and domicile of the guarantor (government or bank) if any? If government, which ministry, or will guarantor be the central bank of the importing country?

Desired final maturity and grace period (often related to the commissioning period of the project)?

How *real* is the chance of obtaining the export order (1 in 3, or 1 in 100)?

7.5. The offer telex

7.5.1. The credit without syndication

Once the information shown in Exhibit 602 has been assimilated by a potential lending bank, it will normally send an *in principle* offer to the exporter, setting out terms and conditions. A sample offering telex from the banker to the seller of capital goods for a straight buyer credit *without* syndication is shown in Exhibit 603.

Exhibit 603: Sample offer telex: non-syndicated buyer credit

Further to our recent discussions we are pleased to confirm that we are prepared to provide the following buyer credit facility on the following terms and conditions:

Borrower:	Latin American Steel S.A.
Guarantor:	Latin American Central Bank.
Amount:	U.S.$ 5,000,000.
Purpose:	To finance the purchase of two specialized cranes to be supplied and manufactured by Europe Steel Ltd.
Drawdown period:	12 months from the date of signing of the Loan Agreement.
Final maturity:	Six years from the date of signing of the Loan Agreement.
Grace period:	24 months from the date of signing of the Loan Agreement.
Repayment:	In nine (9) approximately equal semi-annual instalments commencing 24 months from the date of signing of the Loan Agreement.
Voluntary prepayments:	At the Borrower's option, upon at least 30 days prior notice on any interest payment date in a minimum amount of and integral multiples of U.S.$ 1,000,000. Prepayments will be applied against scheduled repayments in inverse order of maturity and a $\frac{1}{4}$% flat penalty assessed on the amount prepaid.
Interest rate:	$1\frac{1}{2}$% per annum (p.a.) over the London Interbank Offered Rate (Libor) as determined by the lender.
Commitment commission:	$\frac{1}{2}$% p.a. on the daily undrawn portion of the commitment from the date of signing of the Loan Agreement until expiry of the drawdown period, payable quarterly in arrears.
Lender:	Prime Eurobank Ltd.
Administration fee:	$\frac{1}{2}$% flat to be paid at signing of the Loan Agreement.
Taxation:	All payments of principal, interest and other amounts payable to the lender in connection with this financing shall be made free and clear of, and without deduction for, any and all present and future taxes, withholdings, duties, charges and other levies of whatsoever nature imposed thereon by the Republic of ___ or any political or taxing authority thereof.
Expenses:	The Borrower will reimburse the lender for all out-of-pocket expenses (including, but not limited to, legal fees) incurred in the negotiation, preparation, maintenance and enforcement of the underlying Loan Agreement upon presentation of a statement of account by the lender.
Documentation:	It would be a condition that the underlying Loan Agreement incorporates clauses currently standard for this type of financing in the international banking markets. Such clauses would include, among others, the following:

        1. Representations and warranties.
        2. Alternative interest rate provisions.
        3. Indemnification against increased costs incurred by the lenders due to changes in law, regulations, etc.
        4. Default, cross-default and *pari passu* provisions (see Exhibit 604).
        5. Conditions precedent to drawing, such as necessary government approvals, legal opinions, etc.
        6. Covenants re. financial information (optional).
        7. *Drawdown only against engineers' Acceptance Certificates.*

Governing law:	The laws of England.

This offer is open for your acceptance for a period of seven days from the date hereof by telex confirmed by letter.

Exhibit 604: Meaning of default, cross-default and *pari passu* provisions

Default:
The default clause gives the lender the right to demand immediate repayment of all amount due (accelerate) if any payment under this loan is not made on time.

Cross-default:
The cross-default clause allows the lender under this loan to accelerate the loan should the borrower not make payment on another obligation that he may have to another lender.

Pari passu provisions:
The *pari passu* provisions are designed to prevent the borrower obtaining credit and giving security of any form to a higher degree than that given to the lender in this particular transaction. The *pari passu* provision ensures that the lender will, during the life of the loan, always be equally secured to other creditors.

Compare with Chapter IX, Exhibit 902 for texts.

7.5.2. The syndicated credit

An example of an offer telex for a syndicated credit to finance an import on a buyer credit basis is shown in Exhibit 605. The key difference between syndicated and non-syndicated offers is that in the syndicated transaction, the financing bank relies on other banks to come into the deal, as the syndicating bank is not willing to provide the whole amount of the operation from its own portfolio, usually for risk considerations. Additionally, the fee structure is somewhat higher, due to the heavy expenses and extra risks involved for a bank arranging such a transaction.

Exhibit 605: Sample offer telex: syndicated buyer credit

Further to our recent telephone discussions we are pleased to confirm that we are prepared to manage the following syndicated loan [*which we will use our best endeavours to complete] on the following terms and conditions [*subject to no material change in market conditions]. (The offer could be a firm underwriting—not on a *best endeavours* basis.)

Borrower:
Aluminium Smelter Corp.

Guarantor:
Ministry of Finance on behalf of the government of Abecazil.

Amount:
U.S.$ 150,000,000.

Purpose:
To provide funds for the purchase of an aluminium smelter from Successful Enterprises Co. Ltd.

Drawdown period:
Four years from the date of signing of the Loan Agreement.

Final maturity:
10 years from the date of signing of the Loan Agreement.

Grace period:
Five years from the date of signing of the Loan Agreement.

Repayment:
In eleven (11) approximately equal semi-annual instalments commencing 60 months from the date of signing of the Loan Agreement.

Voluntary prepayments:
At the Borrowers Option, upon at least 30 days prior notice on any interest payment date in a minimum amount of and integral multiples of U.S.$ 10,000,000. Prepayments will be applied against scheduled repayments in inverse order of maturity and $\frac{1}{8}$% flat penalty assessed on the amount prepaid.

Interest rate:
One per cent (1%) per annum over the London Interbank Offered Rate (Libor) as determined by the Agent, rounded up to the nearest $\frac{1}{8}$% p.a. of the rates quoted by a selected group of prime reference banks.

Cancellation of commitment:
At the option of the borrower at any time during the availability period in the minimum amount and integral multiples of U.S.$ 10,000,000.

Commitment commission:	$\frac{1}{2}\%$ p.a. on the daily undrawn portion of the commitment from the date of signing of the Loan Agreement until expiry of the drawdown period, payable quarterly and in arrears on the date of expiry of the availability period.
Manager:	Efficient Bank, Zurich.
Management fee:	1% flat to be paid at signing of the Loan Agreement. A portion of this fee (to be determined) will be paid by us to other lenders as a participation fee.
Agent:	Efficient Bank, London Branch.
Agency fee:	U.S.$15,000 per annum.
Taxation:	All payments of principal, interest and other amounts payable to the lenders or the Agent in connection with this financing shall be made free and clear of, and without deduction for, any and all present and future taxes, withholdings, duties, charges and other levies of whatsoever nature imposed thereon by the Republic of Abecazil or any political or taxing authority thereof.
Documentation:	It would be a condition that the underlying Loan Agreement incorporates clauses currently standard for this type of financing in the international banking markets. Such clauses would include, among others, the following:

1. Representations and warranties.
2. Alternate interest rate provisions.
3. Indemnification against increased costs incurred by the lenders due to changes in law, regulations, etc.
4. Default, cross-default and *pari passu* provisions.
5. Conditions precedent to drawing such as necessary government approvals, legal opinions, etc.
6. Covenants re. financial information.
7. *Drawdown only against engineers' Acceptance Certificates.*

Governing law:	The laws of England.
English lawyers:	Fast, Simple, Accurate & Co., London.

This offer is open for your acceptance for a period of 30 days from the date hereof by telex confirmed by letter.

* Phrases used when the offer is *not* underwritten by the managing bank or group of managing banks.

7.6. How does the seller get paid?

This is a key question, and it is important that the loan documentation is so worded that the proceeds of the buyer credit can only be used to finance the sale of the company's exports. Thus, the importer/borrower cannot use the funds for any other purpose, for example, to purchase the goods of a competitor. The best way to cover this difficulty is to include in the buyer credit agreement which runs parallel to the commercial contract, a clause which clearly defines a valid claim under the loan agreement. A sample of a typical valid claims clause is shown in Exhibit 606.

Exhibit 606: Form of a valid claim under a buyer credit

From time to time the Supplier may make claims to the lenders in the manner hereinafter specified and (importer) hereby agrees that the claims so made shall constitute Valid Claims by the Supplier against (importer). A Valid Claim shall be made in respect of sums due under Article . . . of the Contract by the submission to the Lenders of a Qualifying Certificate in the form set out in Appendix . . . hereto.

A sample clause from a Eurodollar buyer credit agreement covering the form of a qualifying certificate is given in Exhibit 607.

Exhibit 607: Form of qualifying (acceptance) certificate

CONTRACT

For the supply to Rapid Transit Railway (Importer/Borrower)
    by ABC Ltd. (Supplier)
    of 300 Freezer Railway Wagons

QUALIFYING CERTIFICATE (SERIAL NO. G/)

To: (Lending Bank)

We hereby certify that:

1. The goods as described below have been delivered in accordance with the Contract entered into between (Importer) and ourselves dated .... 1980 to the value shown in the invoices listed below.
2. The figure shown in Column 3 below is the Contract Price of the relevant goods.
3. The sum claimed does not include any amounts which have already been claimed under any other certificate.
4. The amount claimed is not in respect of any matter currently the subject of an accountant's report or of arbitration as specified in paragraphs 12 and 13 respectively of the Buyer Credit Agreement nor to the best of knowledge and belief will it be the subject of such report or arbitration.
We attach hereto
 (a) Certificate of Acceptance (or Engineer's Certificate) as Exhibit "C" to the Contract or Certificate of Completion and Inspection as Exhibit "D" to the Contract.
 (b) Receipt of the Forwarding Agent at FOQ Dunkirk and/or the Storage Receipt as Exhibit "F" to the Contract or Certificate of Storage as Exhibit "E" to the Contract.
 (c) Invoice(s) with two copies. The amount stated in the invoice(s) shall represent the value of the delivered number of sets of Goods at the Contract Price state in Article 2(a) of the Contract.
We request that you pay us the amount claimed below:

1	2	3
Description of Goods	Invoice No.	Contract Price $
		_____
TOTAL		_____

The amount claimed under this Certificate is $ of the amount in total shown in column 3 above.

       Signed ....
       For (Supplier)

       Date ....

7.7. The delivery period

One of the key difficulties in financing projects is the delay between the signing of the first protocol on the intention to conclude a contract, and the conclusion of an actual commercial contract. There is a further time lag from the signature of the loan agreement to the commencement of construction of the machinery to be shipped and its ultimate delivery when final payment for the goods is due. Sometimes 5–10% of the contract value is held back by the buyer for six to 24 months after final delivery pending satisfactory post delivery and running performance of the capital goods.

 The buyer credit is well suited to cover these difficult gaps. First, the period between the signing of a protocol, when the project seems fairly sure to go ahead, and the signing of the commercial contract, can be covered by informal indication of interest from the exporter's bank. This indication will say that the lender will, if the exporter obtains the contract, probably be prepared to provide direct finance to the buyer or to arrange a larger syndicated credit to cover the buyers needs, but without a formal commitment. His proposal would be subject to changes in market conditions.

When the actual commercial contract is signed, it will generally make mention of the buyer credit in one of the clauses of the commercial contract, usually that covering financial arrangements. When the commercial contract is actually signed, and preferably on the same day, the buyer credit agreement should also be signed, formally committing the lending bank(s). From that time, it is normal for the buyer to pay *commitment commission* to the lending bank or group of lending banks for the privilege of the banks allocating resources which commit them firmly to the eventual financing of the sale of the goods on their delivery. A commitment fee is sometimes charged from the date of telex commitment by the lending bank, since conclusion of final loan agreement wording could take many months to complete, and the bank may receive no other reward for its commitment for this time.

Thus, the buyer, as long as he is dealing with high quality lenders, can be certain that he will have sufficient funds to meet his obligations under the commercial contract on delivery. The lending banks can also earn the necessary reward for holding themselves ready to finance the sale of the goods upon delivery, thereby avoiding the temptation to commit funds to other project financings.

Commitment fees (see section 8.4) on the unused portion of a facility vary, and depend on market conditions, but are normally around $\frac{1}{2}\%$ per annum. One of the advantages of the Euromarket is that the commitment period can be long, and has been known to stretch to periods of up to five years, although this would be for major transactions such as nuclear power plants or for integrated suburban subway systems. Generally, delivery period for a U.S.$ 5 million equipment sale would be one to two years, quite an acceptable commitment period for a buyer credit. This presents an advantage over forfaiting or the Eurobond market when financing the sale of capital goods, since the financing can be tied in advance to the delivery of the goods.

8. Costs

There are basically four types of charge involved in the arrangement of a buyer credit.

8.1. Interest rate

The interest rate determines the main cost of a buyer credit. In the Euromarket, the interest rates are determined by demand for, and the supply of, a particular currency for certain maturities of funds at any particular time. Currency is an important determinant of the basic interest rate. Exhibit 608 illustrates some typical interest rates for the six-month Eurocurrency offered rates for the major currencies over recent years.

It can be seen that the interest rates in Deutschemarks or Swiss francs would have provided a much lower cost than borrowings on a buyer credit basis in U.S. dollars or sterling over recent years. However, the relative disadvantages of borrowing in an appreciating currency such as the Deutschemark and the Swiss franc (as they were in the late 1970s) must be considered, for the penalties often outweigh the advantages of benefiting from a low-interest cost.

8.2. Margin or spread

Since banks fund themselves in the Euromarket at roughly the rates set out in Exhibit 608, they must add an increment, known as a margin or spread, to this cost of funds to earn a profit. The spread reflects credit risk in relation to the loan's maturity, scarcity value of loans issued by a particular borrower, a bank's eagerness to bid aggressively to support an exporting client, collateral business possibilities, and other real or subjective influences present in any lending rate pricing decision.

At present, the lowest to highest range of spreads paid on buyer credits on a roll-over basis is $\frac{1}{2}\%$ p.a., up to $1\frac{3}{4}\%$ p.a. for quasi-governmental or private borrowers negotiating buyer credits, depending on the various factors mentioned in the preceding paragraph. Spreads for fixed rate credits are usually somewhat higher since the lenders often assume an interest rate risk in such an arrangement.

8.3. Fixed rate borrowing

Buyer credits in the Euromarkets are not generally provided on a fixed rate basis—one of their serious disadvantages—since lenders are usually not prepared to commit themselves to a fixed rate of interest payable after a delivery date which may be several years ahead, when interest rates may

Exhibit 608: Short-term Eurocurrency interest rates, 1977–80 (Wednesday figures)

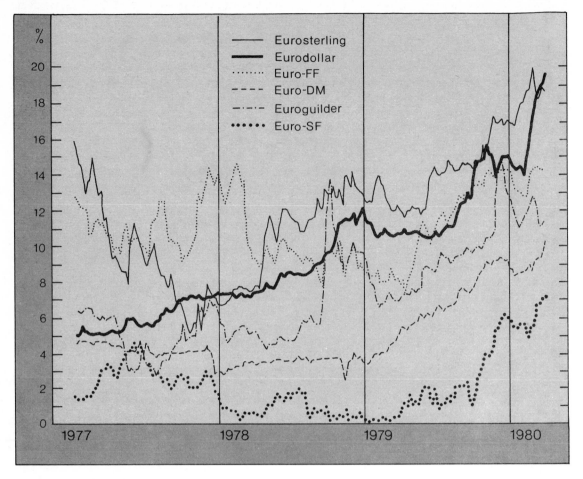

Source: OECD.

be substantially higher. This would produce a loss to the lending bank, if it had committed to a low fixed rate and then had to fund at higher rates at the time of delivery of the goods and actual disbursement of the loan.

8.4. Commitment fee

As already mentioned, a buyer credit with a certain lead time requires a related commitment by a lending bank. Banks will not provide committed finance without the payment of some commission for holding their portfolio available and having to refuse other transactions in the meantime. The commitment fee, therefore, has to be regarded as another cost. Commitment fees are about $\frac{1}{2}\%$ p.a., but on occasions have been known to go down to $\frac{3}{8}\%$ p.a. or up to $\frac{3}{4}\%$ p.a., depending on the particular project, market conditions, the quality of the borrower and the length of the commitment period.

Commitment fees are usually charged from the date of signature of the loan agreement until completion of the drawdown on the amount *undrawn*. The commitment fee is usually payable quarterly or semi-annually in arrears.

8.5. Management fees

A buyer credit is a complex arrangement requiring detailed loan documentation. It is far more complicated than supplier credit and forfaiting. Loan documentation has to be tied in with the commercial contract, involving the lending bank in time consuming work, for which a management fee is usually charged on a buyer credit.

The fee can vary from $\frac{1}{2}\%$ flat up to 2% flat or even more, depending on the complexity of the transaction, the quality of the borrower and the size of the credit. Obviously the larger the credit, the smaller the percentage management fee, since the absolute level of funds paid becomes

100

extremely high on, for example, a U.S.$ 500 million project. But since the amount of work involved for a bank arranging and financing a buyer credit is more or less the same whether the credit is for U.S.$ 1 million or U.S.$ 20 million, the management fee for smaller transactions may seem relatively high, particularly if expressed as a flat amount, reflecting the time spent by the bank arranging the financing.

Syndications of buyer credits also increase their management fees and related out-of-pocket expenses in line with the complexity of the transaction.

9. Calculations: the typical U.S.$ 10 million buyer credit

In summary, the following factors should be taken into consideration when working out the cost of a U.S.$ 10 million buyer credit.

Interest rate:	Floating Libor, usually on a three- or six-month basis plus margin ($\frac{3}{4}$%–$1\frac{3}{4}$% p.a.), payable in arrears on rollover dates (see Exhibit 608).
Commitment fee:	$\frac{1}{2}$% p.a. on undrawn portion of the facility, payable semi-annually in arrears.
Management fee:	$\frac{1}{2}$% flat payable at signing (1% flat, if syndicated).
Agency fee or administration fee:	U.S.$ 2,500 p.a. (U.S.$ 5,000 if syndicated) payable at signing and then annually.
Legal and out-of-pocket expenses:	U.S.$ 5,000 (U.S.$ 15,000 if syndicated) payable within 30 days of signing.

Thus, for a U.S.$ 10 million non-syndicated transaction with a drawdown period of one year, final maturity of six years and a grace period of two years, giving an average life of facility of four years, the interest charge, assuming a 9% Libor average throughout (+1% margin), could be calculated as follows, not taking into account d.c.f. factors:

Commitment fee: ($\frac{1}{2}$% p.a.)	U.S.$ 25,000 (assuming drawdown is gradual and mean delivery period is six months)
Management fee: ($\frac{1}{2}$% flat)	U.S.$ 50,000
Agency fee or administration fee: (U.S.$ 2,500 p.a.)	U.S.$ 6 × 2,500 = U.S.$ 15,000
Legal and other out-of-pocket costs:	U.S.$ 5,000
Total	U.S.$ 95,000

Interest rate (including 1% margin):	10% p.a.
Divide fees and costs over average life of loan (not facility):	$\dfrac{\text{U.S.\$ 95,000}}{3\frac{1}{2} \text{ years}}$ = U.S.$ 27,142·86 = 0·271% p.a.
Therefore, total interest cost:	= 10·271% p.a.

10. Recent developments

The concept of a buyer credit finance from the Euromarkets is now a well-established one. Recent developments include the provisions of a *wider range of currencies* in buyer credits, and the ready availability of a *wider range of banks* to come into financing buyer credits. At one time most of the banks providing funds for any particular export financing operation were in the Euromarket centres, like London or Luxembourg, but today, as projects become larger and more complex, and other financial centres such as Panama, Bahrain, Hong Kong and Singapore have become more active, there has been a tendency to syndicate larger operations among banks located in these financial centres, close to importers. They often have a better knowledge of local conditions and the buyer/borrower.

Another interesting development has been the linking of buyer credits to government-backed export credits, so that such export credits can cover the bulk of the sale of equipment, but the buyer credit from the Euromarket can cover that portion which was perhaps produced in a third country. To complete a whole financial package for an importer, a portion of the downpayments and local costs can also be funded in parallel to a government-backed buyer credit through a Eurocurrency buyer credit.

11. Advantages and disadvantages

11.1. Advantages

Flexibility is the great advantage of buyer credit from the Euromarket, and is reflected in the following:

11.1.1. Currencies
A buyer credit can be made available in any number of currencies: U.S. dollars, pounds sterling, Swiss francs, Deutschemarks, French francs, Canadian dollars, Dutch guilders, Italian lire; in fact, in any currency available in the Euromarket for more than three-month periods.

11.1.2. Term
The period of a Eurobuyer's credit can be from three years up to 10 years and, exceptionally, up to approximately 15 years, depending on the project and, more importantly, the creditworthiness of the buyer and the interest rate margin he is willing to pay.

11.1.3. Possible extended commitment period
The period of commitment in syndicated buyer credits or for straight buyer credits can be long. It can be as short as six months or up to five years. In this respect it is more appropriate to capital goods export financings than are bond issues, private placements or forfaiting. These require relatively quick payout, although a recent development, the deferred payment bond, has stretched the payout period for bond issues to over six months, which could increase their applicability to buyer credits.

11.1.4. Flexible interest rate basis
Buyer credits are usually on a floating rate basis (although they can very occasionally be on a fixed rate basis). Thus, from the point of view of interest rates, there is generally a change every three or six months in the basic interest rate determined by market forces. The spread above the basic interest rate is fixed at the beginning of the transaction and stays constant, but the spread only covers a minor part of the interest cost, the actual funding cost being far more important in determining total interest cost. This variation can be an advantage, if the buyer credit is arranged when interest rates are high. If interest rates subsequently fall the borrower will benefit from the floating rate structure. On the other hand, a floating rate could increase interest costs substantially if there were a sudden rise in rates.

11.1.5. Management fees
As far as fees are concerned, buyer credits are more expensive than forfaiting, where management fees are not usually charged, but far cheaper than bond issues and private placements where the total fee, including management fee, underwriting fee and selling commission can add up to $2\frac{1}{2}\%$ flat, although it is often nearer 2%, depending on currency and market.

11.1.6. Speed
One of the advantages of a buyer credit, particularly if provided by only a single bank, is that it can, under special circumstances, be arranged in a matter of days, although usually the time required is at least two weeks. Larger syndicated credits require a longer time before coming to fruition, generally about two to three months, due to the uncertainties of syndication, complicated loan documentation and, for larger deals, the requirement to issue an information memorandum about the borrower and the project being financed.

There is generally no need for the listing of buyer credit arrangements with any stock exchange, and there is also no *absolute* necessity for the provision of an information memorandum, which is almost always required with a public bond issue and is also sometimes required with a private placement.

For smaller transactions, however, forfaiting would provide an even more rapid form of export financing.

11.1.7. Non-recourse finance
Another advantage for the exporter in a buyer credit arrangement is its non-recourse nature. Since the relationship is between the importer and the lending bank(s), the exporter's credit lines are not affected by the provision of a buyer credit to cover his sales.

102

11.1.8. Continuous nature of the market

An important advantage of buyer credits is that the medium-term bank lending market which provides them, being dependent on floating rate interest structures, tends to operate even in times of turmoil in the capital markets. Thus, whereas in the bond and private placement market there tend to be extremely rapid and unpredictable changes in the investors' appetite for issues of a particular currency or term, the medium-term syndicated or direct buyer credit market has, since the mid-1960s, been consistently available to provide funds for buyer credit operations. In making this statement, it is assumed that the country risk in question is seen as an acceptable one by lending bankers.

Forfaiting has the slight disadvantage of being a rather narrow market, which means that should several tranches of paper covering several export transactions come to the market at the same time, there is an oversupply of paper which may prevent the successful placement of a forfaiting transaction by an exporter. He can, of course, hold the paper until market conditions change in his favour to complete his financing. The medium-term buyer credit market tends to have great depth and it takes unprecedented demands (U.S.$ 200–U.S.$ 1,000 million) for credit for a particular buying country to fully employ its resources to the exclusion of new buyer credits.

11.2. Disadvantages

11.2.1. Use of bank lines

A disadvantage, from the importer's point of view, of buyer credit is that the banks providing the credit will regard his facility as using part of his lending limit for the particular importer/buyer.

11.2.2. Cost

A disadvantage of buyer credits, which are usually at floating rates, is that the cost of interest cannot be determined at the outset as it can be with forfaiting, with the fixed rate bond market or with the private placement market. These instruments, whether issued in New York, London or Zurich, are usually at fixed rates, although floating rating transactions have become more common in the past few years, particularly in the Eurobond market.

For an importer trying to determine the total cost of a project, this can be a serious weakness of the buyer credit.

11.2.3. Laborious documentation

The relationship between the lenders and the borrower in a buyer credit arrangement can be an extremely complex one. If the transaction is syndicated, the complexity is even greater, since the documentation has to cover the role of the agent, the inter-relationship between the lending banks, as well as their direct relationship with the importer or borrower. With forfaiting, such complex documentation problems do not arise.

11.2.4. Size of transaction

Complex buyer credit arrangements are not really suitable for transactions under U.S.$ 1 million. Forfaiting or other forms of supplier credit, where the debt instrument is more likely to be a simple series of bills of exchange or promissory notes, would be far more appropriate.

CHAPTER SEVEN
Leasing

Charles J. Gmür

1. Introduction

Leasing as a means of trade financing is being increasingly stressed by leasing companies operating nationally and internationally. This has come about because producers of capital goods find that the financing assistance they can offer clients helps in the marketing of their products *vis-à-vis* those of their competitors. However, companies with a high technical know-how frequently do not have staff experienced in financial matters. It would, therefore, be a difficult and risky undertaking for them to offer their clients financing by themselves. This is the role for leasing companies.

2. Definitions

2.1. What is leasing?

In a leasing arrangement, an investor (the user) does not buy a product himself, but buys the use of it against payment of a monthly rental fee to a leasing company (the lessor), which owns the product. Leasing substitutes an actual investment by a simple rental relationship over a fixed period of time.

The supplier of the good, i.e., the producer or trader, can be, but does not necessarily have to be, the lessor. In *operating leasing* it will normally be the producer who himself offers his product for lease, together with his technical services and possibly continuous replacement by up-dated products. In *capital leasing*, or *finance leasing*, a triangular relationship is set up between the seller of the article, the buyer who becomes the lessor, and the leasing party, the lessee. It is this kind of leasing which is most commonly discussed in trade financing. It is solely a financial set-up with no technical obligations of the lessor towards the lessee, as in operating leasing.

As an example to explain the three-party relationship, consider company ABC Ltd. which produces a specific machine tool which is of interest to XYZ-Works Ltd. Instead of selling the equipment on credit to XYZ-Works Ltd., who are short of liquid funds, ABC Ltd. will sell the machine tool to a leasing company on a cash basis. This company will lease the equipment to the user of the machine tool, in this instance XYZ-Works Ltd., and be repaid by rental payments, including amortization, interest and a leasing contract fee.

2.2. Domestic leasing

The most common type of leasing is domestic leasing, where the lessor and lessee are domiciled in the same country. It may be a company seeking finance for its investment programme which

Exhibit 701: A leasing relationship

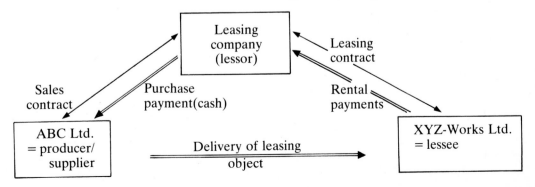

contacts its bankers and is directed by them to a leasing company. Or it may be a seller, using his existing contacts with a leasing company, who initiates a new lease.

Domestic leasing occurs in the *long-life consumer goods* industry as well as in the *capital goods* industry. However, the most commonly leased item is a capital good, which thereby generates an income to pay for itself over its economic life. During the past 10 years, the leasing of *real estate*, mostly factory, service or administration buildings and warehouses, has also become popular. This leasing of immovables is often done in the form of *sale-and-lease-back*. The future lessee constructs the building, sells it to the leasing company and leases it back. In addition to industry and business, *communities* have also started to use leasing for investments. Depending on national legislation, this clientele should become of growing importance in the leasing business.

In Europe, leasing experienced a rapid expansion during the 1970s, particularly during the last three years of the decade. It has found broadest acceptance, however, in the U.S. where between 18 and 20% of investments, including construction, have been financed by leasing. In Europe, the role of leasing is more modest. Whereas in the U.K. leasing is used in about 11% of all domestic investments, continental Europe shows the following estimated percentages: France 9%, West Germany 5%, Switzerland 3–4% and Austria 2–3%.

The high percentage of leasing in the United States is explained by the tax system of the country. *Leveraged capital leasing* makes use of an investment tax credit and involves banks in the leasing business. In leveraged leasing the simple triangular relationship is considerably enlarged. A lease underwriter will initiate and structure the transaction, and the lessee will order the leasing object, leased to him by the owner/lessor. The latter will invest only about 25 to 40% of the cost of the equipment and take up a non-recourse loan for the remaining 60 to 75% from a lender, who will receive in return a charge on both the leasing object and on the rent payments due from the lessee. Since the owner/lessor has all of the tax benefits associated with ownership of the equipment, he can offer his lessee cheaper leasing conditions than his own refinancing costs. Both owner and lender will use trustees, normally commercial banks, as intermediaries. Additional parties in the relationship are the vendor of the equipment and legal counsels to the parties involved. Leveraged leasing allows marginally profitable, capital-intensive companies to enter the capital markets for medium- to long-term, fixed-rate 100% financing at an effective cost well below that which a company would have to pay on a straight-debt issue of similar terms. Attempts have been made to introduce leveraged leasing in a simpler form to the U.K. and Germany, but tax regulations make this kind of domestic leasing less interesting than in the U.S.

2.3. Leasing of international goods

The object to be leased does not necessarily have to be used within national borders. This would be the case, for instance, with means of transport such as containers, trucks, railway carriages, ships and aircraft, but could also occur with construction machinery or, more important nowadays, oil prospect drilling rigs and platforms. This poses an additional risk for the leasing company, who might find it more difficult to establish its rights of ownership in the case of non-fulfilment of the leasing contract by the lessee. However, if the equipment can be internationally registered, as in the case of aeroplanes (in the national air traffic register), or ships (through Lloyds insurance register), such leasing does not pose too many problems.

One common problem is that of owner's liability. If, for example, an aeroplane has been leased, the lessor as owner of the plane could be made responsible for any damages caused by an accident. Imagine the plane crashing on Wall Street, New York. There would be a flood of claims against its owner by individuals, companies, the city and the state. To avoid the accumulation of such risks, the lessor forms individual companies for each item of leased equipment, thereby limiting possible claims to that particular firm. This is already practised in the leasing of aeroplanes, tankers and nuclear power-stations, for example.

2.4. Cross-border leasing

In domestic leasing, at least two parties in the leasing triangle belong to the same country, the lessor and the lessee. However, should a British exporter sell his product to a British leasing company, which then leases the equipment to a foreign lessee, leasing is done across borders: lessor and lessee come from different countries.

Cross-border leasing takes the place of an export transaction. The goods are shipped to the foreign country but remain the property of the domestic leasing company. This creates many legal and tax problems. In most cases, at the end of a leasing period, the equipment is bought by the lessee at a low price. The item is thus finally exported, although it has been in the possession of the importer for some time. The question of when custom duties have to be paid, and on what value, is one of the inherent problems of cross-border leasing. Another one is tax payment. If there are tax agreements between the two countries of the lessor and lessee, the lessor can probably avoid double taxation. Further complications arise in connection with value-added taxes which are deductable within the national tax system but not across borders. Other problems could arise, for instance, out of fiscal schemes for permitted depreciations. The leasing company has to take into consideration all such foreign regulations when calculating its rental fees.

In addition to all these fiscal problems, cross-border leasing may be hampered by legal uncertainties. Will the rights of ownership of the leasing company be honoured in the case of the lessee's default or bankruptcy? Some countries still consider leasing as a special way of purchasing on credit. The leasing company, therefore, would have only the same legal status as other lenders to the company. Moreover, cross-border leasing to socialist countries, though frequently discussed, founders on the regulations governing ownership of the means of production.

Even if all the legal and fiscal problems can be solved, there still remain currency problems. In which currency should the rental payments be effected? If the leasing contract provides for payment in the foreign currency, it is the leasing company which has to cover the currency risk by equivalent refinancing. Then there is the additional risk of interest fluctuations. If the leasing payments are made in the lessor's domestic currency, the lessee runs the risk that his leasing payments might become more expensive following a devaluation of his national currency against the foreign one.

Last but not least, cross-border leasing makes it difficult to monitor the foreign lessee. Before any leasing contract can be signed, a thorough investigation of the foreign customer will be made. And during the leasing period, economic and financial changes in the foreign country should be carefully monitored.

Cross-border leasing incurs large costs and encounters strong competition from local leasing companies, which can operate with all the advantages of the simpler domestic leasing. As a result, there are few cross-border contracts. There is a simpler way to perform an international leasing transaction.

2.5. International leasing

International leasing is leasing used in international trade but is not exactly the same as cross-border leasing. The difficulties inherent in the differing national fiscal and legal systems for lessor and lessee, characteristic of cross-border leasing, are avoided in international leasing. An internationally operating leasing company is a member of an international association of leasing companies, or has its own subsidiaries abroad.

An international leasing arrangement can be initiated by exporter or importer. An importer, for instance, contacts his leasing company which finds, with the help of its foreign associate, an exporter willing to supply the equipment. This exporter might sell the goods directly to the foreign leasing company, or he might sell them to his national leasing company which would then sell them on to its partner company in the lessee's country. Associates in an international chain of leasing companies may arrange with their partners for a commission to be paid for their assistance; but some also cooperate for free.

Within the European Economic Community, legal and fiscal systems will probably converge to a large degree, and encourage the creation of more international leasing companies, with their own subsidiaries in different countries.

3. Application

Leasing requires a contract. The first step towards setting up a contract will be made by:

a. The supplier: he wishes to sell his product and sees in leasing the means of achieving this with more certainty and speed.

b. The lessee: he wants to buy certain equipment and sees in leasing the means to do this with few financial pressures.

c. The bank of the lessee: the former is interested in the commercial success of the latter. Where it considers leasing to be the most advantageous possibility, it will advise the customer accordingly, and put him into contact with a leasing company.

d. The leasing company: it knows the requirements of its customers and keeps in close contact with them.

A leasing company will need to examine the solvency of any future lessee, the reliability of the supplier and the risk on the leased product. The lessee will be asked to fill in a leasing application (see

Exhibit 702). The leasing company will also need to know whether the leased product will help the lessee to increase his cash flow, etc.

Exhibit 702: Application for leasing in Switzerland

Applicant ....
Company ....
Address ....
....Tel. No. ....Telex No. ....
Persons to be contacted ....
Industry ....
Legal status and share capital ....
Commercial register ....
Date of foundation of company ....
Bankers ....
Balance sheets available (for last three years) ....
Do leasing contracts already exist? ....
With whom? ....
Remarks ....

Leasing goods item
Capital goods item to be leased ....
   (Please submit prospectus etc.)
Price ....
Where will the item be placed? ....
Seller ....
Producer ....
Purpose of utilization ....
Date of delivery ....
Insurance covered/not covered ....

Requested leasing duration .... years.......................
Date................................... Signature ....
Please send together with balance sheets and other material to:
                      CS Leasing Ltd.
                      P.O. Box
                      8021 Zurich
                      Switzerland

In the process of investigating the lessee, the leasing company will have to find out whether its customer will be able to make the contractal rental payments. Besides analysing his actual financial situation, it will also make some estimates about his future position. The lessee will, therefore, be asked to submit his balance sheet and his profit and loss accounts for the past three years, in addition to his budget plans for the years to come. He may also be asked whether he has already contracted other leasing arrangements, because in many countries leasing obligations do not show in the balance sheet or profit and loss account. The most advantageous leases are offered when the leased equipment finances itself through its productive use.

The leasing company will also need to have details of the kind of equipment being asked for. Whereas in the English-speaking countries many leasing companies specialize in, and buy, certain products, in continental Europe the goods to be leased are normally not in stock at the leasing company and have to be bought from a supplier. In most cases, supplier and lessee have already agreed on all details of the equipment, including delivery and installation. The leasing company will have to check whether the supplier can fulfil his obligations regarding quality, delivery and service, and whether and for how long the equipment will increase productivity in the customer's company. Having been told the purchase price and the desired period for a lease, the lessor can calculate the cost of the lease, and submit an offer to his customer (see Exhibit 703). In continental Europe, leasing is usually based on a 95–100% amortization of the leased object, though non-full pay-out contracts also exist. The rental payments will depend on the length of the lease—in Switzerland many contracts are signed for five years—and on the amortization percentage (see section 4).

If the customer agrees to the leasing conditions offered to him, lessor and lessee will sign the leasing contract which is done by way of sending back a signed copy of the offer.

Exhibit 703: Letter from CS Leasing to customer

January 20, 1981

Swiss Industrial Company,
P.O. Box,
8600 Duebendorf,
Zurich,
Switzerland

Dear Sirs,

Re: Leasing Offer

Referring to your leasing application we are pleased to submit
to you the following leasing offer:-

Leasing Item :	Machine Sulzer 75608
Price :	Swfr 500,000
Producer :	Sulzer Winterthur
Invoices :	Must be made out to us - CS Leasing Ltd
Firm duration of leasing contract :	3 or 4 years
Beginning of contract :	April 1, 1981
Monthly leasing payment :	3 years : 3.065%, 4 years : 2.371% of the invoice value payable on the first day of each month (total 36 or 48 payments)
Contract fee :	0.5% fee to be paid at conclusion of contract.

This offer is for financial leasing. All the expenses, maintenance
and premiums are to be born by you. Furthermore, our general leasing
conditions apply.

This offer is valid for acceptance until February 10, 1981.

Should you wish to accept this offer, please sign and return the
enclosed copy.

Yours faithfully,
CS Leasing Ltd.

4. Costs

In finance leasing, the lessee will be asked to insure the leasing object and to cede all rights to the
lessor. It is the rule in finance leasing that the lessee pays for service, maintenance and repair. The
actual leasing costs consist of:

a. a small fee due when signing the contract, calculated as a percentage of the purchase value; and

b. the monthly lease instalments.

Exhibit 704: Monthly rentals with various interest rates—basis 1

Basis: —Full amortization during lease period.
—Payments in arrears.
—Monthly rentals as percentage of purchase price.

36 months	48 months	60 months	72 months	84 months	Interest rate p.a.
%	%	%	%	%	%
2·997	2·303	1·887	1·610	1·413	5
3·008	2·314	1·899	1·622	1·425	$5\frac{1}{4}$
3·020	2·326	1·910	1·634	1·437	$5\frac{1}{2}$
3·031	2·337	1·922	1·646	1·449	$5\frac{3}{4}$
3·042	2·349	1·933	1·657	1·461	6
3·054	2·360	1·945	1·669	1·473	$6\frac{1}{4}$
3·065	2·371	1·957	1·681	1·485	$6\frac{1}{2}$
3·076	2·383	1·968	1·693	1·497	$6\frac{3}{4}$
3·088	2·395	1·980	1·705	1·509	7
3·099	2·406	1·992	1·717	1·522	$7\frac{1}{4}$
3·111	2·418	2·004	1·729	1·534	$7\frac{1}{2}$
3·122	2·430	2·016	1·741	1·546	$7\frac{3}{4}$
3·134	2·441	2·028	1·753	1·559	8
3·145	2·453	2·040	1·766	1·571	$8\frac{1}{4}$
3·157	2·465	2·052	1·778	1·584	$8\frac{1}{2}$
3·168	2·477	2·064	1·790	1·596	$8\frac{3}{4}$
3·180	2·489	2·076	1·803	1·609	9
3·192	2·500	2·088	1·815	1·622	$9\frac{1}{4}$
3·203	2·512	2·100	1·827	1·634	$9\frac{1}{2}$
3·215	2·524	2·112	1·840	1·647	$9\frac{3}{4}$
3·227	2·536	2·125	1·853	1·660	10
3·238	2·548	2·137	1·865	1·673	$10\frac{1}{4}$
3·250	2·560	2·149	1·878	1·686	$10\frac{1}{2}$
3·262	2·572	2·162	1·891	1·699	$10\frac{3}{4}$
3·274	2·585	2·174	1·903	1·712	11
3·286	2·597	2·187	1·916	1·725	$11\frac{1}{4}$
3·298	2·609	2·199	1·929	1·739	$11\frac{1}{2}$
3·310	2·621	2·212	1·942	1·752	$11\frac{3}{4}$
3·321	2·633	2·224	1·955	1·765	12
3·333	2·646	2·237	1·968	1·779	$12\frac{1}{4}$
3·345	2·658	2·250	1·981	1·792	$12\frac{1}{2}$
3·357	2·670	2·263	1·994	1·806	$12\frac{3}{4}$
3·369	2·683	2·275	2·007	1·819	13

Notes: $A = K_o \times \dfrac{1}{\dfrac{1 - \dfrac{1}{(1 + i)^n}}{i}}$

K_o = purchase value.
A = annuity, i.e., monthly linear lease payment.
$\dfrac{1}{a_n}$ = annuity factor, i.e., periodic payment necessary to pay off a loan of \$1.
n = lease period (usually in months).
$a_n = \dfrac{1 - v^n}{i}$ = present value of one per period, i.e., what \$1 payable periodically is worth today.
V^n (discount factor) $= \dfrac{1}{(1 + i)^n}$ = present value, i.e., what \$1 payable in the future is worth today
i = monthly interest.

In most comprehensive sets of tables, the annuity factor $(\frac{1}{a_n})$ can be found for all yields and periods in question, either directly or by interpolation, under the heading "Annuity worth \$1 today. Period payment necessary to pay off a loan of \$1".

Source: CS Leasing Ltd., Zurich.

The *fee* at the beginning of the lease is a commitment fee. It is also intended to cover the costs of a leasing contract, and it is the first payment from the lessee. In the early days of leasing, the leasing charge or fee was a few per cent of the leased equipment. Leasing companies engaged in financial leasing nowadays demand a very small charge of about 0·5–1%, and many of them have abolished the charge altogether.

The calculation of the *monthly leasing payments* is based on the refinancing costs to the lessor and a spread covering the amortization, his cost of administration and collection, a management fee and a risk premium. Exhibits 704–8 show, for different monthly payments, expressed as a percentage of the purchase value, the equivalent interest rate. Depending on whether the payment is payable at the beginning or the end of the month, the percentage is lower or higher for the same interest rate. Such tables are of interest to every lessee who wants to compare his leasing cost with the cost of other forms of financing.

Exhibit 705: Monthly rentals with various interest rates—basis 2

Basis: —Full amortization during lease period.
      —Payments in advance (payable at beginning of month).
      —Monthly rentals as percentage of purchase price.

36 months	48 months	60 months	72 months	84 months	Interest rate p.a.
%	%	%	%	%	%
2·985	2·293	1·879	1·604	1·408	5
2·995	2·304	1·890	1·615	1·419	$5\frac{1}{4}$
3·006	2·315	1·901	1·626	1·430	$5\frac{1}{2}$
3·016	2·326	1·913	1·638	1·442	$5\frac{3}{4}$
3·027	2·337	1·924	1·649	1·454	6
3·038	2·348	1·935	1·660	1·465	$6\frac{1}{4}$
3·048	2·359	1·946	1·672	1·477	$6\frac{1}{2}$
3·059	2·370	1·957	1·683	1·489	$6\frac{3}{4}$
3·070	2·381	1·969	1·695	1·501	7
3·081	2·392	1·980	1·707	1·512	$7\frac{1}{4}$
3·091	2·403	1·991	1·718	1·524	$7\frac{1}{2}$
3·102	2·414	2·003	1·730	1·536	$7\frac{3}{4}$
3·113	2·425	2·014	1·742	1·548	8
3·124	2·436	2·026	1·754	1·560	$8\frac{1}{4}$
3·135	2·447	2·037	1·765	1·573	$8\frac{1}{2}$
3·145	2·459	2·049	1·777	1·585	$8\frac{3}{4}$
3·156	2·470	2·060	1·789	1·597	9
3·167	2·481	2·072	1·801	1·609	$9\frac{1}{4}$
3·178	2·493	2·084	1·813	1·622	$9\frac{1}{2}$
3·189	2·504	2·095	1·825	1·634	$9\frac{3}{4}$
3·200	2·515	2·107	1·837	1·646	10
3·211	2·527	2·119	1·849	1·659	$10\frac{1}{4}$
3·222	2·538	2·131	1·862	1·671	$10\frac{1}{2}$
3·233	2·550	2·143	1·874	1·684	$10\frac{3}{4}$
3·244	2·561	2·154	1·886	1·697	11
3·255	2·573	2·166	1·898	1·709	$11\frac{1}{4}$
3·266	2·584	2·178	1·911	1·722	$11\frac{1}{2}$
3·277	2·596	2·190	1·923	1·735	$11\frac{3}{4}$
3·289	2·607	2·202	1·936	1·748	12
3·300	2·619	2·214	1·948	1·761	$12\frac{1}{4}$
3·311	2·631	2·227	1·961	1·774	$12\frac{1}{2}$
3·322	2·642	2·239	1·973	1·787	$12\frac{3}{4}$
3·333	2·654	2·251	1·986	1·800	13

Source: CS Leasing Ltd., Zurich.

Exhibit 706: Monthly rentals with various interest rates—basis 3

Basis: —Partial amortization of 90% during lifetime of the leasing contract.
—Payments in advance.
—Monthly rentals as percentage of purchase price.

36 months	48 months	60 months	72 months	84 months	Interest rate p.a.
%	%	%	%	%	%
2·728	2·106	1·733	1·485	1·308	5
2·739	2·117	1·745	1·497	1·321	$5\frac{1}{4}$
2·751	2·129	1·757	1·509	1·333	$5\frac{1}{2}$
2·762	2·141	1·769	1·522	1·345	$5\frac{3}{4}$
2·774	2·153	1·781	1·534	1·358	6
2·786	2·165	1·793	1·546	1·371	$6\frac{1}{4}$
2·797	2·177	1·805	1·559	1·383	$6\frac{1}{2}$
2·809	2·189	1·818	1·571	1·396	$6\frac{3}{4}$
2·821	2·201	1·830	1·584	1·408	7
2·833	2·213	1·842	1·596	1·421	$7\frac{1}{4}$
2·844	2·225	1·854	1·609	1·434	$7\frac{1}{2}$
2·856	2·237	1·867	1·621	1·447	$7\frac{3}{4}$
2·868	2·249	1·879	1·634	1·460	8
2·880	2·261	1·891	1·646	1·473	$8\frac{1}{4}$
2·891	2·273	1·904	1·659	1·486	$8\frac{1}{2}$
2·903	2·285	1·916	1·672	1·499	$8\frac{3}{4}$
2·915	2·297	1·929	1·685	1·512	9
2·927	2·310	1·941	1·697	1·525	$9\frac{1}{4}$
2·939	2·322	1·954	1·710	1·538	$9\frac{1}{2}$
2·951	2·334	1·966	1·723	1·551	$9\frac{3}{4}$
2·963	2·346	1·979	1·736	1·564	10
2·975	2·359	1·992	1·749	1·578	$10\frac{1}{4}$
2·987	2·371	2·004	1·762	1·591	$10\frac{1}{2}$
2·999	2·383	2·017	1·775	1·604	$10\frac{3}{4}$
3·011	2·396	2·030	1·788	1·618	11
3·023	2·408	2·043	1·801	1·631	$11\frac{1}{4}$
3·035	2·421	2·055	1·815	1·645	$11\frac{1}{2}$
3·047	2·433	2·068	1·828	1·658	$11\frac{3}{4}$
3·059	2·446	2·081	1·841	1·672	12
3·071	2·458	2·094	1·854	1·686	$12\frac{1}{4}$
3·083	2·471	2·107	1·868	1·699	$12\frac{1}{2}$
3·095	2·483	2·120	1·881	1·713	$12\frac{3}{4}$
3·107	2·496	2·133	1·894	1·727	13

Source: CS Leasing Ltd., Zurich.

5. Advantages of leasing

5.1. General remarks

Leasing is a medium- to long-term means of financing. It is an alternative to financing out of equity. It is probably somewhat more expensive than a simple purchase, but has the advantage that payments are due only with the return on the investment. Leasing can be tailored to the needs of the lessee, by making the rental payments progressive or declining, by adjusting the leasing period, and by agreeing on full or only partial amortization (non-full pay-out) leasing. Leasing combines early investment with late payment.

When leasing, there is no risk that the leasing contract could be cancelled by the financing party as, for instance, in short-term credits (on a current account basis). There is also no risk for the lessee that interest rates' rise, rising costs or inflation could alter the leasing terms. Cost calculation and budgeting can thus be based on solid evidence.

112

Exhibit 707: Monthly rentals with various interest rates—basis 4

Basis: —Partial amortization of 80% during lifetime of the leasing contract.
—Payments in advance.
—Monthly rentals as percentage of purchase price.

36 months	48 months	60 months	72 months	84 months	Interest rate p.a.
%	%	%	%	%	%
2·471	1·918	1·586	1·366	1·209	5
2·483	1·930	1·599	1·379	1·222	5¼
2·496	1·943	1·612	1·392	1·236	5½
2·509	1·956	1·625	1·406	1·249	5¾
2·521	1·969	1·638	1·419	1·262	6
2·534	1·982	1·652	1·432	1·276	6¼
2·546	1·995	1·665	1·445	1·289	6½
2·559	2·008	1·678	1·459	1·303	6¾
2·572	2·021	1·691	1·472	1·316	7
2·585	2·034	1·704	1·485	1·330	7¼
2·597	2·047	1·717	1·499	1·344	7½
2·610	2·060	1·731	1·512	1·357	7¾
2·623	2·073	1·744	1·526	1·371	8
2·636	2·086	1·757	1·539	1·385	8¼
2·648	2·099	1·770	1·553	1·399	8½
2·661	2·112	1·784	1·567	1·413	8¾
2·674	2·125	1·797	1·580	1·426	9
2·687	2·138	1·811	1·594	1·440	9¼
2·700	2·151	1·824	1·608	1·454	9½
2·712	2·164	1·838	1·621	1·468	9¾
2·725	2·178	1·851	1·635	1·482	10
2·738	2·191	1·865	1·649	1·497	10¼
2·751	2·204	1·878	1·663	1·511	10½
2·764	2·217	1·892	1·677	1·525	10¾
2·777	2·231	1·905	1·691	1·539	11
2·790	2·244	1·349	1·705	1·553	11¼
2·803	2·257	1·933	1·718	1·568	11½
2·816	2·271	1·946	1·733	1·582	11¾
2·829	2·284	1·960	1·747	1·596	12
2·842	2·297	1·974	1·761	1·611	12¼
2·855	2·311	1·987	1·775	1·625	12½
2·868	2·324	2·001	1·789	1·640	12¾
2·881	2·338	2·015	1·803	1·654	13

Source: CS Leasing Ltd., Zurich.

5.2. Balance sheet considerations

In many countries, since the leased machines and equipment are not capitalized in the balance sheet, and corresponding rental obligations do not appear on the liabilities side, the balance sheet of a company obtaining its equipment through leasing looks very different from that of a company which purchases the product and takes up corresponding finance.

Since the balance sheet of a lessee is lighter than that of a company which has purchased with borrowed funds, the lessee has a higher borrowing capacity. Leasing is therefore different to equipment purchase on credit (supplier credit) or to drawing a bank loan. Leasing encroaches only slightly upon existing credit limits, and represents in effect a broadening of the avenues available to a company seeking external finance.

In contrast to the traditional bank loan, leasing procures 100% finance. It thereby helps to conserve liquidity which can be put to other uses, for example, into development and marketing.

Exhibit 708: Monthly rental with various interest rates—basis 5

Basis: —Partial amortization of 70% during lifetime of the leasing contract.
—Payments in advance.
—Monthly rentals as percentage of purchase price.

36 months	48 months	60 months	72 months	84 months	Interest rate p.a.
%	%	%	%	%	%
2·214	1·730	1·440	1·247	1·110	5
2·227	1·744	1·454	1·261	1·124	$5\frac{1}{4}$
2·241	1·757	1·468	1·275	1·138	$5\frac{1}{2}$
2·255	1·771	1·482	1·289	1·152	$5\frac{3}{4}$
2·268	1·785	1·496	1·304	1·167	6
2·282	1·799	1·510	1·318	1·181	$6\frac{1}{4}$
2·295	1·813	1·524	1·332	1·195	$6\frac{1}{2}$
2·309	1·827	1·538	1·346	1·210	$6\frac{3}{4}$
2·323	1·841	1·552	1·360	1·224	7
2·337	1·854	1·566	1·375	1·239	$7\frac{1}{4}$
2·350	1·868	1·580	1·389	1·253	$7\frac{1}{2}$
2·364	1·882	1·594	1·403	1·268	$7\frac{3}{4}$
2·378	1·896	1·609	1·418	1·282	8
2·391	1·910	1·623	1·432	1·297	$8\frac{1}{4}$
2·405	1·924	1·637	1·447	1·312	$8\frac{1}{2}$
2·419	1·938	1·651	1·461	1·326	$8\frac{3}{4}$
2·433	1·952	1·666	1·476	1·341	9
2·447	1·966	1·680	1·490	1·356	$9\frac{1}{4}$
2·460	1·980	1·694	1·505	1·371	$9\frac{1}{2}$
2·474	1·995	1·709	1·519	1·386	$9\frac{3}{4}$
2·488	2·009	1·723	1·534	1·400	10
2·502	2·023	1·737	1·549	1·415	$10\frac{1}{4}$
2·516	2·037	1·752	1·563	1·430	$10\frac{1}{2}$
2·530	2·051	1·766	1·578	1·445	$10\frac{3}{4}$
2·543	2·065	1·781	1·593	1·460	11
2·557	2·079	1·795	1·608	1·475	$11\frac{1}{4}$
2·571	2·094	1·810	1·622	1·490	$11\frac{1}{2}$
2·585	2·108	1·824	1·637	1·505	$11\frac{3}{4}$
2·599	2·122	1·839	1·652	1·520	12
2·613	2·136	1·853	1·667	1·536	$12\frac{1}{4}$
2·627	2·151	1·868	1·682	1·551	$12\frac{1}{2}$
2·641	2·165	1·883	1·697	1·566	$12\frac{3}{4}$
2·655	2·179	1·897	1·712	1·581	13

Source: CS Leasing Ltd., Zurich.

5.3. Tax considerations

The tax advantages of leasing depend on the country's national tax system. When the investor buys the equipment, he will be allowed, in most cases, to deduct the interest on loans and the depreciation from his taxable income in accordance with tax allowance schemes. When leasing he may be allowed to deduct the total rental payments. So, there might be an interesting shift in the timing of these deductions.

5.4. Valuable alternative

Leasing is a new means of trade financing, and is therefore a sometimes difficult alternative to more traditional alternatives. However, it provides a useful alternative approach.

6. An example of a leasing contract

The text of a leasing contract used by a U.K. company is shown in Exhibit 709.

BOWMAKER LEASING PLAN

ORIGINAL

THE COPYRIGHT
OF THIS
DOCUMENT IS
RESERVED

(B)

L 1. L
(Amd. 17)

NAME AND ADDRESS OF HIRER (*In block letters please*)
Firms please state (1) *trading style and*
(2) *full names of proprietors/partners*

Br. No.	Office use only—Agmt. No.		
		LL	

Postcode   Tel. No.

THE SCHEDULE

FULL PARTICULARS OF GOODS:
(Serial Nos. and Regn. Nos. and accessories must be stated)

Primary hiring period [   ] months

Total rentals payable during primary hiring
period (exc. VAT) ..   .. **£**

[   ] rental(s) paid prior to signing this

Agreement (exc. VAT) totalling   ..   .. **£**

followed by [   ] rentals (exc. VAT) of.. **£**

payable in advance the first due on

_____ 19___
(being ONE MONTH after the date of this
Agreement) and thereafter on the same day of
each succeeding month.

Secondary hiring period

Yearly rentals (exc. VAT) of   ..   .. **£**
the first due on

_____ 19___

VAT is payable on all rentals at the rate from time to time in force.

Assuming that VAT remains at the rate of [   ] %:

MOTOR VEHICLES

Date first Reg.	Make and Model	Regn. No.	Chassis No.

SITING ADDRESS(ES) OF GOODS (see clause 3(a) below)

(i) the total rentals payable prior to
signing including VAT will be   **£**

(ii) the total Primary hiring period rentals
including VAT will be   ..   **£**

Mark selected
method of payment   through post [ ]   over bank counter [ ]   by Direct Debiting Mandate [ ]
with X

Refund percentage _____ (see clause 10 below)

SIGNATURES TO AGREEMENT

(1) Witness to
signature of Hirer_____

Address_____

Occupation_____

(2) Witness to (Second witness required in Scotland only)

signature of Hirer_____

Address_____

Occupation_____

NOTE: My/Our attention was drawn to Clause 11 below

SIGNATURE
OF HIRER_____

Signature for and on behalf of Bowmaker Leasing Limited

_____ Date_____

TERMS OF AGREEMENT

This Agreement is made between BOWMAKER LEASING LIMITED of Bowmaker House, Christchurch Road, Bournemouth, BH1 3LG (hereinafter called "the Owner") of the one part and the Hirer named above of the other part whereby the Owner agrees to let and the Hirer agrees to hire the goods specified in the Schedule above (hereinafter called "the goods" which expression shall also include any accessories replacements renewals or additions thereto and in the event of more than one item of goods being the subject of this Agreement shall where the context so admits include each and any of such item of goods) for the Primary period stated in the said Schedule and on the terms set out below.

1.   The hiring shall commence on the date on which this Agreement is signed by or on behalf of the Owner and unless determined by the Hirer or the Owner in accordance with the provisions hereof shall continue for the Primary hiring period specified in the Schedule above and thereafter in accordance with Clause 9 hereof.

2.   (a)   The Hirer having before the signing of this Agreement paid the rental(s) referred to in the Schedule above together with the appropriate VAT thereon shall unless the hiring shall in the meantime have been duly determined in accordance with the provisions hereof pay the rentals for the remainder of the Primary hiring period as set out in the Schedule above

(b)   The Hirer shall with each rental or other payment payable hereunder pay to the Owner VAT on the amount of such rental or other payment at the rate from time to time in force

(c)   All rentals and other payments hereunder are to be paid to the Owner at Bowmaker House, Christchurch Road, Bournemouth, BH1 3LG but should the Hirer make any payments by post or to any other person for transmission to the Owner they shall be at the risk of the Hirer and shall only be credited to the Hirer as and when received by the Owner. In default of punctual payment (but without prejudice to the Owner's rights hereunder) the Hirer shall on demand pay interest on any overdue rentals or other payments at the rate of 4 per cent. per annum over Finance House Base Rate from time to time.

Exhibit 709: A U.K. leasing contract (continued)

Terms of Agreement—*continued*

3. The Hirer shall

(a) keep the goods in good order repair and condition at the siting address(es) specified in the Schedule above or at such other address(es) as shall be agreed in writing by the Owner and be responsible for all risks of whatsoever kind fire included and in the case of a motor vehicle the Hirer shall ensure that the same has the routine maintenance and service called for by the manufacturer's recommendations at the intervals recommended by the manufacturer. If and whenever any service maintenance repair or replacement of parts is required it shall be carried out at the expense of the Hirer and in the case of a motor vehicle such service maintenance repair or replacement of parts shall be carried out by an authorised agent of the manufacturer of such motor vehicle provided that the Hirer shall not have or be deemed to have any authority to pledge the Owner's credit for the repair of the goods or to create a lien thereon in respect of such repairs or for any other purpose or thing whatsoever

(b) pay any licence duties fees insurance premiums road tax and registration charges payable in respect of the goods and if any such duties fees premiums road tax or charges shall be paid by the Owner (the Owner being hereby authorised to pay the same on behalf of the Hirer) the Hirer shall repay the same to the Owner forthwith

(c) neither use nor permit the goods to be used for any purpose for which they are not designed or reasonably suitable nor permit them to be used in contravention of any statute or statutory regulations for the time being in force, nor during the hiring take or send or permit to be taken or sent the goods out of the British Isles (save with the previous written consent of the Owner) and in the case of a motor vehicle not use the same for racing or pacemaking nor for competing in any rally

(d) allow the Owner or its duly authorised representative at all times to have access to the goods to inspect the condition thereof and within ten days after notice in writing from the Owner of any want of repair or injury in or to the goods to make good the same to the satisfaction of the Owner

(e) repay to the Owner forthwith on demand all expenses costs or charges incurred in ascertaining the whereabouts of the Hirer or the goods or in recovering or endeavouring to recover possession of the goods from the Hirer or any other person firm or company

(f) forthwith (unless otherwise agreed in writing by the Owner) insure the goods and during the currency of this Agreement keep them insured in their full replacement value against all insurable risks and without any excess or restriction (and in the case of a motor vehicle shall insure and keep insured the same comprehensively) under a policy issued by a reputable insurer and notify the insurer of the interest of the Owner in the goods and produce such policy and the latest premium receipt to the Owner upon demand. In the event of the Hirer returning the goods to the Owner or the Owner recovering possession of the same the interest of the Hirer in any insurance effected hereunder shall absolutely vest in the Owner who shall be entitled to the full benefit of such insurance including any claims thereunder which may be outstanding at the time of such return or recovery of possession

(g) in the case of a motor vehicle hold the registration document(s) to the Owner's order and on the expiry or termination for whatever reason of the hiring deliver up such registration document(s) to the Owner or such other person as the Owner may stipulate

(h) in the case of a motor vehicle pay all parking fines and other penalties in respect of the same and in the event of the Owner being required for whatever reason to pay such fines or other penalties on demand reimburse the Owner for all such amounts that it shall have been required to pay

(i) fully indemnify the Owner against any claims loss or costs arising out of any breach of the obligations of the Hirer under this Agreement (whether under this Clause 3 or otherwise).

4. The Hirer shall not agree the settlement of any claim under any insurance effected under Clause 3(f) hereof in respect of the goods without the concurrence of the Owner. The Hirer shall instruct the Insurer that any moneys receivable under any such insurance pursuant to a total loss claim shall be paid by the Insurer to the Owner and the Hirer hereby irrevocably appoints the Owner as its agent for claiming and/or receiving such moneys and authorises the Owner to give a good discharge to the Insurer for such moneys. In the event of all the goods being so damaged as to give rise to a claim under such insurance upon a total loss basis then the Hirer shall be entitled to terminate the hiring created hereby on payment to the Owner of such sum as will together with the amount received by the Owner from the Insurer equal the balance of the rentals which remain to be paid during the balance of the Primary hiring period (less an allowance as referred to in Clause 7 on any rentals not accrued due at the date of payment by the Hirer). In the event of some or one item only of the goods being so damaged as to give rise to a claim under such insurance upon a total loss basis then the rentals payable during the balance of the Primary hiring period shall be reduced by such amount as the Owner shall, in its absolute discretion, consider appropriate after taking into consideration any moneys received by the Owner from the Insurer in respect of such total loss.

5. Except with the previous consent in writing of the Owner the Hirer shall not attempt to assign sub-let pledge mortgage or charge the goods nor part with the possession or the control of the goods or the benefit of this Agreement nor allow any other person or persons to obtain any lien or charge upon the goods nor do or allow to be done any other thing which will tend prejudicially to affect the ownership of the Owner and the goods shall at all times remain the property of the Owner and nothing herein contained shall be construed to imply that ownership of the goods will or may pass at any time to the Hirer.

6. If the Hirer shall

(a) make default in punctually paying any of the rentals or

(b) commit any act of bankruptcy or have a receiving order made against him or if a judicial factor, liquidator or trustee shall be appointed on any portion of his estate or effects, or if he shall convene any meeting of creditors or make a deed of assignment or arrangement or compound with his creditors or (being a company) shall pass a resolution for winding-up or have a petition for winding-up presented or have a receiver appointed or suffer an execution of any legal diligence or

(c) have any execution or distress levied or allow the goods to be poinded or seized under any distress execution or other process or

(d) fail to observe and perform any of the terms conditions and stipulations on his part herein contained or

(e) do any act or thing which in the Owner's opinion may prejudice or jeopardise its rights of ownership of the goods

then it shall be lawful for the Owner (but without prejudice to any other rights it may have hereunder) forthwith to terminate the hiring and thereupon any consent by the Owner to possession of the goods by the Hirer shall forthwith cease. A demand by the Owner for the return of the goods or a notice by it terminating the hiring hereunder shall be sufficiently made if given orally to the Hirer by a duly authorised representative of the Owner or in writing left at or sent by prepaid post addressed to the Hirer's last known address or to his address shown in the Schedule above. For the purpose of retaking possession of the goods the Owner may enter any premises occupied by or under the control of the Hirer where the goods may be or be supposed to be and this clause shall be construed as a licence to enter in a lawful manner any premises of the Hirer and to remove the goods the Owner making good any damage occasioned by such entry and removal.

7. Should the hiring be terminated by the Owner in accordance with the provisions of Clause 6 hereof then the Hirer shall remain liable to pay to the Owner (i) all arrears of hire rent (ii) any other sums due hereunder up to the date of the receipt of the goods by the Owner (iii) by way of liquidated damages for breach of the provisions of this Agreement such further sum (if any) as shall be necessary to make the amount paid by way of rentals plus the arrears of hire rent due under (i) above equal to the full amount of the rentals that would have been payable if the hiring had continued for the Primary hiring period specified in the Schedule above, less a rebate calculated at the rate of 4 per cent. per annum on such rentals that would not at the date of payment have accrued due (iv) all sums payable under Clause 3(i) above.

8. The Hirer may terminate the hiring by giving not less than one month's notice in writing to expire on or at any time after the expiration of the Primary hiring period specified in the Schedule above and upon such termination the Hirer shall return the goods to the Owner to such place as the Owner shall reasonably appoint in good order, repair and condition (fair wear and tear excepted). Such termination shall be without prejudice to the rights of the Owner in respect of the agreements on the part of the Hirer herein contained.

9. If the hiring shall not have been terminated at the expiration of the Primary hiring period by the Owner or by the Hirer in accordance with the provisions hereof then it shall continue for a Secondary hiring period from year to year upon the terms and conditions herein contained and subject to any statutes and regulations for the time being in force and the Hirer shall pay to the Owner in advance the yearly rentals specified in the Schedule above applicable during the Secondary hiring period the first such rental being payable on the day following the expiration of the Primary hiring period and subsequent rentals on the same day in each succeeding year.

10. If the Hirer terminates the hiring in accordance with Clause 8 above the Owner shall upon sale of the goods make a cash allowance by way of refund of rentals equivalent to the percentage specified in the Schedule above of the net proceeds of sale of such goods exclusive of VAT received by the Owner. The decision whether a sale can reasonably be effected and the terms of any such sale shall be entirely at the discretion of the Owner and the granting of any such allowance will be conditional upon (a) there being no change in existing relevant legislation and (b) the Hirer having strictly performed and observed all agreements on the part of the Hirer contained in this Agreement and any document ancillary hereto and also any other agreement made by the Hirer with Bowmaker Limited or any subsidiary company of Bowmaker Limited.

11. The Hirer acknowledges that the Owner is not a dealer or expert in the goods. The Owner does not give make or agree to any condition warranty term stipulation or representation express or implied (whether by statute or otherwise) or in any other way arising as to the state condition quality or (if not new) the age of the goods or as to their fitness for any purpose (whether of the Hirer or any other) and any such condition warranty term or stipulation is hereby excluded.

12. In the event of two or more persons constituting the Hirer the obligations of such persons shall be joint and several.

13. Any dealer or manufacturer by or through whom this transaction may have been introduced negotiated or conducted is not an authorised agent of the Owner except insofar as he is deemed to be an agent of the Owner by virtue of the provisions of the Consumer Credit Act 1974 and except as aforesaid should the word "agent" have been or be used in connection with this transaction it shall be construed in a descriptive sense only and not as implying any legal relationship.

CHAPTER EIGHT
Forfaiting

Charles J. Gmür

1. Introduction

Forfaiting has been known for about 20 years. In the late 1950s and early 1960s, when the seller's market for capital goods gradually changed into a buyer's market, importers increasingly demanded credit periods extending beyond the traditional 90 or 180 days. Additionally, with the expansion of worldwide trade, the exporter was confronted with credit demands from countries in Eastern Europe and the Third World—countries which were difficult to assess at that time. Heavy investment commitments by Western expert firms prevented them from financing such medium-term supplier credits out of their own funds, and the existing banks were unable to offer the services the exporters desired. This was the situation where forfaiting appeared, providing a medium-term refinancing of suppliers' credits, freeing the supplier from the risks attached to such credits by using the form of non-recourse financing.

In the 1970s, forfaiting was often chosen for small or medium sized project financing. In each project somebody has to bear the risks. If the risk-taking party is good, the financing can take place without recourse, as described in this chapter.

2. What is forfaiting?

Forfaiting is the term generally used to denote the purchase of obligations falling due at some future date, arising from deliveries of goods and services—mostly export transactions—without recourse to any previous holder of the obligation. By including the non-recourse clause, all risks and collection difficulties are passed on to the purchaser of the claim (the forfaiter) who pays the exporter cash after the deduction of his interest charge (the discount). The word *forfaiting* comes from the French *à forfait*, and thus conveys the idea of surrendering rights, which is of fundamental importance in forfaiting. This expression becomes *Forfaitierung* in German, *le forfaitage* in French, *la forfetizzazione* in Italian and *la forfetización* in Spanish.

Financing instruments in forfaiting usually take the form of bills of exchange and promissory notes, but also include, less commonly, book debts, deferred payment rising from letters of credit, and other forms of obligation. The predominance of promissory notes and bills of exchange is explained by their long history as a means of trade financing, and their inherent simplicity. They are easily transferable, and a broadly internationalized legal framework rules out many uncertainties.

Forfaitable claims normally carry a security in the form of an *aval* or an unconditional irrevocable and freely transferable guarantee of a bank, acceptable to the forfaiter. Since the foreign importer and debtor of the claim is normally unknown and not assessable to the purchaser of the obligation, the forfaiter can only rely on this form of bank guarantee as his sole security in the event of non-payment by the obligor. Any recourse to bill is ruled out by the without-recourse clause. Therefore, the fulfilment of this condition, i.e., the providing of a bank guarantee or aval, is of utmost importance in view of the non-recourse aspect of the forfaiting business.

Forfaiting is possible in any currency in which the forfaiter can obtain congruent refinancing over the credit period. As forfaiting normally covers medium-term periods of three to five or maybe up to seven years, the main currencies used are those of the Euromoney market, accompanied by the respective national currency of the forfaiter. Short-term financing up to one year sometimes offers the possibility of including other foreign currencies.

Each forfaiter has to impose his own limits, determined largely by market conditions for his refinancing and for selling the claim to possible investors, and by his own assessment of the risks involved in a particular transaction. Once he has decided to take over an obligation, the procedure is simple and quick. The exporter receives immediate cash, being the face value of the bills or notes reduced in advance by the interest (discount) for the whole period of the credit. For the exporter, this means the conversion of a credit-based sale into a cash transaction. His sole responsibilities lie in the satisfactory manufacture and delivery of the goods and the correct drawing up of the obligation. This last point, along with the fixed rate interest charged at the outset for the whole of the transaction, makes forfaiting an attractive service for the exporter.

3. Forfaiting compared with other means of financing

Forfaiting combines several banking techniques. It has been described as being roughly halfway between the normal Eurobank lending business and Eurobond business on the one hand, and, between traditional trade financing (by short-term discount of trade drafts) and international factoring on the other. There are elements of these business activities in forfaiting, but by and large, forfaiting is a unique form of trade financing.

Forfaiting shares the following similarities with other classical forms of international finance:

— Forfaiting is normally done at fixed interest rates, as are Eurobonds.
— Forfaiting is normally medium-term finance, involving a series of half-yearly maturing notes or bills. This is a term structure similar to normal Eurocurrency credit.
— In most cases, forfaiting assumes foreign bank or government-related risks, comparable again to the Eurocurrency lending market.
— Forfaiting is based on discounting trade bills or promissory notes, as is the traditional business of bill discounting.
— Forfaiting relies on papers associated with most international trade transactions, as does classical trade financing. Financial credits can be covered by non-recourse financing, but require a different procedure (see Exhibit 801).
— Forfaiting transactions can be of any size—from Swfr100,000 up to Swfr100 millions— covering export deals as large as those seen in the syndicated Eurocurrency banking market (see Chapter VI).
— Forfaiting is related to capital goods finance, as are medium-term government export credits.
— Forfaiting means the purchase of claims from the exporter as does factoring.
— Forfaiting assumes the risks of international lending from the exporter in a way similar to some governmental export schemes or international insurance.
— Forfaiting transactions are of investment interest to banks, institutions and individuals, and thus compete with other investments in giving a high yield.

Exhibit 801: Dealing in financial paper and trade paper

	Non-recourse dealing in financial paper	Non-recourse dealing in trade paper
Specific name	Without recourse financing; (French: *financement sans recours*), (German: *Ohne-Regress Finanzierung*).	Forfaiting; (French: *le forfaitage*), (German: *Forfaitierung*).
Reason for borrowing	Creation of working capital.	Financing of genuine trade transactions.
Borrower	The issuer of the obligation.	The buyer of the goods (usually foreign).
Lender	The bank or finance company and/or its investment clients.	The seller of the goods (exporter) who is freed of his credit obligations by selling the bill or note.
Liquidation of the claim	—	Sale of undisputable claim by the vendor (usually the exporter) to the forfaiter.
Instrument of credit	Promissory notes preferred for loans and private placements, with the formulation based on the *Code Napoléon*: "I promise to pay against his promissory note . . ."	Formerly predominantly bills of exchange (drafts); now, increasingly promissory notes, issued in payment of goods and services, as well as for project financing. Here it is understood that: —problems which have a bearing on the commercial contract, i.e., the underlying transaction, must be sorted out between the buyer and seller;

Instrument of credit (contd)		—where the claims to be forfaited are not in the form of a bill or promissory note, the indisputability of the claim, i.e. no liens or counterclaims, must be expressly stated.
Characteristics of the obligation	Usually in round amounts, issued to the order of the lender, with the effective clause where necessary. (The effective clause is necessary when the currency of the obligation is not the currency of the place of payment.)	Usually in irregular amounts, maturing semi-annually, issued to the order of the exporter, with effective clause where necessary.
Payout	As soon as transaction is satisfactorily completed, i.e., after the checking of the validity of the signatures by the lender, and clarification of foreign exchange and tax problems; transfer of the proceeds to the borrower's bank account in his country (in foreign or local currency): —with deduction of discount where agreed, —in full, where notes are issued for interest as well as capital, —the nominal amount, where notes contain the clause "plus interest at x% p.a."	Usually after shipment of goods. Checking of legality of the obligations and validity of the signatures by the bank or the forfaiter; delivery of the bills endorsed, either to order or in blank, without recourse to the exporter. Delivery of goods may take place several weeks or months later; payout under deduction of discount takes place only exceptionally before shipment, against a performance bond issued by the exporter's bank.
Repayment	Usually in equal annual or semiannual instalments after three, six or 12 months or after two, three, four or five years, or in one amount after a fixed credit period.	Invoice price divided into semi-annual instalments, the first payable six months after delivery, the last after three, five or exceptionally seven years.
Primary trading	*Sale*: to a bank, a finance company or a broker for placement; the notes are usually passed on. *Buyer* (investor): acquires obligation from trustworthy institutions who arrange a clean execution of the transaction.	Basically unsuitable for general trading, but possible in certain cases: *Sale*: if necessary to a bank, a finance company or investment client. Obligations are usually not passed on by a forfaiter, but may be sold by means of a participation letter from a trustworthy forfaiter. *Buyer*: is usually content with a participation letter from the forfaiter or bank. The forfaiter takes the responsibility for checking the legality of the transaction.
Secondary trading	Possible; payment to the principals (directly or through trustworthy brokers).	Less suitable; is nevertheless practised in exceptional cases. Payment to the current principals (directly or through trustworthy brokers). Trade often undesired by obligor.
Important markets	Developed particularly in New York; now also in London, Geneva, etc.	Developed in Zurich; now also in West Germany, London, etc.
Practitioners	Trustworthy brokers, financiers or bankers.	The forfaiter directly or the exporters bank through which the documents usually pass.
Dealers remuneration	—As principal for his own account: the difference between purchase and sale. —As principal for the account of a third party: a normal commission. —As broker between two parties: an agreed fee.	As with financial paper.

119

Recourse	The commercial, political and transfer risks are assumed by the purchaser. Recourse is not possible. If purchase contract is not completed, a declaration of the invalidity of the financing is not to be excluded.	As with financial paper.

Although forfaiting has many characteristics in common with other finance business, it is clearly different. Forfaiting has been adapted in a unique way to the needs of exporters who want quick financial assistance without complicated legal documentation, want to avoid all the risks involved in the case of a supplier's credit, without loosing the opportunity of offering a medium-term credit to their customers, and want a refinancing that is discreet and without publicity.

4. The forfaiter as banker and insurer

What are the risks undertaken by the forfaiter?

4.1. Commercial risk

The commercial risk concerns the possible inability, or unwillingness, to pay on the part of the obligor or guarantor. With state guarantees, the commercial risk is identical to the political risk.

4.2. Political and transfer risk (also called country risk)

The political risk encompasses extreme military or political measures in the country of the obligation or guarantor, which prevent payments of external obligations. The transfer risk relates to the inability or unwillingness of countries or official bodies to effect payments in the currency agreed upon (including moratorium).*

4.3. Currency risk

This embraces variations in the exchange rates between local and foreign currency when the invoices are denominated in a currency different from that of the exporter or of the holder of the obligation (the forfaiter).

Since these risk are not insured, it is the forfaiter's function to evaluate them in each case, and to decide whether he is willing to assume them.

This brings us to the crucial matter of credit policy. The golden rule is that risks must be assessable. The forfaiter will only engage in credit periods which keep the risk within foreseeable bounds. The commercial risk is limited by a bank aval or guarantee. The currency risk is covered by the forfaiter's acceptance of bills denominated only in those currencies in which congruent refinancing is available through the Euromarket. But in the case of the economic and political situation in the debtor country, the forfaiter has to assume the full risk. He will include a risk premium into the discount rate, and make appropriate reserves. Following all the developments in international politics and foreign economies is of paramount importance to the forfaiter. Developments, such as those in Iran, have shown how rapidly a country risk may change.

Risk premiums in the discount rates applicable to forfait paper do not necessarily compare with the ratings established in other markets. For example, high Eurocredit demands may give rise to Eurospreads, while the same paper, being rather rare in the forfaiting market, might still compare with countries of a much lower country-risk ranking. An example would be Brazilian paper for sometime in 1980. On the other hand, a country with a good standing on the Eurocredit market might qualify as difficult in legal matters and procedures, and therefore be ranked among high country risks. Restriction on the transferability of documents might also drive up the discount rate.

While these might be justifiable differences in Eurocredit spreads, forfaiting rates of different forfaiters normally remain within reasonable bounds. In large transactions partly or wholly traded to other forfaiters or investors, there is an international competitive market which prevents an exporter from finding himself confronted with uncertain market conditions. The forfaiter as his financier and insurer will be able to give him a well-based offer.

5. The mechanics and elements of forfaiting

Some of the elements which make forfaiting possible and at the same time determine its cost, are examined in this section. These elements are: the instruments used in financing, the means of securing a claim and ensuring its free negotiability, and the cost components.

---

* For more information, see *Country risk: how to assess, quantify and monitor it*, Euromoney Publications, 1979, and Finanz AG Zurich Publication No. 10.

5.1. Instruments used in financing

Instruments which embody the claim in an easily comprehensible form, without any additional documents or clauses, are to be found in forfaiting. The most usual instruments are promissory notes (see Exhibit 802) and bills of exchange (see Chapter II). Book claims (accounts receivable items) can be taken into consideration, as can other forms of claims such as documentary credits with deferred payments. The instruments must be in a form which makes them readily negotiable. A promissory note issued by the importer best fulfils the requirement of negotiability as, unlike bills of exchange (accepted drafts), there is no problem of the forfaiter having to relieve the drawer (exporter) of liability. Should the claim take the form of a bill of exchange, it can only be sold by the exporter if the forfaiter in a written confirmation expressly excludes his legal right of recourse against the drawer. Such an agreement is, however, not covered by the law governing bills of exchange and can, therefore, be accepted only if concluded with a first-class financial institution.

Many of the national laws governing promissory notes and bills of exchange are based on the Geneva Convention of 1930 (Uniform Law for Bills of Exchange and Promissory Notes) or are similar to it. The promissory note and bill of exchange offer certain legal security. They are increasingly used as instruments of medium-term credit or investment; in earlier days, they were principally a means of payment.

If the bill is not in the currency of the country of payment, the word "effective" should be written before the amount in letters, or else the payment of the claim in the currency of the importers country, converted at the relative rate, cannot in the terms of the uniform law be refused by the creditor. The effective clause serves to reduce the currency risk (see Exhibit 802).

Exhibit 802: International promissory note

International PROMISSORY NOTE

....
(place and date of issue)   (currency and amount in figures)

On..(date) fixed

for value received I/we ....(names of maker(s))

promise to pay *against this promissory note* to the

order of ....(name of beneficiary)

the sum of ....(amount in letters)

effective payment to be made in...(type of currency) only,

without deduction for and free of any tax, impost, levy or duty

present or future of any nature under the laws of..(country of maker(s))

or any political subdivision thereof or therein.

This promissory note is payable at...(domicile)   (signature of maker(s))

Book claims and letters of credit with deferred payments are generally less negotiable, since the underlying transactions tend to be more complex, demanding an intimate knowledge by all parties of the legal and business practices prevalent in the debtor country. Both forms necessitate greater attention to detail than is the case with bills of exchange or promissory notes; furthermore, a book claim's indisputability, i.e., the absence of counter claims, must be expressly stated. (For exclusion of drawer's liability under English law, see Chapter XI, section 1.3.)

5.2. How are payments guaranteed?

The guarantee and the aval serve mainly to enhance the negotiability of the claim and to limit the commercial risk. The simple guarantee (*Bürgschaft*) is less common.

5.2.1. Guarantee

The guarantee usually takes the form of a separate document in which each maturity, i.e., the relevant capital amount plus the interest charged to the importer, is mentioned. Both public companies and banks can be acceptable as guarantors.

    a. Government or state guarantees

        Such guarantees are usually linked to the satisfactory completion of the underlying commercial contract; as a result, they differ little from a simple guarantee. With this type of guarantee, it is vital for the forfaiter to establish that the underlying commercial contract has been fulfilled to the letter, and that the guarantee is unconditionally and irrevocably in force and valid.

    b. Bank guarantee

        These guarantees are usually given in an abstract form, that is to say, without any legal connection to the underlying transaction. The guaranteeing bank commits itself unconditionally and irrevocably to the payment of the claim. Often the guaranteeing bank is one and the same as the importer's own bank. The bank should be of reasonable size and international standing. The guarantee can only be given by an internationally recognized bank established in the country of the currency of the claim. Bank guarantees are usually freely transferable, unless non-transferability is expressly stated.

5.2.2. Aval

The preferable and practical form of securing a claim is the payment guarantee by way of an aval. It is a promise to pay, written directly by using the wording "per aval" plus signature onto the document, representing an unconditional and irrevocable guarantee of payment. Through it, the free negotiability of the claim is ensured. With bills of exchange (drafts) it is necessary to stipulate that the aval is given on behalf of the drawee (see also Chapter XI, section 1.6.)

5.2.3. Legal difficulties

The best forms of guarantee are those which are unconditional, irrevocable and fully transferable, thereby securing the claim and ensuring that it is freely negotiable. However, it must be said that the legal interpretation of the aval and the guarantee are not the same in all countries. Sometimes, in non-European countries, the legal opinion is based on the original intentions of the contracting parties, thereby possibly calling into doubt the unconditional aspect of the guarantee. Such transactions should stipulate under the laws of which country the guarantee is enforceable, and in the country in question an unconditional guarantee should be recognized as such between a forfaiter and the guaranteeing bank.

6. The conclusion of a forfaiting transaction

6.1. General information

The course of a forfaiting transaction is determined by the specific requirements of the client as well as the peculiarities of individual transactions; no general formula can be laid down. Nevertheless, a logical sequence of steps from first enquiry to cash payout can be described on the basis of general experience.

6.1.1. The parties involved

The enquiry can come directly from the exporter. The discounting of the paper is then carried out by the forfaiter as principal, i.e., he purchases for his own account and at his own risk. Alternatively, the enquiry can come from the exporter's own bank, the latter taking in the paper and passing it on to the forfaiter as principal, or agent; where he acts as agent, it is the duty of the forfaiter to check that the documentation is in order. It is possible that the forfaiter, for reasons of business policy or country limits, re-discounts the paper without recourse with a third party. The forfaiter's profit usually consists of the difference between the buying and selling rate. This rediscounting should be carried out first and foremost to improve the forfaiter's risk distribution and not with the intention of carrying out risk-free business for its own sake; it offends against good business practice when a buyer claims to act for his own account but in fact passes on the paper to a third party (see Exhibit 801).

The forfaiter should ensure that all problems relating to the underlying transaction are resolved between exporter and importer by the time of discount. Should the enquiry from the exporter be of a general nature, then his exact financing requirements must be ascertained; here, the advisory role of the forfaiter comes into play to assist the exporter in selecting the appropriate form of finance. If the discounting of obligations under exclusion of all risks is required, then the possibility of forfaiting arises.

6.1.2. Preliminary offer

In most cases the exporter will wish to know the possible costs of financing (see section 6.4). This would normally be when the commercial contract relating to the export of goods is being prepared by the exporter and importer. At such an early stage, not all of the details of the transaction are known or fixed to enable the forfaiter to issue a binding offer. (For the details, see section 6.2: information checklist.) Nevertheless, the forfaiter will be in a position to answer the exporter or his bank's—usually telephone—enquiry, by giving an approximate non-binding discount rate. This allows the exporter to adjust his price structure accordingly (see Exhibit 803).

6.2. Information for a firm offer

At a later stage in the transaction, when the details necessary for forfaiting are known, the exporter will require a firm offer from the forfaiter. The following information is important before a firm offer can be issued; and before making a firm commitment, the forfaiter needs to know the following:

— the currency, amount and period to be financed;
— the exporting country;
— the name and country of the importer;
— the name and country of the guarantor;
— the form of debt to be forfaited (e.g., promissory notes, bills of exchange etc.);
— the form of security (e.g., aval or separate letter of guarantee);
— the repayment schedule (i.e., amounts and maturities of the bills);
— the nature of the goods to be exported;
— the date of delivery of the goods;
— the date of delivery of the documents;
— the necessary authorizations and licences (e.g., import licences, transfer authorizations, etc.);
— the place of payment of the promissory notes or bills of exchange.

6.3. Receipt and verification of documentation by the forfaiter

If the firm offer is accepted by the exporter or his bank, both parties are mutually committed. The presenter of the documentation is committed to deliver it in good order and on time. The forfaiter is committed to the purchase of the claims at the agreed rate. The verification of the trade paper and other documents (type of instrument of finance, security and negotiability, import licences or other authorizations) plays an especially important part at this stage of the transaction. The verification of signatures appearing on the documents is of paramount importance (see section 6.3.1). Once the presented documents have been checked and found to be in order, both the risks and benefits of the claims are taken over by the forfaiter. Even in the case where the presenter of the documents is an agent or a broker, the forfaiter must see to the verification of the documents himself, notwithstanding that their validity has been confirmed by the counter-party. Whenever a bank is presenting documents to a forfaiting institution, part of the documentation is probably confirmed as being valid. The forfaiter then checks the remaining part.

6.3.1. Signature verification

Sometimes uncertainties arise in connection with the verification of signatures. When the forfaiter is unable himself to check the signatures on documents passed to him, as is often the case, he can only purchase the paper without recourse when the signatures have been clearly confirmed to him. It is therefore important for the exporter that the bank (usually his house bank), through which the whole documentation is passed, confirms the signatures on the paper. When the forfaiter must himself seek confirmation of signatures from the guaranteeing bank, the exporter runs the risk of having to wait for payment until the confirmation arrives.

Another solution would be an immediate payout made under the proviso that the validity of the signatures be confirmed.

Signature confirmations given by banks are as follows:

1. "We hereby confirm the authenticity of the signature of . . . . and that the persons signing are authorized to commit the company" (follows authorized signature of verifying institution).
2. "The signature of . . . . compares favourably with the specimen on file" (follows authorized signature of verifying institution).

Exhibit 803: Forfaiting rates

These are indicative rates for the purchase of medium term trade paper without recourse (½–5 years) as of November, 1980.

Debtor country (importer's territory)	**Final maturity** (½ yearly instalments)	**Commitment fee** (until pay-out)	**Swfr forfait rates** (approx. disc. % p.a.)		**U.S.$ forfait rates** (approx. disc. % p.a.)		**DM forfait rates** (approx. disc. % p.a.)	
			3 years*	5 years*	3 years*	5 years*	3 years*	5 years*
	approx. years:							
Argentina	5	1% p.a.	6⅝	6⅝	12½	11⅝	9	8½
Australia	5	1% p.a.	6¼	6¼	12¼	11¼	8⅝	8¼
Austria	5	1% p.a.	6	6⅛	12⅛	11⅛	8½	8⅛
Belgium	6	¾% p.a.	6¼	6¼	12¼	11¼	8⅝	8¼
Brazil	5	1‰ p.m.	7⅜	7⅛	13⅛	12⅛	9⅝	9⅛
Bulgaria	5	**	7⅝	7⅜	13⅜	12¼	9⅞	9⅜
Canada	6	¾% p.a.	6	6⅛	12⅛	11⅛	8½	8⅛
Chile	3	1‰ p.m.	6⅝	6⅝	12½	11⅝	9	8½
China	5	1% p.a.	6¼	6¼	12¼	11¼	8⅝	8¼
Colombia	3	**	7⅛	7	12⅞	11⅞	9⅜	8⅞
Czechoslovakia	5	**	7⅛	7	12⅞	11⅞	9⅜	8⅞
Denmark	5	1‰ p.m.	6¼	6¼	12¼	11¼	8⅝	8¼
Ecuador	3	**	7⅜	7⅛	13⅛	12⅛	9⅝	9⅛
Finland	5	1% p.a.	6⅜	6⅜	12⅜	11⅜	8¾	8⅜
France	6	¾% p.a.	5⅞	5⅞	11⅞	11	8¼	7⅞
Germany, East	5	**	7⅛	7	12⅞	11⅞	9⅜	8⅞
Germany, West	6	¾% p.a.	5⅞	5⅞	11⅞	11	8¼	7⅞
Great Britain	5	1% p.a.	6	6⅛	12⅛	11⅛	8½	8⅛
Greece	5	1‰ p.m.	6⅝	6⅝	12½	11⅝	9	8½
Hong Kong	5	1‰ p.m.	6⅜	6⅜	12⅜	11⅜	8¾	8⅜
Italy	5	1‰ p.m.	6¼	6¼	12¼	11¼	8⅝	8¼
Japan	6	¾% p.a.	5⅞	5⅞	11⅞	11	8¼	7⅞
Korea (South)	3	**	8	7¾	13⅝	12½	10⅛	9⅝
Kuwait	5	**	6⅜	6⅜	12⅜	11⅜	8¾	8⅜
Malaysia	3	**	7⅛	7	12⅞	11⅞	9⅜	8⅞
Mexico	5	1‰ p.m.	6⅜	6⅜	12⅜	11⅜	8¾	8⅜
New Zealand	5	1% p.a.	6⅜	6⅜	12⅜	11⅜	8¾	8⅜
Netherlands	6	¾% p.a.	6	6⅛	12⅛	11⅛	8½	8⅛
Norway	5	1% p.a.	6	6⅛	12⅛	11⅛	8½	8⅛
Panama	3	**	7⅝	7⅜	13⅜	12¼	9⅞	9⅜
Peru	3	**	7⅝	7⅜	13⅜	12¼	9⅞	9⅜
Philippines	3	**	7⅝	7⅜	13⅜	12¼	9⅞	9⅜
Portugal	5	1‰ p.m.	6⅝	6⅝	12½	11⅝	9	8½
Romania	5	**	7⅜	7⅛	13⅛	12⅛	9⅝	9⅛
Saudi Arabia	5	**	6⅜	6⅜	12⅜	11⅜	8¾	8⅜
Singapore	5	1‰ p.m.	6⅜	6⅜	12⅜	11⅜	8¾	8⅜
South Africa	3	1‰ p.m.	6⅝	6⅝	12½	11⅝	9	8½
Spain	5	1‰ p.m.	6⅜	6⅜	12⅜	11⅜	8¾	8⅜
Sweden	5	1% p.a.	6	6⅛	12⅛	11⅛	8½	8⅛
Switzerland	6	¾% p.a.	5⅞	5⅞	11⅞	11	8¼	7⅞
Taiwan	3	1‰ p.m.	6⅝	6⅝	12½	11⅝	9	8½
Tunisia	5	1‰ p.m.	7⅛	7	12⅞	11⅞	9⅜	8⅞
United Arab Emirates	5	**	7⅛	7	12⅞	11⅞	9⅜	8⅞
U.S.A.	6	¾% p.a.	5⅞	5⅞	11⅞	11	8¼	7⅞
U.S.S.R.	5	**	6⅝	6⅝	12½	11⅝	9	8½
Venezuela	5	1% p.a.	6⅜	6⅜	12⅜	11⅜	8¾	8⅜
Yugoslavia	3	**	8	7¾	13⅝	12½	10⅛	9⅝

* Basis 365/360, 3 years: average 1¾ years (6 half-yearly instalments); 5 years: average 2¾ years (10 half-yearly instalments).
** Delivery within 1 month.

Source: Finanz AG Zurich.

In the first case, the confirming party takes full responsibility for validity whilst in the second case, which is more usual, the verification is without full responsibility. The forfaiter must decide in this second case whether he wishes to obtain a binding confirmation from the guarantor. In the case of documents with a non-binding signature confirmation ("the signature compares favourably with the specimen on file"), the forfaiter should only pay out to trustworthy sellers of paper.*

6.4. Financing considerations

6.4.1. Cost elements

The most important elements of cost in fixing a forfaiting rate are the cost of refinancing, and a margin to cover the risks assumed and the administration.

    a. Refinancing costs
        The level of these costs, which are the largest component of a forfaiting rate, is determined by the cost of money in the Euromarket for the congruent refinancing period.

    b. Margin
        The margin differs from debtor country to debtor country, and consists of administrative costs and a risk or insurance premium element. The size of the insurance premium is subject to change. The experiences and views of financial institutions which are active in the Euromarket are especially important in judging the country risk (see section 4.2).

The calculation of the cost from the above factors gives the forfaiting rate *on a yield basis*. Since an *à forfait* purchase is carried out by deducting the interest in advance, this yield rate must be converted into the appropriate *discount rate* (see Exhibit 804). Even trading in forfaiting paper always takes place on the basis of discount rates. This convention has come into being not only because the commercial discount is a generally well-known calculation method, but also because the discounting method has traditionally been applied to bills.

If a credit of $100,000 is to be made by discounting a financial bill, then the face value of the bill must be increased in such a way that the payout is $100,000; discount rates apply to the future value of an obligation, whereas yield rates apply to the present value, i.e., the capital. The yield rates express the relationship of interest to payout and are usually reckoned on the same compounding basis as current account interest; thus, on a credit of $100,000, the interest payable quarterly represents a true yield.

Occasionally, a forfaiting rate is also quoted to a client in terms of yield, in order to permit comparison with other forms of finance which are expressed on this basis. The difference between discount and yield rates grows with increasing credit periods and increasing rates (see Exhibit 804).

Other factors in the cost, independent of the discount rate but which nevertheless appear in the discount calculations, are the commitment commission and the so-called days of grace.

    a. Commitment fee
        This is a fee charged for the period between the issuing of a firm offer and delivery of the paper, when the paper is not immediately available for discounting. The fee is expressed in percent per annum or per mille per month, and is calculated on the nominal value to be forfaited. Since forfaiting rates are fixed, a commitment period of several months represents a substantial increase in interest rate risk for the forfaiter.

    b. Additional cost caused by the days of grace
        A number of days are added to each maturity in order to compensate for the loss of interest due to payment and transfer delays. The number of grace days varies from country to country and depends on the forfaiter's experiences with obligors in the debtor country concerned. Account is also taken of maturities falling on official holidays, since legally, collection takes place on the next working day (see Exhibit 810).

6.4.2. Credit period and repayment

The final maturity of a series of bills does not normally exceed five years; the fixed rate nature of forfaiting transactions means that any extension of credit period over these limits would involve a considerable interest rate risk. Moreover, this limit corresponds to the recommendations of the Berne Union, which agreed that periods of credit given should relate to the economic life of the capital goods financed. Repayments are usually made at six-monthly intervals, with the first payment six months from delivery of the goods. Amounts are normally unequal since they include interest on the declining balance, although equal instalments on the annuity basis may be calculated.

6.4.3. Calculation conventions

In the Euromarket (international transactions) interest numbers corresponding to the exact days of

---

* The text has been taken from Crédit Suisse publication 47II.

Exhibit 804: Discount and yield rate differential

Relation between discount and yield for a single maturity. Yield with three-monthly compounded interest adjustment.

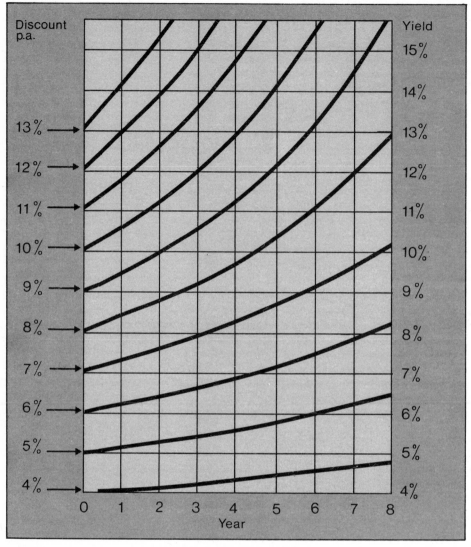

Source: Finanz AG Zurich.

the month are used. Conversion to a per annum rate is carried out on the 360-day year basis. It is normal to express this convention by the notation 365/360; the calculation method should be expressly stated with every offer and discount statement (see Exhibit 805).

6.5. Discount and payout

The next stage of the transaction is the discounting of the individual amounts, thus producing the payout and the amount which will be credited to the exporter. Interest for the whole life of the claims is deducted in advance. The basis, from which this interest is deducted, is the total amount which becomes due in the future (100%) (see Exhibits 805–807).

— Export of machinery.
— Value of the goods to be exported (contract price): U.S.$500,000.
— Credit period: five years.
— Repayments: in 10 semi-annual instalments (capital and interest); first instalment six months after delivery.
— Interest agreed between exporter and importer (internal interest) $10\frac{1}{2}\%$ p.a., calculated on the open credit balance, i.e., to each maturity interest is added on the outstanding balance, thus making: Invoice amount (credit amount): U.S.$ 644,375
— Forfaiting rate: $9\frac{1}{4}\%$ straight discount p.a.
— Days of grace: five.
— Payout: U.S.$ 487,132 (see discount statement in Exhibits 806 and 807).

126

Exhibit 805: Country calculation conventions (in local currency)

Country	Days	Year	Notation	Calculation int. numbers	Calculation of discount
U.S., France and others	Exact number of days	360 days	365/360	$N = \dfrac{V.t^*}{100}$	$D = \dfrac{N.d^*}{360}$
U.K.	Exact number of days	Exact number of days	365/365	$N = \dfrac{V.t^*}{100}$	$D = \dfrac{N.d}{365}$
Germany, Belgium, Switzerland, Scandinavia	The month at 30 days	360 days	30/360	$N = \dfrac{V.t}{100}$	$D = \dfrac{N.d}{360}$

V = nominal value of bill   t = the month at 30 days
t* = exact number of days   d = discount rate (% p.a.)
N = discount numbers   D = discounted amount
* This method is used for currency in London as well as for forfaiting worldwide.

Source: Finanz AG Zurich.

Exhibit 806: Discount statement

	Amounts[1]	Due dates	Days (+5)[2]	Interest numbers[3]
	76,250·—	26.1.80/28.1.80 (+2)[4]	191	1,456·38
	73,625·—	26.7.80/28.7.80 (+2)[4]	373	2,746·21
	71,000·—	26.1.81	555	3,940·50
	68,375·—	26.7.81/27.7.81 (+1)[4]	737	5,039·24
	65,750·—	26.1.82	920	6,049·00
	63,125·—	26.7.82	1,101	6,950·06
	60,500·—	26.1.83	1,285	7,774·25
	57,875·—	26.7.83	1,466	8,484·48
	55,250·—	26.1.84	1,650	9,116·25
	52,625·—	26.7.84	1,832	9,640·90
Total of face value[5]	644,375·—			61,197·27
Minus 9¼% discount p.a.[3]	157,242·99			
Payout value 26.7.79	487,132·01			

Notes: [1] Contract value $500,000; internal interest of 10½% p.a. on the average life (2¾ years) gives $144,375; nominal value is therefore $644,375.
[2] Five days of grace are added to each maturity.
[3] For calculation method see Exhibit 804: calculation methods and notation.
[4] For maturities falling on a Saturday (+2) or Sunday (+1) value date is the next working day. See Exhibit 810.
[5] Corresponds to sum of all future values (=100%).

6.5.1. Adjustments for financing costs and down-payments

6.5.1.1. *Financing costs*

Whenever the invoice amount has to be adjusted to cover the interest difference caused by the fact that the discount rate differs from the interest agreed by exporter and importer, the following formula has to be applied which gives the sale price multiplier:

$$X = \frac{1}{\left(1 + \dfrac{p \times al}{100}\right) \times \left(1 - \dfrac{d \times AL}{100}\right)}$$

where   X   = multiplier.
       p   = interest rate, calculated on the outstanding balance in percent p.a.
       al   = average life of the credit.
       d   = discount rate.
       AL   = average life of the bills.

Exhibit 807: Computer print of discount statement shown in Exhibit 806 (with net amount of each maturity)

Discount statement

Regarding:	Export of machines	
Our reference:	FZ 8'000	
Conditions:	—Discount rate	9.25% p.a.
	—Day of grace	5
	—Calculation basis	365/360
	—Value date	26.7.79

Nominal amounts[3] U.S.$	Maturities (+Sa., Su., holidays)	Days[1]	Value of discount[4] U.S.$	Discounted value (net value) U.S.$
76,250·00	26.1.80+2[2]	191	3,742·07	72,507·93
73,625·00	26.7.80+2	373	7,056·24	66,568·76
71,000·00	26.1.81	555	10,124·90	60,875·10
68,375·00	26.7.81+1	737	12,948·04	55,426·96
65,750·00	26.1.82	920	15,542·57	50,207·43
63,125·00	26.7.82	1,101	17,857·80	45,267·20
60,500·00	26.1.83	1,285	19,975·50	40,524·50
57,875·00	26.7.83	1,466	21,800·39	36,074·61
55,250·00	26.1.84	1,650	23,423·70	31,826·30
52,625·00	26.7.84	1,832	24,771·76	27,853·24
644,375·00[5]	Total		157,242·97[6]	487,132·03

In our example, the average life of the credit is $2\frac{3}{4}$ years (five-year credit with equal semi-annual instalments), and the average life of the bills, owing to the declining nominal values:

$$\frac{N \times 100}{V \times 360} = 2,638,098 \text{ years (numbers calculated as in Exhibit 806)}$$

N = discount numbers.
V = nominal value of bills.

Therefore:

$$X = \frac{1}{\left(1 + \frac{10\frac{1}{2} \times 2\frac{3}{4}}{100}\right) \times \left(1 - \frac{9\frac{1}{4} \times 2,638,098}{100}\right)}$$

$$= \frac{1}{(1 \cdot 28875) \times (0 \cdot 755976)}$$

$$= 1 \cdot 026416$$

The contract price is raised to U.S.$513,207·90 and thereby takes into account the interest paid by the buyer as well as the cost of finance:

Contract price	U.S.$ 513,207·90
Plus semi-annual interest at $10\frac{1}{2}$% p.a. on the declining balance	U.S.$ 148,188·80
Total nominal value of bills	U.S.$ 661,396·70
Minus discount at $9\frac{1}{4}$% p.a. on the nominal amount (average life: 2·638098 years)	U.S.$ 161,396·70
Net amount	U.S.$ 500,000·00

6.5.1.2. Down payments

It is usual practice, where export deliveries are made on credit, for the importer to agree to a down payment. Therefore, our above-mentioned formula has to be completed by a *down payment factor* (DP):

$$X = \cfrac{1}{\left(1 - \cfrac{DP}{100}\right) \times \left(1 + \cfrac{p \times al}{100}\right) \times \left(1 - \cfrac{d \times AL}{100}\right) + \cfrac{DP}{100}}$$

Continuing our example and including a down-payment of 20% the calculation becomes:

$$X = \cfrac{1}{\left(1 - \cfrac{20}{100}\right) \times \left(1 + \cfrac{10\frac{1}{2} \times 2\frac{3}{4}}{100}\right) \times \left(1 - \cfrac{9\frac{1}{4} \times 2{,}638{,}098}{100}\right) + \cfrac{20}{100}}$$

$$= \cfrac{1}{(0{\cdot}8 \times 1{\cdot}28875 \times 0{\cdot}755976) + 0{\cdot}2}$$

$$= 1{\cdot}021022 \text{ (multiplier)}$$

The invoice price, therefore, need only be raised to U.S.\$ 510,510·80. The recalculation gives:

Sales price × multiplier	U.S.\$ 510,510·80
Less down-payment 20%	U.S.\$ 102,102·15
Credit amount	U.S.\$ 408,408·65

Interest of $10\frac{1}{2}\%$ p.a. is charged on this amount and bills issued, which are discounted as follows:

Amounts (U.S.\$)	Days (see Exhibit 806)	Interest numbers
62,282·30	191	118,959
60,138·16	373	224,315
57,994·01	555	321,867
55,849·87	737	411,614
53,705·73	920	494,093
51,561·58	1,101	567,693
49,417·44	1,285	635,014
47,273·29	1,466	693,026
45,129·15	1,650	744,631
42,985·15	1,832	787,488

	Amounts (U.S.\$)	Interest numbers
	526,336·68	4,998,700
Less $9\frac{1}{4}\%$ p.a. discount	128,438·83	
Payout (present value)	397,897·85	
Plus down-payment	102,102·15	
Cash value of goods	500,000·00	

Normally the net payout is transferred to the exporter's bank account. The discount of the transaction and the transfer of the payout are immediately advised (usually by telex) to the exporter or the presenter of the documents. (Examples and formulas in this section are taken from Crédit Suisse Publication 47, II.)

6.6. Letter of confirmation of the forfaiter

The confirmation that the transaction has been concluded is sent by letter, with all details such as the form which the claims take, security and negotiability, points which have been confirmed by the counter-party and all other important agreed conditions. The exporter is normally requested to indicate his agreement with the contents of the letter. By doing so, the purchase/sale contract of the financial transaction is concluded.

Exhibit 808: Situation before forfaiting

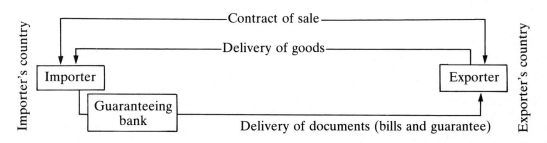

Exhibit 809: Situation after forfaiting

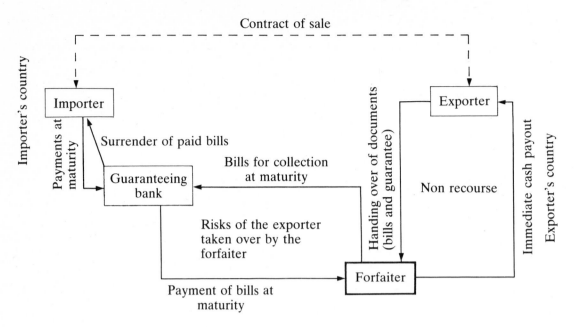

7. Dealing in forfaited claims

7.1. Difference between dealing in financial and trade paper

The principal differences and similarities between dealing in forfait paper (non-recourse dealing in *trade* paper) and dealing in financial paper (non-recourse dealing in *financial* paper) are shown in Exhibit 801.

7.2. Investing in forfaiting paper

Any claim which a forfaiter purchases becomes his property completely. As they normally take the form of bills or notes, they are easily negotiable and are therefore relatively liquid assets. Thus, the criteria for their being instruments of investment are fulfilled. Forfaiting's primary function is to be a means of finance, but it has a secondary function as a means of investment, providing an alternative to private placements. The forfaiting market is equally a credit and investment market.

The attractiveness of investing in forfaiting paper lies in the fact that often a relatively higher yield can be reached, compared with other medium-term investment instruments with comparable security and currency. This relatively higher yield should be seen in relation to the risk which an outsider to the market assumes when he turns to a forfaiting or finance house not internationally recognized and trustworthy; this is because the resale of forfaited claims always takes place without recourse.

A prerequisite of investment in forfaiting paper as opposed to in quoted securities is a certain experience of the market; the rules of the market are not embodied in law to the same extent as in bond trading, for example (bond agreement, stock exchange registration, etc.). In addition, the denomination of bonds and private placements is more uniform, and changes in creditworthiness of the obligor as well as market conditions are reflected in the corresponding variations in market price. Investment in forfaiting paper is more suited to investors with a strong capital base, since usually only relatively large tranches are made available to investment clients.

Since the forfaiting market is restricted, and confusing to outsiders, the investor should always seek the assistance of a trustworthy institution. For institutional investors, the forfaiting market holds advantages from the point of view of portfolio diversification. Institutional investors have a preference for prime names, since they are held responsible for funds entrusted to them in a fiduciary capacity; they should, therefore, take sufficient advice to be able to keep the risk within reasonable bounds. In addition, a trustworthy forfaiter will protect his client when rediscounting and withhold the exporter's name from the market by holding the paper in his own safekeeping and carrying out administrative and collection duties usually free of charge on behalf of the investor.

When paper is bought or sold it is important to establish whether the purchaser is acting as principal, agent or broker.

8. Market trends and outlook

The demand for forfait finance is related to the level of interest rates in as much as the demand is high at a time of rising interest rates, since forfaiting is done with fixed rates. At times of falling interest rates and of high liquidity, demand for forfaiting is smaller and less paper comes to the market.

Changes in interest rates are just one of a number of influential factors. The demand for this type of finance is greatly affected by the need of companies to substitute their medium-term risk-related claims for cash. This risk-assuming function of the forfaiter aids the development of a diversified industrial sector, represented to a large extent by the small and medium-sized companies of the

Exhibit 810: Days to be taken into account when discounting

(Sa = Saturday,   Su = Sunday)

	1982		1983		1984		1985		1986		1987		1988		1989		1990		1991		1992	
	Sa	Su	Sa	Su	Sa	Su	Sa	Su	Sa	Su	Sa	Su	Sa	Su	Sa	Su	Sa	Su	Sa	Su	Sa	Su
JANUARY	2	3	1	2		1	5	6	4	5	3	4	2	3		1	6	7	5	6	4	5
	9	10	8	9	7	8	12	13	11	12	10	11	9	10	7	8	13	14	12	13	11	12
	16	17	15	16	14	15	19	20	18	19	17	18	16	17	14	15	20	21	19	20	18	19
	23	24	22	23	21	22	26	27	25	26	24	25	23	24	21	22	27	28	26	27	25	26
	30	31	29	30	28	29					31		30	31	28	29						
FEBRUARY	6	7	5	6	4	5	2	3	1	2		1	6	7	4	5	3	4	2	3	1	2
	13	14	12	13	11	12	9	10	8	9	7	8	13	14	11	12	10	11	9	10	8	9
	20	21	19	20	18	19	16	17	15	16	14	15	20	21	18	19	17	18	16	17	15	16
	27	28	26	27	25	26	23	24	22	23	21	22	27	28	25	26	24	25	23	24	22	23
											28										29	
MARCH	6	7	5	6	3	4	2	3	1	2		1	5	6	4	5	3	4	2	3		1
	13	14	12	13	10	11	9	10	8	9	7	8	12	13	11	12	10	11	9	10	7	8
	20	21	19	20	17	18	16	17	15	16	14	15	19	20	18	19	17	18	16	17	14	15
	27	28	26	27	24	25	23	24	22	23	21	22	26	27	25	26	24	25	23	24	21	22
					31		30	31	29	30	28	29					31		30	31	28	29
APRIL	3	4	2	3		1	6	7	5	6	4	5	2	3	1	2		1	6	7	4	5
	10	11	9	10	7	8	13	14	12	13	11	12	9	10	8	9	7	8	13	14	11	12
	17	18	16	17	14	15	20	21	19	20	18	19	16	17	15	16	14	15	20	21	18	19
	24	25	23	24	21	22	27	28	26	27	25	26	23	24	22	23	21	22	27	28	25	26
			30		28	29							30		29	30	28	29				
MAY	1	2		1	5	6	4	5	3	4	2	3		1	6	7	5	6	4	5	2	3
	8	9	7	8	12	13	11	12	10	11	9	10	7	8	13	14	12	13	11	12	9	10
	15	16	14	15	19	20	18	19	17	18	16	17	14	15	20	21	19	20	18	19	16	17
	22	23	21	22	26	27	25	26	24	25	23	24	21	22	27	28	26	27	25	26	23	24
	29	30	28	29					31		30	31	28	29							30	31
JUNE	5	6	4	5	2	3	1	2		1	6	7	4	5	3	4	2	3	1	2	6	7
	12	13	11	12	9	10	8	9	7	8	13	14	11	12	10	11	9	10	8	9	13	14
	19	20	18	19	16	17	15	16	14	15	20	21	18	19	17	18	16	17	15	16	20	21
	26	27	25	26	23	24	22	23	21	22	27	28	25	26	24	25	23	24	22	23	27	28
					30		29	30	28	29							30		29	30		
JULY	3	4	2	3		1	6	7	5	6	4	5	2	3	1	2		1	6	7	4	5
	10	11	9	10	7	8	13	14	12	13	11	12	9	10	8	9	7	8	13	14	11	12
	17	18	16	17	14	15	20	21	19	20	18	19	16	17	15	16	14	15	20	21	18	19
	24	25	23	24	21	22	27	28	26	27	25	26	23	24	22	23	21	22	27	28	25	26
	31		30	31	28	29							30	31	29	30	28	29				
AUGUST		1	6	7	4	5	3	4	2	3	1	2	6	7	5	6	4	5	3	4	1	2
	7	8	13	14	11	12	10	11	9	10	8	9	13	14	12	13	11	12	10	11	8	9
	14	15	20	21	18	19	17	18	16	17	15	16	20	21	19	20	18	19	17	18	15	16
	21	22	27	28	25	26	24	25	23	24	22	23	27	28	26	27	25	26	24	25	22	23
	28	29					31		30	31	29	30							31		29	30
SEPTEMBER	4	5	3	4	1	2		1	6	7	5	6	3	4	2	3	1	2		1	5	6
	11	12	10	11	8	9	7	8	13	14	12	13	10	11	9	10	8	9	7	8	12	13
	18	19	17	18	15	16	14	15	20	21	19	20	17	18	16	17	15	16	14	15	19	20
	25	26	24	25	22	23	21	22	27	28	26	27	24	25	23	24	22	23	21	22	26	27
					29	30	28	29							30		29	30	28	29		
OCTOBER	2	3	1	2	6	7	5	6	4	5	3	4	1	2		1	6	7	5	6	3	4
	9	10	8	9	13	14	12	13	11	12	10	11	8	9	7	8	13	14	12	13	10	11
	16	17	15	16	20	21	19	20	18	19	17	18	15	16	14	15	20	21	19	20	17	18
	23	24	22	23	27	28	26	27	25	26	24	25	22	23	21	22	27	28	26	27	24	25
	30	31	29	30							31		29	30	28	29					31	
NOVEMBER	6	7	5	6	3	4	2	3	1	2		1	5	6	4	5	3	4	2	3		1
	13	14	12	13	10	11	9	10	8	9	7	8	12	13	11	12	10	11	9	10	7	8
	20	21	19	20	17	18	16	17	15	16	14	15	19	20	18	19	17	18	16	17	14	15
	27	28	26	27	24	25	23	24	22	23	21	22	26	27	25	26	24	25	23	24	21	22
							30		29	30	28	29							30		28	29
DECEMBER	4	5	3	4	1	2		1	6	7	5	6	3	4	2	3	1	2		1	5	6
	11	12	10	11	8	9	7	8	13	14	12	13	10	11	9	10	8	9	7	8	12	13
	18	19	17	18	15	16	14	15	20	21	19	20	17	18	16	17	15	16	14	15	19	20
	25	26	24	25	22	23	21	22	27	28	26	27	24	25	23	24	22	23	21	22	26	27
			31		29	30	28	29						31			30	31	29	30	28	29

manufacturing industry which have an innovative product range. In these days of rapid structural economic changes, with the accent on foreign markets, providing risk capital is of vital importance to those companies which find themselves on the threshold of internal reorganization and adaptation. Forfaiting offers the possibility of financially weathering this period of transition. It is for this reason that forfaiting can be called an innovative form of finance. The forfaiting market will probably never take on huge proportions: it is likely to remain relatively small (at present $\frac{1}{4}\%$ of world trade) but all the more efficient for it. The last two decades laid the foundations for this.

For legal considerations, see Chapter XI, section 1: Forfaiting.

CHAPTER NINE
Bonds, private placements and Eurocredits

Giles Clarke

The development of trade has been dependent upon the different kinds of financing available to the exporters and importers. The development of the Eurodollar bond market has provided a source of money for marketers of capital goods which has enabled them to make substantial investments in plant and machinery with the firm knowledge of budgeted return over a period of time irrespective of the rate of inflation in any given country or the appreciation or depreciation of any given currency. It is a particular characteristic of the Eurodollar market that it is open to a number of different industrial organizations more easily comprehensive to the Eurobond or international investor.

1. History of the Eurobond market

The forerunners of present day Eurobond issues were bond issues offered by governments in a foreign capital market and sold entirely (at least theoretically) within such a market. In particular, the most immediate antecedents were foreign issues in the U.S. domestic capital market, to which European governments turned after World War II. Access to the market was relatively simple, its supervisory body, the Securities and Exchange Commission (SEC), having dispensed with its most onerous disclosure requirements for such issuers. Capital was available in significant amounts and the U.S. dollar was a currency of denomination acceptable not only to the borrowers and the domestic investors, but also to foreign investors—as important factor for the future direction of international financing. It was soon recognized that a great proportion of foreign bonds issued in New York was flowing back through the European financial centres to individual and institutional investors scattered around the world. These were attracted by the quality of the paper, the currency in which it was denominated, and the fact that it was listed on a stock exchange in bearer form and that payments were made free of the withholding taxes, normally imposed in the issuer's country of origin. New York was, in effect, providing a means through which borrowers of diverse nationality, who had in common a high credit standing, could issue debt securities with particular characteristics to widely dispersed *retail* investors.

In 1963, foreign issues in the New York market were singled out by the Kennedy administration as making an important contribution to the U.S. capital account deficit which the administration was seeking to redress. Its answer, the imposition of the interest equalization tax (IET), made it impracticable for foreign borrowers to issue bonds in New York by making such bonds unattractive to domestic investors through yield-reducing fiscal penalties: if domestic investors would not buy the paper (unless induced to do so by the compensation of a higher coupon, which was unacceptable to the issuer) then the New York Stock Exchange would not list it, since one of its requirements for the listing of an issue was that at least 20% of it should be held by U.S. residents. The natural response to this manoeuvre was to relocate the base of such financing operations to the European financial centres and tap the investment demand of international investors directly by offering the bonds to a wide group of financial institutions through which this demand was channelled—especially the Swiss banks, as a result of their management of international investment portfolios. This development was made inevitable by the fact that no other single domestic capital market was capable of providing funds in the size, with the regularity and with the ease of procedure desired. The first international issue, launched in Europe in 1963 after the introduction of the IET in the United States, and which can be therefore considered to mark the opening of the public Eurobond market, was, not surprisingly, for a government institution—Autostrade, guaranteed by IRI (the Italian state-holding company). Public sector financing continued to constitute almost all public Eurobond issuing activity until 1965. In that year, the concern of the U.S. authorities to check capital outflows from the country, the same concern which had given birth to the IET, led to a voluntary programme of restraint (which became mandatory in 1968) on the export of capital by U.S. industry to fund its international expansion; the resultant entry of U.S. corporations into the public Eurobond market broadened access to this type of financing and the U.S. corporations were soon joined by public European corporate borrowers. Today, the public Eurobond market caters to a diverse range of borrowers from all parts of the world, issuing debt securities in amounts of between $15 million and $500 million at one time and for maturities ranging up to 20 years. The volume of public Eurocurrency debt issues at the end of 1979 amounted to approximately $14·1 billion equivalent.

2. Characteristics of public Eurobond issues

Public Eurobond issues quickly acquired distinguishing characteristics which remain fundamentally unchanged today and may be summarized as follows:

2.1. Market Place

There is no single market place. Various centres, of which London, Amsterdam, Brussels, Dusseldorf/Frankfurt, Luxembourg, New York, Paris, Zurich/Geneva, Singapore and Hong Kong are the most important, provide the technical facilities and channel the funds. The degree to which any given centre provides technical services or funds varies with each issue and depends on such factors as the country of origin and quality of the borrower, the currency of denomination of the issue, the stock exchange (if any) on which the issue is to be listed and the location of the managers, in particular the lead manager, of the syndicate of financial institutions through which the bonds are sold. The market is really a massive telephone and, perhaps more important, telex network connecting banks and other financial institutions throughout Europe, the Middle East, the Far East, the U.S. and Canada.

2.2. Currency

The currency of denomination of an issue can be, and often is, foreign to the borrower or investors, or both. The choice of a so-called *guest currency* will vary according to which currencies are acceptable at the time of issue to both sides of the transaction—acceptable both in terms of underlying strength (or weakness, as viewed from the borrower's standpoint) and rate of interest.

2.3. Distribution

The placing of issues is spread over a wide number of countries, though the extent of the distribution will naturally vary from issue to issue, depending on factors such as the currency of denomination, the credit of the borrower and whether the issue is public or private.

2.4. Payments

Payments on bonds are made through banks (*paying agents*) located in the financial centres of Europe and the country of the currency in which the bonds are denominated. Payments are invariably made free of withholding taxes imposed at source in the issuer's country of origin (though this exemption may not be valid for bondholders who are nationals of, or resident in, the issuer's country), issuers being liable either to bear the burden of any such withholding taxes that may be imposed or to redeem the issue.

2.5. Form

Eurobonds are usually in denominations of $1,000 or equivalent and are almost without exception in bearer form. Retail Eurobond investors have shown their strong preference for bearer paper by ignoring issues of registered bonds, which have been consequently very few in number and have been taken up mainly by banks.

2.6. Legal covenants

Eurobonds are rarely secured by specific assets of the issuer, since the fact that the bonds are in bearer form and widely dispersed would make such security difficult to administer. Instead, bondholders are customarily protected by a legal covenant known as the *negative pledge*, according to which the borrower undertakes that he will not secure present or future indebtedness without granting the same security, equally and rateably, to that debt to which the negative pledge applies, which ensures that bonds will continue to enjoy equal status with the issuer's other indebtedness (see Exhibit 902 on p. 139).

2.7. Listing

With the exception of Euro-Dutch guilder issues, virtually all Eurobond issues are listed on one or more stock exchanges, usually London or Luxembourg.

2.8. Secondary market

Secondary market trading activity in issues, with the partial exception of Eurobonds denominated in Deutschemarks, generally does not take place on the stock exchange on which the issues are listed, but in an international *over-the-counter* market, consisting of financial institutions around the world linked by telephone and telex. The foundations of the secondary bond market are the so-called market makers—dealers who actively buy and sell bonds as principals (i.e., take positions in the paper), rather than as agents or brokers.

2.9. Summary of characteristics of public Eurobond issues

A summary of these characteristics is given in Exhibit 901, with the costs and commissions shown at the end.

3. Development of the public Eurobond market

3.1. Size

The aggregate annual volume of Eurobond issues, starting with $800 million equivalent in 1963, had risen to $6·99 billion by 1975 and was $14·1 billion in 1979. As the Eurobond gained credence as a secure investment medium (defaulted issues, totalling roughly $170 million, represent an insignificant fraction of the total volume issued) with a sufficient degree of liquidity ensured by an increasingly sophisticated, over-the-counter secondary market, an ever growing number of investors have entrusted a significant proportion of their surplus liquidity to this market. A cross-section of end-buyers of bonds from a new issue today might include a private individual whose money is handled on a discretionary basis by a bank, the pension fund of an international company, an insurance company with long-term foreign currency liabilities and a central bank. An important aspect of this market is the relatively high proportion of bonds placed with individual investors and, conversely, the relatively low institutional participation compared with most domestic capital markets.

There has been not only a sharp increase in the aggregate volume of new issues in each year since the inception of the Eurobond market, but also an equally dramatic increase in the size of individual financings. Whereas even at the beginning of the present decade the average size for a Eurobond issue was in the $10–25 million range, during the past couple of years financings of $100 million and over have been common occurrences in the market, which has absorbed, for example, a $350 million financing for the Commonwealth of Australia, $500 million for Royal Dutch Shell, $300 million for Citicorp and $300 million and $500 million branches, sold a fortnight apart, for the European Economic Community.

3.2. Maturity

The Eurobond market was, in its early years, truly a long-term market, with issuing activity concentrated in the 10- to 15-year maturity range; medium-term financings, with maturities of 10 years and under, accounted in 1969, for instance, for only 14% of all new issues. In 1973–74, however, under the impact of inflation and high short-term interest rates, the focus was suddenly shifted to the shorter end of the conventional maturity range and in 1974 medium-term bonds represented 69% of new issue activity. In 1979, renewed concern in the international investment community over the high levels of inflation resulted in medium-term issues accounting for in excess of 75% of all Eurobond issuing activity.

(A note on market terminology: although *bond* is used as the generic term for all types of securities issued in the market, in order to differentiate between paper of varying maturities, medium-term securities, with maturities of under eight years, are often referred to as *notes* and longer-term securities as *bonds*.)

Exhibit 901: Characteristics of public Eurobond issues

Syndication: Managed, underwritten and sold through an international syndicate of banks.

Principal amount: Amounts generally range from $25 million to $100 million, although issues as large as $500 million have been completed for a few borrowers.

Form and denomination: Negotiable bearer instruments issued generally in denominations of $1,000 each.

Maturity: Maturities typically range from five to 15 years. Maturities of over 10 years are only possible under favourable market conditions for prime borrowers.

Amortization: In medium- and long-term fixed rate issues, amortization through a sinking fund or purchase fund is common. Floating rate notes normally do not include purchase or sinking fund provisions, unless market conditions are unfavourable.

Optional redemption: Most issues provide for early redemption after several years at the option of the issuer. At the end of the non-call period, the issue becomes callable, generally at premia declining to par over the call period. Optional redemption privileges vary with market conditions and quality of issuer.

Application of funds: No restrictions.

Taxation: Interest is customarily paid free of withholding taxes imposed by the issuer's country of origin. In the event that payments become liable to withholding tax, the borrower normally has the option either to pay additional amounts so that the net sum received by the bondholders equals the amount receivable under the terms of the bonds, or to redeem the bonds, usually at par.

Listing: Usually London or Luxembourg.

Secondary market: Secondary market dealers buy and sell fixed rate bonds as principals and make two-way markets based on quoted prices plus accrued interest. The spread between bid and asked prices is generally $\frac{1}{2}$% of principal, but can vary with market conditions.

Governing law: U.K. or U.S. law.

Terms and covenants:
(a) Negative pledge;
(b) *Pari passu* provisions (see Exhibit 902);
(c) Withholding tax indemnification (see Taxation above);
(d) Cross-default provisions (see Exhibit 902);
(e) Covenants contained in domestic debt, as appropriate;
(f) Floating rate issues only: alternative provisions for the calculation of the rate of interest.

Costs and commissions: Total commissions (*gross spread*) are usually:
  —2% for five-year maturity;
  —$2\frac{1}{4}$% for seven-year maturity;
  —$2\frac{1}{2}$% for longer maturities.
The gross spread is sometimes reduced for especially large issues.
The total commissions are divided into:

(a) a management fee for the manager's services in structuring and leading the issue;
(b) an underwriting commission for the underwriters' market risk;
(c) a selling concession for the institutions actually making sales. A reallowance may be given to other dealers, payable out of the selling concession.

Typical initial expenses to be borne by a first-time issuer of Eurobonds would range from roughly $155,000 to $250,000. This amount would include reimbursement of the managers' expenses; printing, delivery and

Costs and commissions: (contd.)	checking costs of bonds; printing and delivery costs of documents; and initial listing fees. In addition, the issuer would be responsible for the fees of its own counsel and accountants, paying agency fees, annual listing and trustee fees and its own out-of-pocket expenses. The expenses incurred for a first issue would be higher than those for subsequent issues.

3.3. Type of borrower

Governments, government agencies, municipalities, industrial corporations, financial institutions.

3.4. Type of instrument

While fixed rate medium- to long-term straight debt offerings constitute the largest proportion of issuing activity, more complex instruments have either been borrowed from national capital markets and adapted for use in the international capital market or invented in this latter market—and have been readily absorbed by investors. Paper can be offered today in the Euromarket covering the whole maturity spectrum, from short-term securities (London dollar certificates of deposit for banks with branches in London—one month to five years—and Eurocommercial paper for corporations— 90 to 270 days—although neither is publicly distributed) to medium- and long-term securities, with retractable or extendable maturities, with equity features (convertible bonds, bonds with warrants attached—usually with maturities of between five and 20 years) and so on. There is, however, a considerable difference between the distribution of short-term and of medium- to long-term securities, in that the former group is privately placed and the latter is generally publicly issued. A sector which falls in the latter category and which has enjoyed particularly rapid development recently is the market for floating rate notes.

3.5. Currency

Though in the initial phase of this market Eurobonds were denominated almost exclusively in U.S. dollars (reflecting the market's New York parentage), since 1963 the choice of currency has diversified widely in the effort to provide at any given time a vehicle reconciling the requirements of borrowers and investors. The U.S. dollar has been joined by the Deutschemark and other leading European currencies (excluding the Swiss franc because Swiss authorities forbid the use of the Swiss franc for Eurobond issues, although they allow foreign borrowers to float Swiss franc issues in their domestic capital market), the Canadian dollar, Middle Eastern currencies (notably the Kuwaiti dinar) and various currency-linked composite units (the most widely recognized being the European unit of account and the International Monetary Fund's special drawing right).

3.5.1. The importance of the U.S. dollar

The U.S. dollar remains the single most important currency in this market, for the following reasons:

a. Owing to the importance of the U.S. economy in world trade and the persistent balance of payment deficit which has characterized it since World War II, U.S. dollar liquidity outside the U.S. is relatively greater than that for any other currency outside its country of origin.

(As a result of (a), the U.S. dollar markets are broadest in terms of the range of investors participating in them and thus in terms of the amount of funds available to potential borrowers.)

b. Dollar deposits represent the most important sector of the Eurocurrency market and an active secondary market in Eurodollar bonds can be maintained, since market makers can easily obtain short-term funds to refinance their positions in bonds. This consideration is of importance to investors concerned about the liquidity of their portfolios and for borrowers whose credit standing is in part a function of the secondary market performance of their paper.

c. The size and timing of bond issues in the Eurodollar sector are subject only to market forces, while issues in other sectors which make a meaningful contribution to overall activity in the Eurobond market are additionally subject to close control by the monetary authorities of the denominating currency's country of origin (for example, in the case of the Deutschemark, public issues must be submitted for the approval of the central capital market committee of the Bundesbank). This considerably reduces the prospective borrower's flexibility on the timing and size of issues denominated in Eurocurrencies other than the dollar.

137

4. Documentation and procedure for a Eurobond issue by ABC Limited

4.1. Documentation

4.1.1. The prospectus

A prospectus is a standard requirement of the leading European stock exchanges for the listing of a debt issue. The prospectus would contain a full description of the history, structure and activities of ABC Limited, including capitalization, audited financial statements, consisting of the latest five-year profit and loss accounts and two-year balance sheets, with explanatory notes thereto and the report of ABC Limited's auditors. Further sections in the prospectus would give details of the terms and conditions of the bonds and certain general information required by the stock exchange on which the bonds would be listed (and in conformity with the requirements of which the prospectus would be drawn up).

The prospectus would be prepared (like all the principal documentation in a Eurobond issue) by the lead manager of the financing in close consultation with the ABC Limited management. The document would, however, remain legally the responsibility of ABC Limited and a statement would be printed on the inside cover of the prospectus to the effect that:

> ABC Limited, having made all reasonable enquiries, confirm that to the best of its knowledge, information and belief the information contained in this Prospectus is true and accurate in all material respects and does not contain any untrue statement of a material fact or omit to state any fact necessary to make the statements herein, in the light of the circumstances under which they are made, not misleading.

The prospectus is virtually finalized before the issue is launched, but is sent out to the underwriters and members of the selling group in preliminary form at the same time as invitations are despatched for the underwriting and sale of the bonds. Because the coupon and issue price for a fixed rate issue are normally not finalized until the end of the selling period, they are not included in the preliminary version of the prospectus. In the case of a floating rate note (FRN) issue the margin over Libor, issue price and minimum interest rate are fixed before the launch of the issue and this information is therefore included in the preliminary prospectus for an FRN issue. The final form of the prospectus is sent out in both cases after the allotment of the bonds.

4.1.2. Legal documentation

4.1.2.1. *The bonds*

The bonds would, in accordance with the almost invariable practice in the international capital market, be issued in bearer form.

The bonds would be printed on security paper with interest coupons attached, would be numbered serially and would have printed on them the terms and conditions of the issue; the final maturity date; details of sinking or purchase fund redemptions (if any) and the provisions for the early redemption of the bonds at the option of the issuer; a list of paying agents through which payments on the bonds would be made available to bondholders; a statement of the law that governs the bonds; and, of great importance, *the legal covenants* to which ABC Limited has agreed for the protection of the bondholders as shown in Exhibit 902. In addition to this information, the bonds in a fixed rate issue would have printed on them the rate of interest, amount of interest and date on which interest is payable and the notes in a floating rate issue would have printed on them the methods of calculating the applicable rate of interest and the interest payment date.

4.1.2.2. *Trust deed or fiscal agency agreement*

All Eurobond issues are governed either by a trust deed, which interposes a trustee (usually a specialized institution) between the issuer and the bondholders for the administration of the provisions of the issue, or by a fiscal agency agreement, under which a bank agrees to act as fiscal agent and is principally responsible for coordinating the technical aspects of payments on the issue. Fiscal agents specifically never assume any trustee functions.

In an issue governed by a trust deed, the trustee technically represents the bondholders, in contrast to a fiscal agent which would act for the issuer; nevertheless, the existence of a trustee brings advantages to the issuer, which become all the more significant with issues of longer maturities:

— A trust deed confers wide discretionary powers upon the trustee to deal with detailed provisions and restrictions in the terms of the bonds which are designed to protect the bondholders. From the issuer's point of view this has the advantage that the trustee may be persuaded to waive, for instance, an event of default which may be only technical in nature.

— If it should become desirable to consider renegotiation of any term of the bonds at any time, information can be disclosed to the trustee and negotiations can be undertaken with it on a totally confidential basis, up to the making of any announcement. Certain changes can usually be made to the terms and conditions of the bonds or the trust deed with the agreement of the trustee and without reference to the bondholders.

— If legal proceedings have to be taken at any time, it is preferable for a single action to be taken by the trustee rather than separate actions by many investors. Under the terms of a trust deed drawn up under English law, bondholders can only initiate proceedings against the issuer through the trustee (which therefore protects the issuer against litigious bondholders).

4.1.2.3. *Paying agency agreement*

This agreement would be drawn up between ABC Limited and the principal paying agent, and would set out the mechanics for payments on the bonds in the major financial centres. This document would be superfluous in the event of the issue being done under a fiscal agency agreement instead of a trust deed.

4.1.2.4 *Agent bank agreement (floating rate issues only)*

This agreement would be drawn up between ABC Limited and the agent bank (normally an institution which is a significant factor in the Eurodollar market) and would set out the mechanics for the agent bank's determination of the interest rate applicable to the floating rate notes for each interest period. Such determination would normally be based on offered quotations made to leading banks by selected prime banks (*reference banks*) in the London market for Eurodollar deposits over the relevant time period, which are collected by the agent bank.

4.1.2.5. *Documents relating to the underwriting and sale of the bonds*

These include: (*a*) *a subscription agreement* which binds the managers, on a joint and several basis, to procure subscribers for, or in default thereof to subscribe, the issue; and (*b*) *an underwriting agreement* (to which the issuer is not a party) which binds the underwriters severally to the managers to purchase if necessary (i.e., if the issue is undersubscribed by the selling group) a certain amount of the issue from the managers. In addition, a number of bonds and financial institutions will be invited into the selling group which allows them to subscribe bonds with no underwriting obligation.

4.1.2.5.1. The subscription agreement

The most important of the documents relating to the underwriting and sale of Eurobonds would be the *subscription agreement* between ABC Limited and the managing banks sponsoring the issue, which would set out their respective contractual liabilities. Under this agreement, the managers would agree to subscribe or procure subscribers for the bonds at a certain price (FRNs are conventionally priced at par), subject to certain warranties and undertakings. Typical warranties would include: that all necessary official consents for the issue of the bonds had been obtained; that

Exhibit 902: Legal covenants for the protection of the bondholders

—*Pari passu provision* and *negative pledge clause*, which would provide that the bonds enjoy, and will continue to enjoy, at least equal status with all other present or future unsecured debt obligations for the indebtedness of others.

—*Withholding and other tax provisions:* that all payments on the bonds to bondholders would be made free of deductions for withholding or other taxes imposed in ABC's domicile. In the event that these payments became liable to tax, ABC Limited would have the option either to pay additional amounts so that the net sum received by the bondholders equalled the amounts specified under the terms of the bonds or, alternatively, to redeem the bonds at par.

—*Events of Default:* on the occurrence of which the immediate redemption of the bonds at par could be demanded by the trustee on behalf of the bondholders, in the case of an issue governed by a trust deed, or by the bondholders themselves, if the bonds were issued under a fiscal agency agreement. These events would include defaults on payments due on the bonds or on any other obligation under the bonds, such defaults continuing for a specified period; default on any other indebtedness or being obliged to repay prematurely any other borrowing on grounds of default thereon (cross-default); and certain other events, including bankruptcy of ABC Limited.

—*Covenants contained in domestic debt*, as appropriate.

the bonds constitute valid obligations of ABC Limited under its legal constitution; that the information relating to ABC Limited given in the prospectus was accurate and there were no facts the omission of which, would, to the knowledge of ABC Limited, make any statement in the prospectus misleading, and that there existed nothing which would, on the issue of the bonds, constitute an event of default under their terms. ABC Limited would also agree to pay the managers the various commissions payable under the terms of the transaction (management fee, underwriting commission and selling concession), to indemnify the managers against any damages caused by breach of the warranties and to reimburse their expenses up to a pre-agreed amount.

The subscription agreement would contain a "force majeure" clause which would provide for termination of the issue between the time of signing of the subscription agreement and the closing date if, in the opinion of the managers of the issue, there had occurred a change in national or international monetary, financial, political or economic conditions or exchange controls or currency exchange rates as would, in their view, be likely to prejudice materially the success of the proposed issue.

4.1.2.5.2. The underwriting agreement

Attached as exhibits to the subscription agreement would be the forms of the *underwriting agreements* and *selling agreements* by which the managers would invite, on behalf of ABC Limited, the underwriters and/or members of the selling group, respectively, to underwrite and subscribe the bonds, on certain terms and conditions. These conditions would contain, *inter alia*, a general prohibition on sales of the bonds in jurisdictions where such sale was not legal.

4.1.2.5.3. Additional documentation

Additional marketing documentation would include telexes inviting banks to participate in the issue as underwriters and/or members of the selling group; a telex notifying the underwriters and members of the selling group of their allotments of bonds; and various covering letters which accompany the preliminary and final prospectuses.

4.1.2.6. *Documents relating to the listing of the bonds*

Listing for most public Eurodollar bond issues is either on the London or Luxembourg stock exchange. Though London listing has always been generally considered to be the more prestigious of the two, until recently there were substantial advantages in terms of cost and flexibility in listing Eurobond issues in Luxembourg. Recently, however, London has revised its requirements and its charges are now approximately the same as those for listing in Luxembourg. Disclosure and other requirements are comparable for the two exchanges.

Whichever stock exchange is chosen for the listing of the issue, the principal document involved would be a letter from ABC Limited to the stock exchange, agreeing to notify the stock exchange of the dates of sinking fund redemptions (if applicable), the amounts of bonds redeemed or purchased in the market and of any other information essentially required to avoid the creation of a false market in the paper, and, in the case of a floating-rate issue, of the interest rate applicable to the FRNs. ABC Limited would also undertake to file their annual reports with, and to pay the annual listing fee to, the stock exchange so long as the bonds were listed on it.

4.1.2.7. *Legal opinions and other closing documents*

Opinions on points of English law confirming that the issue of the bonds and the documentation relating to the issue has satisfied in every respect the requirements of the English legal systems in so far as they affected the transaction would be prepared by independent lawyers and delivered to the managers. The completion (*closing*) of the transaction would be conditional on the delivery of satisfactory legal opinions, as well as other documents, including: a certificate of officers of ABC Limited stating that there had been no material adverse change affecting ABC Limited between the date of the signing of the subscription agreement and the closing date, and that all representations and warranties given in the subscription agreement were still correct at the closing date; and a letter from ABC Limited's auditors stating that there had been no material adverse change in the financial condition of the company between the date of the signing of the subscription agreement and the closing date.

4.2. Public Eurobond issue procedure

The normal timetable for an issue can be divided into three phases:

    a. *Preparation of the documentation* and the application for the necessary consents for the issue, which for a first-time borrower normally require two to three weeks, but which for subsequent issues can often be reduced to a few days.

b. *Underwriting and sale of the bonds*—the selling period—culminating in the signing of the subscription agreement and the allotment of the bonds, which occupy approximately seven to 10 days.

c. *Closing period* of 10 to 14 days, ending with the payment of the proceeds of the issue to the borrower and the delivery of the bonds to the managers.

An issue can, therefore, be completed in a time span of roughly seven weeks, but this can be significantly reduced if by so doing advantage can be taken of a market. Exhibit 903 gives a list of required documentation for the public issue of Eurobonds.

Exhibit 903: Required documentation for the public issue of Eurobonds

Proceedings by the borrower

—*Resolution of the borrower* approving and authorizing the issue and sale of the bonds, the form and execution of the subscription agreement, the trust deed and paying agency agreement (or fiscal agency agreement), the listing of the bonds on the London or Luxembourg Stock Exchange and related matters.

Underwriting and marketing arrangements

—*Subscription agreement*, which is to be signed by the borrower and each of the managers, setting out their contractual liabilities.

—*Underwriting agreement* between the managers and underwriters setting out their contractual liabilities.

—*Selling agreement* between the managers and selling group members setting out their contractual liabilities.

—*Preliminary prospectus* to be prepared and sent out to underwriters and selling group members on the same day as the invitation telexes are sent out to the above.

—*Invitation telex* sent by CSFB (Credit Suisse First Boston) as lead manager on behalf of the managers from London to prospective underwriters inviting them, on behalf of the borrower, to participate in the issue.

—*Invitation telex* sent by CSFB on behalf of the managers from London to prospective selling group members inviting them, on behalf of the borrower, to participate in the issue.

—*Covering letter* from CSFB on behalf of the managers to prospective underwriters transmitting copies of the preliminary prospectus and the underwriting agreement with attached selling agreement.

—*Covering letter* from CSFB on behalf of the managers to prospective selling group members transmitting copies of the preliminary prospectus and the selling agreement.

—*Delivery instruction form* (to be completed by selling group members).

—(Fixed-rate issues only) *Telex* sent by CSFB on behalf of the managers from London the day prior to the signing of the subscription agreement *advising the underwriters* of the terms of offering of the bonds. This telex requests the underwriters' confirmation of their acceptance of the terms.

—*Telex* sent by CSFB on behalf of the managers from London on the day of the signing of the subscription agreement *to selling group* members giving allotments and payment instructions and requesting delivery instructions for the bonds.

—*Final prospectus* dated the day of the signing of the subscription agreement sent out to selling group members.

Trust deed or fiscal agency agreement

—*A trust deed* would be between the trustee and the borrower. It would contain the detailed terms and conditions of the bonds and would set out the limits of the trustee's powers and its discretion in enforcing them. Since a trustee does not act as the principal paying agent (unlike a fiscal agent), a separate paying agency agreement between the borrower and the principal paying agent would be required in conjunction with a trust deed.

—*A fiscal agency agreement* would be between the borrower and the fiscal agent. Because the fiscal agent acts as the principal paying agent, the fiscal agency agreement sets out the contractual obligations between the borrower and the fiscal agent on payments on the bonds.

Paying agency agreement (issues governed by a trust deed only)

—*A paying agency agreement* would be between the principal paying agent and the borrower. It would set out the contractual obligations of the principal paying agent and the borrower with regard to payments on the bonds.

Agent bank agreement (floating rate issues only)

—An *agreement* between the borrower and the *agent bank* setting out the mechanics for the agent bank's periodic determination of the rate of interest.

Closing

—*Certified copies of the board minutes* of the borrower authorizing the issue.

—*Certificate* of an officer of the borrower stating that there has been no material adverse change affecting the borrower between the date of the signing of the subscription agreement and the closing date and that all representations and warranties given in the subscription agreement are still correct at the closing date.

—*Instructions* from the managers to the closing bank instructing it to pay funds to the borrower.

—*Letter* from the borrower *ordering delivery* of the bonds to the managers.

—*Cross receipt acknowledging receipt* of the proceeds of the issue by the borrower and receipt of the bonds (for distribution to the allottees) by the managers.

Legal opinions and comfort letters

—*Opinion of counsel* to the borrower.

—*Opinion of counsel* to the managers.

—*Letter from the auditors* of the borrower stating that they have no reason to believe that the *prospectus is not accurate* in all material respects and that there has been no material adverse change in the financial condition of the borrower between the date of the latest financial statements contained in the prospectus and the date of the prospectus except as set forth in the prospectus.

—*Letter from the auditors* of the borrower stating that there has been no material adverse *change* in the financial condition of the borrower between the date of the signing of the subscription agreement and the closing date.

4.2.1. The preparation of the issue

Once a company has decided to proceed with an issue and has given a mandate to the lead manager of the prospective financing, the lead manager sends out a team to the company's offices for initial discussions, during which central points relating to marketing policy and documentation are determined. When these points have been settled and appropriate legal counsel appointed, the initial phase of the transaction opens with the commencement of preparatory work on the documentation, especially the prospectus. When drafts of the prospectus and trust deed (or fiscal agency agreement), the paying agency agreement (if appropriate), the agent bank agreement (in the case of a floating rate issue only) and the subscription agreement have reached a satisfactory stage, appropriate institutions are asked to act as trustee (or fiscal agent), principal paying agent (if appropriate) and agent bank (for a floating rate issue only) and the stock exchange on which the bonds are to be listed is also contacted. In the case of a London listing, the services of a firm of London stockbrokers are used for liaison with the stock exchange and in the case of a Luxembourg listing, the services of a Luxembourg bank are used. In order to restrict to the minimum the number of institutions which know about the issue, the prospective management group and particularly the underwriters and selling group members, as well as the reference banks, are approached only immediately prior to the launching of the issue.

Throughout this period, the lead manager keeps a careful check on conditions in the market. If these conditions are favourable when the documentation is seen to be approaching its near-final form, then the penultimate preparatory steps for the launching of the issue are taken. The lead manager has a final discussion with the borrower on the maturity, size and coupon parameters for an issue under the then-prevailing market conditions, and once the borrower has indicated his final preferences, the lead manager proceeds to invite a select group of banks to participate in the management of the issue. These co-managers will have been chosen after close consultation between borrower and lead manager on the basis of criteria including, in order of priority:

— Proven placing capability—the ability to place with retail (individual and institutional) investors sizeable amounts of bonds from new issues; the managers will take substantial underwriting commitments (usually aggregating about 40–50% of the issue) and so effectively lay the foundation for the success or failure of the offering.
— Experience in the management of Eurobond issues.
— Commitment to the secondary bond market, which will support the bonds after their issue.
— Geographic location (so that the issue effectively draws on the investment demand of the world's major sources of funds).

The final stages of the critical path to the launching of the issue are: the receipt of all official consents and authorizations for the issue; the approval of the board of directors of the issuer; the acceptance of the invitations extended to the prospective co-managers; and the approval of the preliminary documentation by all parties concerned. In the case of a fixed rate issue, a final discussion between borrower and managers is sometimes held to determine what coupon and issue price levels should be indicated on the invitation telexes; when these points are agreed, the issue is ready for launching.

4.2.2. The selling period

The market is notified of the bond issue by the lead manager sending out telexes to prospective underwriters and members of the selling group, inviting the former institutions to participate in the underwriting of the issue and both groups to participate in the selling of the bonds, on the basis of the indicated terms and the provisions of the underwriting and selling agreements, respectively. The underwriters are selected primarily by the lead manager but in consultation with the borrower and the co-managers and include banks with consistent placing capability. The selling group is chosen entirely by the lead manager and includes banks whose placing capability is less than that of the underwriters, but would nevertheless have been proven by past performance to be significant. A further consideration taken into account when selecting a bank for inclusion and determining the seniority of its position in the syndicate is its ability to place the type of paper being issued, e.g., some banks are stronger in the placement of short-term paper than long-term paper, while others are the converse; some perform well in floating rate note issues and less well in convertibles.

The adoption of the classical broad configuration for the syndicate of managing, underwriting and selling institutions enhances not only the possibility of achieving wide distribution of the bonds but also the process of familiarizing the international financial community with the issuer's credit.

The sending of the telexes to the prospective underwriters and selling group members is followed immediately by the mailing of the preliminary version of the prospectus together with the relevant agreements; these actions mark the beginning of the selling period. The banks making up the management, underwriting and selling groups now contact their investor clients and solicit subscriptions. The selling period lasts up to 10 days and a deadline is set at the end of the period for each member of the syndicate to register with the lead manager the extent of its interest in subscribing bonds from the issue.

Approximately four days after the launch, the lead manager will have received replies from the underwriters indicating their willingness to underwrite the issue, subject in the case of a fixed rate issue to their acceptance of final terms.

Approximately one week later, the lead manager will have received from both the underwriters and selling group members indications of their interest in subscribing the issue. The lead manager, in consultation with the co-managers, then evaluates the degree of interest, taking into account both the quantity and the quality of demand for the issue (the lead manager's experience is crucial at this point since it will know which banks have good retail demand as opposed to those which take the bonds onto their own books either for subsequent resale or for immediate disposal into the secondary market).

At a formal pricing meeting held in the case of a fixed rate issue, which would usually take place in the lead manager's offices, the managers recommend to the borrower the terms on which the issue should be priced which, when finally agreed, are telexed to the underwriters who are asked to confirm their underwriting commitments. This confirmation is received the following day. In the knowledge that the issue is fully underwritten, the subscription agreement is signed at a formal meeting by the borrower and the managers.

During the same day, allotments of bonds are telexed to those banks in the syndicate which submitted indications of interest, together with a request for immediate confirmation of acceptance of the allotment and payment instructions. This telex is confirmed by letter, accompanied by the final version of the prospectus. Stabilization provisions may be invoked by the lead manager depending upon the interpretation of the book (subscriptions) for the issue. The stabilization operation is naturally beneficial to the issuer, but its expense is borne by the underwriters.

If not already finalized, during approximately the next 10 days the rest of the documentation is completed and the trust deed (or fiscal agency agreement), paying agency agreement (if appropriate), and agent bank agreement (in the case of a floating rate issue) are signed by the relevant parties; the bonds are printed and their listing is confirmed. During this period, the managers reserve the right under the terms of the subscription agreement to cancel the issue if there occurs, in their opinion, "such a change in national or international financial, political or economic conditions or currency exchange rates as would be likely to prejudice materially the success of the operation". Such a provision (known as a *force majeure* clause) covers contingencies such as a crisis in the international money market but, to the best of our knowledge, has never been exercised.

4.2.3. The closing period

Thereafter, payment is made by the allottees for the bonds into a subscription account, opened in New York by the lead manager, in which the subscription moneys are held pending transfer to the borrower at the closing. (In the case of a fixed rate issue, payment is made by allottees into the subscription account in New York clearing house funds one day prior to the closing, while in the case of a floating rate issue, such payment is made on the day of the closing.)

In the case of a floating rate issue, two business days before the closing, the agent bank will have contacted the reference banks for the determination of the interest rate applicable to the FRNs during the first interest period. This rate—like all subsequent rates so determined—is published by the agent bank in a leading financial journal (e.g., the *Financial Times* in London).

The closing meeting is attended by representatives of the borrower, the lead manager and the legal advisers. At the closing, confirmation is received that all the required documents have been executed and the bonds have been listed and that the legal opinions and no-change certificates are delivered.

With these conditions satisfied, the proceeds of the issue are transferred by the lead manager to the account of the borrower and simultaneously therewith the bonds are transferred by the borrower to the lead manager, for delivery to the allottees. A majority of the allottees will have instructed the lead manager to have their bonds delivered into one of the two European bond clearing systems, Euroclear (Brussels) or Cedel (Luxembourg).

These actions mark the completion of the issue (the bonds being formally issued at the time of the simultaneous interchange of issue proceeds and bonds), which is normally recorded in the European financial press the next day by a tombstone advertisement (Exhibit 904). Subsequently, bound volumes are prepared which contain all major documents relating to the issue of the bonds and are an important reference in the preparation of future issues.

5. Timetable for a public Eurobond issue

Document preparation normally takes two to three weeks; the selling period requires seven to 10 days; and two weeks would elapse before the closing of the issue and the receipt of funds. Thus, from the date of the initial decision to undertake an issue to the closing date of the issue, six to seven weeks typically elapse.

The days referred to in this timetable include business days only and all times given are local London times.

Fixed rate issue/Floating rate issue

Day −15 to Day −1: *Preparation of the documents* and application for all necessary official consents. A team from CSFB, as lead manager to the issue, would join the borrower to discuss documentation and the structure and timing of the issue.

Day −1: All official consents to have been received and offering documentation finalized. Final discussion of terms, market conditions and launch possibilities to take place between CSFB and the borrower.

Day 1: Acceptances of co-managers, reference banks, trustee and principal paying agent (or fiscal agent), and agent bank (floating rate issues only) to have been received.
CSFB to send out:
— *press release* announcing launch of the issue to leading newspapers;
— *underwriting invitation telex;*
— *selling group invitation telex;*

This announcement appears as a matter of record only

Minolta

Minolta Camera Co., Ltd.

(Minolta Camera Kabushiki Kaisha)

U.S. $30,000,000
7¼ per cent. Convertible Bonds 1995

Daiwa Europe N.V.

Credit Suisse First Boston Limited

The Taiyo Kobe Bank (Luxembourg) S.A.

Berliner Handels- und Frankfurter Bank

Crédit Lyonnais

DBS-Daiwa Securities International Limited

Kleinwort, Benson Limited

Kuwait Foreign Trading Contracting & Investment Co. (S.A.K.)

Smith Barney, Harris Upham & Co. Incorporated

Union Bank of Switzerland (Securities) Limited

Westdeutsche Landesbank Girozentrale

Algemene Bank Nederland N.V.	Amsterdam-Rotterdam Bank N.V.	Arab Financial Consultants Company S.A.K.
Banca del Gottardo	Banco di Roma	Bank Julius Baer International Limited
Bank of Tokyo International Limited	Banque Nationale de Paris	Banque de Neuflize, Schlumberger, Mallet
Banque de l'Union Européenne	Barclays International Group	Baring Brothers & Co., Limited
Bayerische Landesbank Girozentrale	BNP-Daiwa (Hong Kong) Limited B.S.I. Underwriters Limited James Capel & Co.	
Cazenove & Co. Commerzbank Aktiengesellschaft	County Bank Limited	Daiwa Overseas Finance Limited
Daiwa Securities Co. Ltd.	Daiwa Securities (H.K.) Limited	DG BANK Deutsche Genossenschaftsbank
Fuji Bank (Schweiz) A.G.	Fuji International Finance Limited	Antony Gibbs & Sons, Limited
Goldman Sachs International Corp.	Hill Samuel & Co. Limited	IBJ International Limited
Istituto Bancario San Paulo di Torino	Japan International Bank Limited	Kredietbank S.A. Luxembourgeoise
Kuwait International Investment Co. s.a.k.	Kuwait Investment Company (S.A.K.)	Manufacturers Hanover Limited
Merrill Lynch International & Co.	Mitsui Finance Europe Limited	Morgan Grenfell & Co. Limited
The National Commercial Bank (Saudi Arabia)	New Japan Securities Europe Limited	The Nikko Securities Co., (Europe) Ltd.
Nomura Europe N.V.	Osakaya Securities Co., Ltd.	Pierson, Heldring & Pierson N.V.
Saitama Bank (Europe) S.A.	Salomon Brothers International	Sanwa Bank (Underwriters) Limited
J. Henry Schroder Wagg & Co. Limited	Société Générale	Société Générale de Banque S.A.
Sumitomo Finance International	Svenska Handelsbanken	Swiss Bank Corporation International Limited
Taiyo Kobe Finance Hong Kong Limited		Vereins- und Westbank Aktiengesellschaft
Vickers da Costa International Limited	J. Vontobel & Co.	Yamaichi International (Europe) Limited

Source: *Euromoney*, November 1980.

— *letter to prospective underwriters* enclosing preliminary prospectus, underwriting agreement, selling agreement and delivery instruction form;
— *letter to prospective selling group members* enclosing preliminary prospectus, selling agreement and delivery instruction form.

Fixed rate issue	**Floating rate issue**
Day 4: Underwriters' preliminary telex replies to underwriting invitation to be received by CSFB.	Underwriters' telex replies to underwriting invitation to be received by CSFB.

Day 6: Countersigned selling and underwriting agreements to be received by CSFB.

| Day 8: —By 15:00 hours indications of interest from selling group members to be received by CSFB.
—At 16:00 hours the managers to meet to review pricing of the issue.
—At 16:30 hours the managers and representatives of the borrower to meet to price the issue.
—At 17:30 hours the printer to be advised of the final pricing details and printing of the final prospectus and subscription documents to commence.
—At 17:30 hours the final terms of the issue to be telexed to underwriters. | —Indications of interest from selling group members to be received by CSFB.

—Printing of final prospectus and subscription documents. |

Day 9: Stock exchange listing(s) to have been granted.

| —By 10:00 hours telex confirmation of acceptance of final terms by underwriters to be received by CSFB.
—*Signing meeting:* Copies of subscription agreement to be signed by the borrower and each of the managers.
—After signing meeting, CSFB to send allotment telexes to allottees.

—Allotment letters and prospectus to be despatched to selling group members by CSFB.
—Press release announcing completion of issue arrangements to be circulated by CSFB. | —*Signing meeting:* Copies of subscription agreement to be signed by the borrower and each of the managers.
—After signing meeting, CSFB to send allotment telexes to allottees.

—Allotment letters and prospectus to be despatched to selling group members by CSFB.
—Press release announcing completion of issue arrangements to be circulated by CSFB. |

Day 10: Acceptance of allotments to be received by CSFB from selling group members.

Day 17: By this date

| —Form of trust deed (or fiscal agency agreement and paying agency agreement) to have been finalized. | —Form of trust deed (or fiscal agency agreement and paying agency agreement and agent bank agreement to have been finalized. |

—Notes to have been delivered, and authenticated (if applicable).

| Day 19: | —Interest rate for first interest period to be determined by agent bank and notified to managers and selling group members. |

| Day 20: —Payment for their allotments to be made in New York clearing house funds in New York by selling group members. | |

| Day 21: | —Payment for their allotments to be made in New York clearing house funds by selling group members. |

146

—Delivery of counsels' opinions to the manager, together with all documentation required by the subscription agreement.

—Delivery to the managers of the bonds by the borrower against payment in New York clearing house funds of the proceeds of the issue by the managers to the borrower.

6. Private placements

The private placement sector, obviously closely linked to the public, has similar characteristics, with the exception that it may or may not be listed on a stock exchange, it may or may not be advertised, it may or may not be entirely underwritten and placed by a single bank, and it is usually denominated in larger amounts than a public issue, such as $5 million. Private placements are also made directly with only one institutional lender, which means that the borrowing may be in the form of a single bond with a value of $50 million or more. Furthermore, private placements are often not widely traded, and sometimes not at all, although the bank arranging the financing is prepared to buy back bonds from those institutions who have acquired them should they wish to sell.

7. Eurocredits

Eurocredits quite often are requested by the buyers of goods in order to pay for shipments of goods in cash. Chapter VI deals with these kind of credits.

CHAPTER TEN
Contract guarantees and international bonding practices

Lode G. Beckers

1. Definition

The practice whereby banks, insurance companies or other financial institutions are requested to guarantee their customers' performance or delivery obligations under a construction or supply contract is well-established. A variety of forms of guarantee issuances has developed over the course of years. However, in recent years this trade-related practice has received more attention, for several reasons:

    i. single contract amounts and associated bonding requirements have increased tremendously, mainly because of the emergence of jumbo-sized hydro-electric projects (in South America) and large-ticket infrastructure projects (in the Middle East);

    ii. for international construction contracts, banks apparently have assumed the role which traditionally—and still so in some home markets—was reserved for surety companies;

    iii. political risk considerations and events in Iran and Iraq have led the involved contract parties and the courts to greater or renewed awareness of the limitations and risks associated with the use of guarantees, bonds, or clean letters of credit as instruments to back-stop someone's completion capability or his compliance with an agreed set of contract terms.

In most Western legal systems, a *guarantee* is defined as a commitment to pay a sum of money in consideration of the non-fulfilment or breach of contractual terms by the account party. The guarantee cannot be called unless there was an actual obligation to pay, to deliver or to perform by the guaranteed party, and unless that party defaults under its primary obligation. Narrowly defined, a guarantee is not a generic concept; it is an ancillary agreement, a form of security, related to another underlying transaction.[1] A *bond* traditionally is issued by surety companies, particularly in the construction industry. By bonding a construction company, the surety company will guarantee correct performance in accordance with the contract terms. Should the contractor fail to perform, the surety company will use its knowledge of market conditions and its technical resources to try and complete the project in lieu of the defaulting contractor. A *letter of credit* is a legal instrument, commonly used by banks in international trade, whereby a bank is committed to the payment of a sum of money, provided the demand to pay is received in good form prior to an expiry date stated in the letter of credit, and provided all terms stipulated in the opening letter of credit are duly complied with. Broadly speaking, a documentary letter of credit calls for the presentation of a valid and genuine set of documents. A *clean* letter of credit does not require such a presentation of invoices or other trade documents and can be made payable on simple demand of the beneficiary. If this right of first demand is not conditioned, and if the call under the clean letter of credit is virtually left to the discretion of the beneficiary,[2] the clean letter of credit offers the beneficiary the advantages of a cheque or a banker's draft, payable upon presentation.[3]

---

[1] See under section 3. Legal nature of contract guarantees.

[2] H. Harfield, *Bank Credits and Acceptances*, New York, The Ronald Press Company, 5th Edition, 1974, p. 30: "A clean irrevocable credit issued to a named beneficiary or assignee may impose no condition other than due presentation of a demand for payment, just a promissory note, although an unconditional promise to pay a certain sum at a specified time and place, imposes the condition of due presentment."

[3] For practical purposes, the term *bonds* will be used as a generic term in this article, although one should be alerted to the shortcomings of such a generalization. The same applies to *contract guarantees*, which is used in a broad sense, thus encompassing the *first demand guarantees* (or letters of credit) as well as the ancillary *guarantees*.

2. Purpose and scope

The expansion of international trade in recent years and the dramatic increase in size and importance of some major markets in the Middle East have highlighted the need for a more precise definition of rights and practices related to bonds and contract guarantees. To provide definite answers for all possible forms of guarantee instruments falls beyond the scope of this chapter. The following paragraphs identify and describe the most common forms of bonds issued in respect of international supply, construction and turn-key contracts, thereby also formulating some practical guidelines as to how to issue and syndicate such bonds. The latter part of the chapter deals with recent developments, problem areas, cost considerations and comparative advantages and disadvantages.

3. Legal nature of contract guarantees

The legal nature and form of the guarantee is an indispensable part of any set of practical guidelines for users, issuers or beneficiaries. Some of these legally-oriented guidelines are formulated in the following paragraphs.

The practice of issuing contract guarantees in connection with construction contracts is widely known and provides a good starting point for a reflection on the legal nature of the involved commitments (see section 3.1. Surety bonds and bank guarantees). Section 3.2. looks in more detail at guarantee features such as the first demand and unconditional character of most internationally issued contract guarantees, distinguishing between letters of credit and bank guarantees. Section 3.3. will draw some conclusions and list some bank policies concerning guarantee issuances.

3.1. Surety bonds and bank guarantees for construction contracts

3.1.1. Preventive and remedial function

Contract guarantees and bonds have the common objective of providing the beneficiary of these guarantees with an additional, tangible assurance that the commercial contract entered into either will yield the expected results (this can be referred to as the *preventive* function of the bond), or that the possible consequences of non-performance, default or dishonesty can be limited, thanks to the committed availability of additional technical, operational or financial resources (the *remedial* function of the bond). From the applicant's point of view, the issued guarantee or bond is an aid, and often a requirement to obtain the contract. The contractor or supplier will, therefore, permit the bond to be issued in a format which confers the majority of rights to the beneficiary, leaving himself with an imbalance between rights and obligations.

3.1.2. Surety bonds

While the predominance of the beneficiary's rights is a frequent feature in international construction bonds, this is not the case for bond issuances related to supply contracts or for domestic issuances of construction bonds in the United States: surety companies, when issuing a bond in favour of a U.S. employer, are committing themselves to indemnify the beneficiary only when the contractor fails to perform. The contractor usually obtains a grace period during which he will attempt to remedy the situation. If the contractor is unable to do this, the surety company may call on other available technical and operational resources. Surety bonds, perhaps because they are by definition conditional, are usually issued for an amount equal to 100% of the contract price. The locally operating U.S. surety company has an obligation towards the employer not merely to make a payment; it is an obligation to perform under the contract, an obligation to achieve the results described and aimed at in the contract. In case of breach of contract by the employer, the surety bond becomes invalid.[4]

3.1.3. International surety bonds

Sometimes, but rarely, contract guarantees for international contracts are issued by surety companies. However, in the case of these international issuances, the required surety bonds are generally worded as a commitment to pay. The issuing surety company enters into a commitment to pay and forfeit a sum of money to the employer. Here, the surety bond is generally payable on demand. On the one hand, this may explain why the percentage value of the required bond is a fraction of the contract value (ranging from 10% to 25%). On the other hand, it also explains why the surety company wants the contractor to deposit or promise to deposit with them liquid funds for

---

[4] McNeill Stokes, *International Construction Contracts, An ENR Book*, New York, McGraw Hill, 1980, pp. 143–4.

an amount equal to the demand bond. The payment obligation is unconditional, because the beneficiary can call the bond upon simple declaration of default by the contractor, i.e., without prior proof of the non-performance of the contractor.

3.1.4. International bank guarantees

The international banking system is considerably more developed than internationally-operating surety companies, and foreign employers are often not very familiar with the suretyship institution as it is known in the U.K. and the U.S. In addition, employers strongly prefer an unconditional commitment to pay to a conditional commitment to perform or to remedy. For these three reasons, the issuance of an unconditional bank guarantee, payable on simple demand, is required for the majority of international construction contracts. The format of the bank or insurance company construction bond is looked at in the next paragraphs. What is important to note at this stage is the payable *on demand* character of the construction bonds, the related *payment* rather than *performance* obligation, and the *absolute* or abstract character of these guarantees as opposed to the subsidiary or *accessory* character of the more limited (domestic) surety bond. Another reason for giving preference to bank-issued construction bonds lies with the account party (the contractor, seller or supplier). Historically, buyers or employers would require their contract parties to make a deposit with their bank, to ensure their satisfactory performance. This practice was costly to the exporter or contractor: the blocked funds, callable on demand by the beneficiary, either meant a drain on liquidity or had to be borrowed from the exporter's or contractor's bank, and were subsequently remitted to the beneficiary's bank. Hence, it is clear why bank guarantees were gradually considered as an acceptable substitute for the blocked deposits.[5] On the other hand, the beneficiary wanted to safeguard his ready access to liquid funds, without need for proof of the other party's non-performance. For that reason, the issued bank guarantees were required to be payable on first and simple demand.[6]

3.2. General considerations concerning contract guarantees

3.2.1. Conditional and unconditional bonds

As mentioned above, surety bonds, as issued in the U.S. market, are usually conditional bonds, because the rights of the beneficiary (and the obligations of the surety company) are dependent on the existence of default or non-performance by the account party. However, for other contract guarantees it is not usually possible to rely on the name the instrument bears to determine the validity and the nature of the legal obligation. The intention of the parties is reflected in the specific wording of the bond or the contract guarantee, and will determine the respective rights and obligations. Using this as a criterion, an unconditional bond or guarantee is a separate legal obligation whereby the issuer commits himself to pay a sum of money to the beneficiary without further examination of the true respect or breach of terms under another contract. Conversely, a conditional bond is an ancillary obligation which, to be callable, needs *proof* of non-performance, rather than a simple declaration of default by the beneficiary or his representative. In the case of an unconditional bond, the *nature* of the obligation is described as *abstract*, or *absolute*. In the case of a conditional bond, the obligation is said to be ancillary, or relative, or *accessory:* one needs to ascertain whether the breach of terms of the *related* construction or supply contract is proven.

Exhibit 1001. Comparison: surety bonds—bank guarantees (simplified case)

	Surety bond	Bank guarantee
Type of obligation	Obligation to perform	Obligation to pay
Usual form	Guarantee	Letter of credit (U.S.)
Strength of commitment	Conditional	Unconditional
Legal nature	Surety	Indemnity
Call is triggered by	Existence of default	Statement
Type of contract	Ancillary relative	Independent absolute

3.2.2. Letters of credit and guarantees

To determine whether a bond is an unconditional or conditional, absolute or relative commitment, it is not sufficient to refer to the terminology. Whereas in most legal systems, two different terms are

---

[5] To look upon guarantee issuances in comparison making a loan highlights the need for taking the involved corporate credit strength as the basis for issuing the bond, rather than the customer's performance capability (see also section 6).

[6] Legal commentators sometimes refer to blocked deposits as a *real security*, and to bank guarantees as *personal security*.

used to distinguish the one type of commitment from the other,[7] it is important to examine the precise wording of the issued bond to determine the nature of the commitment.

In this context, the use of the expression *letter of credit* as a substitute term for *unconditional guarantee* needs explanation. In the U.S., nationally chartered banks are not permitted to issue guarantees on the letterhead of their head offices.[8] When requested to issue an unconditional commitment, payable on first demand, they will issue a letter of credit. This is an independent contract between issuing bank and beneficiary. A dispute about payment cannot be resolved by reference to another contract. Because the bank's reputation and obligation to pay is irrevocably committed, business practice and the U.S. Comptroller of the Currency's interpretative ruling[9] have carefully defined which rules should be adhered to in order to safeguard the true character of a letter of credit:

i. The bank's obligation to pay must be *unconditional.* Payment will be made on demand, on presentation of a draft, or on presentation of a set of pre-agreed documents, but there is no need to examine the actual existence or non-existence of facts, and no need to refer to debatable elements of another contract. There can be a simple reference to the existence of another contract, but not to the existence of any particular fact related to that contract which can be interpreted as the incorporation of a condition into the letter of credit.

ii. The letter of credit should carry a specific *expiry date.*[10]

iii. The letter of credit should state the *maximum amount* of the bank's commitment.

iv. The account party must have entered into an *unconditional obligation to reimburse* the bank.[11]

The latter condition is of particular importance to issuing banks, who may sometimes face a request to issue an unconditional letter of credit, while themselves benefiting only from a more restrictive right of recourse on the account party. The bank will remain committed to the beneficiary in an unconditional way.

While the distinction between the two concepts, i.e., the absolute character of a letter of credit and the relative, ancillary character of a guarantee, is clear, in the real world this character can be blurred. Harfield puts this as follows: ". . . the inclusion of conditions and language generally found in trust indentures, underwriting agreements, or term loan contracts, is an invitation to misconstruction that may well be irresistible to a court"[12] and ". . . contracts characterized as letters of credit may be so drawn as in fact to be ancillary to other contracts or relationships, and contracts characterized as guarantees may be so drawn as to be independent of any other agreement, relation or condition".[13] In other words, it is the specific wording that determines whether a bond or guarantee was intended to have the force and character of a payment instrument.

3.2.3. First demand guarantees and irrevocable letters of credit

These are the extreme forms under which an unconditional commitment will appear. The payment instrument character of a contract guarantee appears most clearly in the case of a first demand guarantee, whereby the bank undertakes to pay at the first (written) request of the beneficiary, either with the presentation of a set of documents of which only the conformity must be examined, or without any further justification. The same applies to irrevocable letters of credit which are issued for the same purpose.[14]

It is misleading to present first demand guarantees as different from documentary guarantees, since the demand guarantee can be payable against simple, undocumented demand or presentation of documents. The latter can be an expert's opinion or an independent authority's certificate. However, when a court judgment or arbitrage council opinion is listed as the required documentation, the demand character of the guarantee becomes questionable because these documents, by their nature, tend to establish *proof* of the default or non-performance, rather than simple declaration or *statement* of non-performance, and to arrive at that *proof* of default, examination of the respect or breach of the terms of *another* contractual relationship is necessary.

---

[7] The following terminology, in French, German, Dutch and English, is used to designate unconditional guarantees: *garantie* (F), *Garantievertrag* (G), contract of indemnity (E), *garantie* (D); to refer to a conditional, ancillary guarantee: *cautionnement* (F), *Bürgschaft* (G), contract of guarantee (E), *borgtocht* (D).

[8] For a commentary on the historic origin of this rule and its proper interpretation, see H. Harfield, *Bank Credits and Acceptances*, pp. 154–67.

[9] No. 7.7016 (12 C.F.R. §7–7016).

[10] Even when the expiry date can be extended at the beneficiary's option.

[11] The comptroller's ruling also adds that the bank should receive a fee in consideration for the issuance of a letter of credit.

[12] H. Harfield, *op. cit.*, p. 176.

[13] H. Harfield, *op. cit.*, p. 164.

[14] They can be issued either directly in favour of the beneficiary, or as a back-stop letter of credit in favour of a bank issuing a first demand guarantee in favour of the beneficiary.

3.2.4. Conclusion

Contract guarantees can take the form of: (i) first demand guarantees, which are unconditional payment instruments, payable on demand or against simple presentation of documents, and which legally can be characterized as an indemnity; or (ii) guarantees in the narrow sense of the expression, whereby the guarantee has a surety or security function (*Sicherheitsfunktion*), and whereby the guarantee is callable only after it is established that non-performance exists.

Whereas in Europe and in overseas markets, the *bonds* and *guarantees* are used as generic concepts for conditional as well as unconditional, ancillary as well as absolute commitments, the U.S. practice is to make a clear distinction between letters of credit (unconditional commitments to pay) and guarantees (a promise to answer for someone else's obligation in case of his default). However, as mentioned before, in practice, as well as semantically and conceptually, there are overlapping areas. This leads to the conclusion that the true nature and strength of the guarantee commitment can only be determined after case per case examination of the terms. On the other hand, when the parties intend to issue a first demand guarantee, the following features should be inserted in an unequivocal way:

— unconditional commitment to pay;
— first demand payment upon beneficiary's request or upon presentation of an agreed set of documents;
— commitment to pay a sum of money rather than a commitment to guarantee another contract party's performance.[15]

3.3 Bank policies with respect to guarantee issuances

a. In the majority of cases, banks will issue unconditional demand guarantees and letters of credit on behalf of their customers. The following cases are *not* in accordance with common commercial banks' policy:
  (1) guarantee issuances which would not be a commitment to make a payment, but merely a joint and several obligation to perform (in legal language: a surety rather than an indemnity, an ancillary commitment rather than an absolute commitment);
  (2) guarantee issuances whereby the issuing bank would have to establish whether default has occurred under the underlying contract.

b. Most banks' policies do *not* encourage:
  (1) guarantees which require the account party's consent prior to making payment (i.e., another form of conditional guarantees), unless specifically agreed by the beneficiary;
  (2) guarantees which carry no firm expiry date;
  (3) guarantees which contain features leading to uncertainties about the maximum amount of the guarantee;[16]
  (4) guarantees which contain overly elaborate[17] documentary requirements, even if the demand nature of the guarantee could be maintained;
  (5) guarantees whereby the extent of the guarantee commitment is not properly matched by the right of recourse on the account party.

c. While observing that banks will prefer to issue contract guarantees (or letters of credit) which are unconditional commitments to make a payment up to a given amount and prior to a stated expiry date, employers (*maîtres d'ouvrage*) seem to have a similar preference. Does this therefore leave the supplier or contractor at the mercy of the beneficiary of the unconditional bond? To a great extent, yes. However, this is an element which supposedly has received proper consideration when evaluating the overall attractiveness of the underlying commercial or industrial transaction. At the same time, history shows that reputable employers or importers do not make their living by the calling of bonds. They are more genuinely interested in performance or delivery rather than in obtaining an amount of cash from the bond issuer.[18] Seen in this broader commercial or trade context, the on

---

[15] If the issuer guarantees the performance of its account party under the contract, the guarantor will have to establish and prove that his customer was in default, i.e., the guarantee becomes a conditional guarantee and pushes the guarantor into an unwanted *suretyship* role. On the other hand, if the issuer guarantees a *good* performance, i.e., the expected *result* of the contract, he can again end up in a suretyship role, unless it is made clear that the guarantor's commitment is clearly limited to the payment of a sum of money.

[16] See section 6.

[17] H. Harfield, *op. cit.*, p. 68: "The same considerations that proscribe incorporation of excessive detail in letters of credit used to finance sales contracts apply with even greater force to the documentary requirement of credits that are payable upon non-performance or inadequate performance of other agreements between account party and beneficiary."

[18] Cases are known, though, of fraudulent actions of obscure middle-men who, through mischievous retention of progress payments, lead their sub-contractors to stop the works on the site, thus generating themselves the causes for claiming advance payment and performance guarantees—which apparently was the fraudulent caller's intention from the outset.

demand payable contract guarantees may appear as less onerous than at first glance. It is somewhat surprising that first demand guarantees, which are the most frequently requested and issued form of contract guarantees, are not more emphatically dealt with in the International Chamber of Commerce Uniform Rules for Contract Guarantees. Article 9 addresses documented calls only, and as far as claims under performance bonds and advance payment guarantees are concerned, suggests as a rule that these claims should only be honoured against "either a court decision or an arbitral award justifying the claim, or the approval of the principal in writing to the claim and the amount to be paid".[19]

4. Types of contract guarantees and practical mechanics

4.1. Most common types of bonds

4.1.1. Bid bonds

The purpose of a bid bond is to ensure that the party to whom a contract is awarded will indeed accept the award the proceed with the execution of the construction, supply or delivery obligation falling under the terms of the awarded contract. The bid bond can be called by the employer (or the buyer or importer) when the contractor (or the exporter) fails to accept the contract award and, consequently, the employer is faced with the additional costs of re-awarding the contract to another party. The employer may have to publish new tender conditions or to examine again the specifications of another party's bid. To cover these costs, the issuance of a bid bond is requested for either a fixed amount of money[20] or a fixed percentage of the submitted bid.[21]

Bid bonds can be requested for publicly tendered contracts as well as privately negotiated contracts, and carry a fixed expiry date. The expiry date usually corresponds to the expected contract award date. However, in the case of sizeable public tenders in the Middle East, it is common practice to leave the extension of the bid bond up to the discretion of the governmental authority involved. And in addition, the same public authority may reserve for itself the right of reducing the amount of the requested bid bond extension, depending on intended changes in the

Exhibit 1002: Bid bond structure

Example of 2% bid bond, issued for six months.

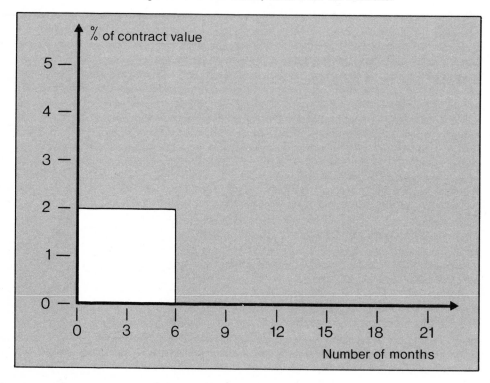

---

[19] *Uniform Rules for Contract Guarantees*, International Chamber of Commerce, Publication No. 325, Paris, 1978, p. 32.

[20] The bid bond is denominated in U.S. dollars or in the contract country's local currency. For major public contracts, a local bank may be required to issue or to advise the bid bond issuance to the contracting authority involved.

[21] For example, this is common practice in the Kingdom of Saudi Arabia, where bid bonds are requested for all publicly tendered contracts. By Royal Decree of April 22, 1977, Article Two, the percentage is fixed at 1–2%.

154

forthcoming contract amount.[22] The bid bond is usually returned to the winning contract party upon the signing of the contract and upon issuance of the performance bond. In principle, all bid bonds covering the unsuccessful bids are returned at the same time. In several cases, the requested wording of the bid bond is not as precise as the legal practitioner would prefer: sometimes, the issuing bank or financial institution is committing its customer to strict compliance with terms of the underlying awarded contract.

Excerpt from bid bond wording, commonly used in the Kingdom of Saudi Arabia
"On the Contractor's failure to fulfil any of the conditions of the Contract as determined by you in your absolute judgement, the Guarantor shall forthwith on demand made by you in writing and not withstanding any object by the Contractor pay you such amount or amounts as you shall require, not exceeding in aggregate the above-mentioned amount of Saudi Riyals . . ."

However, the sanction following the non-compliance or failure to sign the awarded contract is less ambiguous; the involved bank or insurance company will pay the mentioned amount of money. Whether, in addition, the defaulting contractor or exporter is at risk of triggering a claim for consequential damages over and above the amount of the bid bond, is an issue of considerable complexity, and not dealt with in this chapter.

4.1.2. Performance bonds

The performance bond has several purposes. It offers the employer an assurance about the creditworthiness of the involved construction company or exporter. When the performance bond is issued by a first-class banking institution or reputable bonding company, the employer may presume that the guarantee or bond has been issued only after a diligent assessment of the contractor's or importer's financial standing, trade reputation and capability to perform successfully under the awarded contract terms.

A second purpose is served in that the performance bond eventually may give access to additional resources should the contractor—or exporter—fail to perform or encounter difficulties in the execution of the contract. A distinction must be made here between performance bonds issued by surety companies, and performance bonds or guarantees issued by banks or other financial institutions. When a surety company issues a performance bond, it commits itself to the good performance of its customer and guarantees satisfactory completion.

Excerpt from performance bond wording as issued by a surety company
". . . Whenever Contractor shall be, and declared by Employer to be in default under the Contract, the Employer having performed the Employer's obligations thereunder, the Surety may promptly remedy the default, or shall promptly:
1. Complete the Contract etc. . . .
2. Obtain a bid or bids (. . .) for completing the Contract (. . .) and make available sufficient funds to pay the cost of completion etc. . . .
3. Pay the Employer the amount required (. . .) to complete the Contract . . ."

Source. International Chamber of Commerce, Brochure on Contract Guarantees, Paris 1978.

When a financial institution issues a performance bond, the employer does not receive a commitment that the works will be completed.[23] The commitment extends only to the payment of a sum of money, often on first written demand, and following the simple notice of malperformance by the contractor or supplier:

Excerpt from performance bond wording as issued by a bank
". . . (A) On the Contractor's failure to fulfil any of the conditions of the Contract (. . .) the Guarantor shall forthwith on demand made by you in writing and notwithstanding any objection of the Contractor pay you such amount or amounts etc. . . . (C) The covenants herein contained constitute unconditional and irrevocable direct obligations of the Guarantor."

Source. *Saudi Arabia and its Construction Industry*, Citicorp International Group, Information Memorandum, May 1978, p. 42.

Performance bonds are usually issued, by definition, until final performance, i.e., until the end of the expected contract period. In the case of a supply-and-install contract, this expiry date is obviously firmer than in the case of construction contracts which are more frequently subject to extensions, variations or alterations. In principle, the performance bond will remain outstanding for its full amount until final completion (see Exhibit 1003).[24]

---

[22] This has been the case for the civil works contract for the University of Riyadh.
[23] See section 3.
[24] Contract parties may agree to partial reduction of the performance bond, e.g., when a project is to be completed in stages.

Exhibit 1003: Performance bond structure

Example of 5% performance bond, issued for two and a half years.

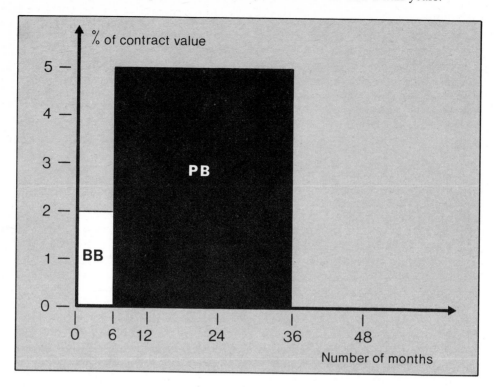

The performance bond is usually issued for a fixed percentage of the awarded contract amount.[25] In most cases of major construction or turn-key contracts, it is replaced with a *maintenance bond* upon its expiry or when the executed works are accepted by the client. However, quite frequently, the banks or financial institutions issuing the performance bond are requested to extend the expiry date of their commitment. This can happen upon a simple request from the beneficiary. This is current practice, for instance, in the major construction markets of the Middle East: the issuing bank cannot refuse[26] the re-issuance or extension provided the request in writing is made prior to the previously stated expiry date:

Excerpt from performance bond, as issued in the Kingdom of Saudi Arabia
". . . (C) . . . No alteration in the terms of the contract or in the extent or nature of the work to be performed thereunder and no allowance of time by you or other forbearance or concession or any other act or omission by you which but for this provision might exonerate or discharge the Guarantor shall in any way release the Guarantor from any liability hereunder."

Source: CIG Information Memorandum, May 1978, p. 42.

The performance bond is often issued by the same bank or financial institution which handled the bid bond. In that respect, the FIDIC (Fédération Internationale des Ingénieurs Conseil) recommended terminology is revealing: they refer to bid bonds as *preliminary bonds* and to performance bonds as *final bonds*. However, in the bank-customer relationship the issuance of these bonds raises rather substantially different questions.

An important consideration of all involved parties, i.e., issuing financial institution, contractor/importer and employer/beneficiary, is to know precisely what is understood by the performance obligation covered by the performance bond: is the guaranteed performance an obligation to construct, or an obligation to operate economically?[27] Is it an obligation to deliver the purchased

---

[25] For example, in Saudi Arabia the percentage is fixed by Royal Decree at 5% for publicly-tendered contracts. The performance bond percentage is sometimes a matter of negotiation and can reflect the respective strength of the employer's or contractor's bargaining position.

[26] A refusal to extend the expiry date is usually sanctioned with a call of the involved bond.

[27] Recent examples are known in the field of hospital construction, whereby the main contract provides for the "construction of the hospital, and its staffing, training and adequate operation during the year following the completion of the construction works . . ."

equipment, or an obligation to install it as well and to operate the assembled plant satisfactorily? Does "satisfactorily" mean "economically" as well? A precise definition of the type of expected performance (construction, supply operation, training, staffing, etc.) may become even more inportant in the future, as turn-key contracts become more frequent, and competitive forces steer contracting parties further towards "successful operation" rather than "successful construction".

4.1.3. Advance payment guarantees (APGs)

In most major contracts, the employer or importer wants to make liquid funds available to his contract party, to permit him to cover the mobilization costs necessary to proceed with the execution of the contract. Usually, the advance payment is intended to be used for the purchase of equipment, the funding of overhead and organization costs and for the financing of all activities (such as the hiring and housing of local or expatriate labour, transportation of a first supply of aggregates, delivery of permits and clearing of duties) which take the contractor or importer to the stage where a first progress certificate or a first set of shipping documents can be produced and presented to the employer.

It is often unclear whether the advance payment guarantee covers the simple making of the advance payment rather than its proper use by the recipient party. In the former case, the advance payment guarantee will be called whenever an amount is still outstanding at the moment of breach of contract or malperformance.[28] In the latter case, there would be a more direct link between the advance payment guarantee issuance and its intended use for mobilization purposes: in other words, the advance payment guarantee would become callable in case of proven improper use, regardless of whether or not doubt has arisen about the ultimate completion capability of the contractor. Suffice it to say at this stage that financial institutions, in accordance with their policy for performance bonds, will usually look upon their liability under an advance payment guarantee as a simple commitment to pay and to restitute the part of the advance payment still due by the contractor.

Exhibit 1004: Advance payment guarantee structure

Example of 20% APG, issued for two and a half years.

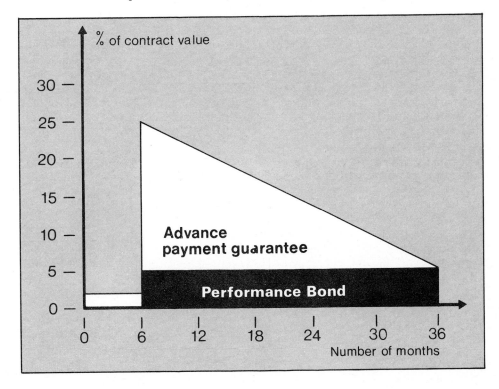

---

[28] This seems to be the interpretation to be given to the advance payment guarantee format requested for public contracts in Saudi Arabia: ". . . On the Contractor's failure to fulfil any of the conditions of the Contract as determined by you (i.e. the employer) in your absolute judgment, the Guarantor shall forthwith on demand (. . .) pay you such amounts etc. . . ." CIBL, Information Memorandum, p. 43.

Whether a bank's advance payment guarantee is outstanding for the entire amount or for a fraction of the initially issued guarantee, depends upon the contractor's performance under the contract. It is common practice to consider a fraction of the progress certificate as representing works or expenses[29] previously covered by the advance payment. This means that as more progress certificates are produced, more evidence is given of the proper use of the advance payment. Consequently, the advance payment can be considered as definitely earned and acquired for these documented expenses, and the advance payment guarantee is then no longer applicable on these portions of the advance payment. Hence, it is common practice to proceed to successive reductions in the advance payment guarantee. The contractor or supplier requests a confirmation from the employer that the amount outstanding under the advance payment guarantee is reduced. The contractor advises his guarantor accordingly, and subsequently obtains relief or proportionate reduction of his recourse obligation to the guaranteeing bank or insurance company.[30] It follows that the advance payment guarantee will be reduced as the contract proceeds. The outstanding amount actually may be reduced to zero prior to final completion of the contract. However, this is not often the case.

Advance payments are made for a lump sum amount of cash, or—less frequently—in kind[31] or for a fixed percentage of the contract. The common practice for public contracts in Saudi Arabia is to make a 20% advance payment. However, in this country as well as in other major markets, the size (or percentage) of the advance payment guarantee is also a reflection of the contractor's or supplier's competitive strength or technological advantage. It is, for example, customary to obtain larger advance payments on projects with a high technological content,[32] and to settle for a 5% or 10% advance payment on award of less sophisticated infrastructure projects. In addition, there usually is a carefully negotiated relationship between the percentage of the requested performance bond, the amount of the advance payment and the agreed contract price.

4.1.4. Retention money bonds (RMBs)

As with the advance payment guarantee, we can look firstly at the purpose of the retention money, and then at the objective aimed at through issuance of a retention money bond. Under most construction contracts, a part of the payment due upon presentation of a duly certified progress certificate is retained by the employer, in order to cover future unforeseeable expenses arising from heretofore untraceable mistakes or faults in the completed construction works (or in export contracts, in the delivered goods or equipment). The fraction of the progress payment thus retained by the employer, the *retention money*, theoretically should go into an escrow account in the name of the contractor or exporter and become available after a given period, usually *one year*, following final completion of the project. This also is usually the moment when final and definite acceptance takes place. It is obvious that the retention money increases over the life of the contract and reaches its maximum upon final completion. The most frequently recurring percentage of the retained progress payment money is 10%.

However, it is not very practical for the contractor whose works are in progress to obtain only a 90% payment on his certificates of progress. What he desires is to obtain payment in full on the valuation of works performed. For that reason, he will request a bank or another financial intermediary to issue a guarantee against which all retained money will be released. The retention money guarantee is usually issued for the full amount of expected final outstandings or for a fixed percentage of the contract. However, the guarantor's actual liability at any point in time is limited to the progress payment fractions effectively released. A glance at Exhibits 1004 and 1005 will help to clarify that APG and RMB outstandings develop in opposite ways: both guarantees or bonds are largely overlapping and thus not cumulative. However, administrative delays in obtaining proper release or reduction in APG outstandings usually lead to a situation in which both guarantees are outstanding for a combined amount larger than the progress state of the construction works (or shipments) would call for.

---

[29] These can be cash outlays or non-cash items such as depreciation relative to equipment acquired with the advance payment.

[30] Sometimes the confirmation of reduction in advance payment guarantees is handled by the issuing bank as an administrative function.

[31] For some hydro-electrical projects in South America, an advance payment may be made in the form of delivery of equipment purchased by the employer. This transaction will be covered by the issuance of an *equipment bond*, which will decrease in accordance with depreciation allowances based on the expected average useful life of the equipment (see section 4.2.4).

[32] Construction of petrochemical plants, turn-key phosphate plants, cement plants, telecommunications systems, etc.

158

Exhibit 1005: Retention money bond structure

Example of RMB building up to 10% over a two and a half year contract period.

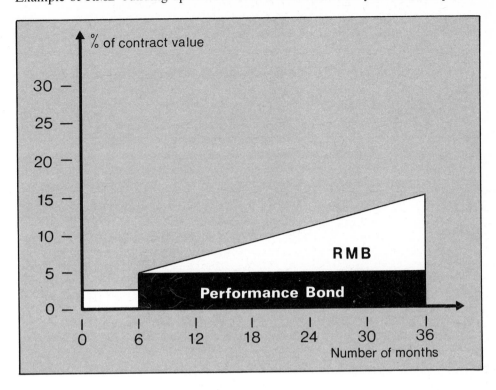

4.1.5. Maintenance bonds

The purpose of the maintenance bond is to prevent a contractor from walking off the construction site as soon as the project is completed and the last progress payment received, leaving it to the client to discover latent faults or defects in workmanship which may not be evident at completion. The maintenance bond is issued at the end of the construction period and will remain outstanding until the end of the maintenance period. This is usually agreed to be one year and in most cases coincides with the final acceptance date of the project.

The question is sometimes asked whether retention money bonds and maintenance bonds are not the same. There are indeed similarities, but basic differences should be highlighted, which may explain why it is possible to encounter a requirement to issue both an RMB and a maintenance bond for one and the same project.

Exhibit 1006: Comparison of RMB and maintenance bond

	Retention money bond	Maintenance bond
When issued	At contract award or upon completion of works	Upon completion of works
Outstanding liability	In accordance with state of works	Full amount of issued bond
Objective	Cover additional costs after completion of project	Cover additional costs after completion of project

The maintenance bond is issued for a fixed percentage of the contract. Requests for extension of the one-year period are not unusual, especially if a problem has arisen and as a result both parties are awaiting the outcome of the related repair works or have submitted the case to court or arbitrage council.

Most often, the maintenance bond is issued at the moment of release and return of the performance bond. In a sense, the maintenance bond replaces the performance bond, albeit often for different amounts. The final outstanding amount of the retention money bond may be converted into a maintenance bond, and this usually for the same amount. Another possibility is to aggregate the final or residual amount of both APG and RMB, and convert these into a one-year maintenance bond upon completion of the contract.

Exhibit 1007: Maintenance bond structure

Example of 12-month 5% maintenance bond issued upon completion and replacing both PB and RMB.

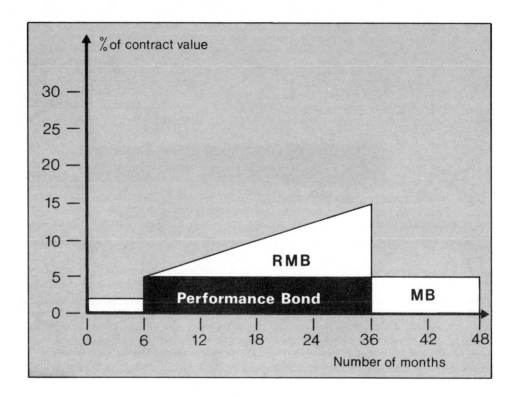

4.1.6. Conclusion

Bid (or *tender*) bonds, performance bonds, advance payment bonds, retention money bonds and/or maintenance bonds are the most frequently occurring types of contract guarantees. Even for these commonly-used bonds, legal or contractual rights and liabilities are not always well-defined and many variations and mutations are adopted and agreed upon when the underlying construction, supply or turn-key contract is negotiated. To keep things simple, it is perhaps preferable to agree on the following basic conclusions before discussing in more detail more complex types of bonds.

    i. The bid bond is usually returned upon award of the contract.

    ii. The performance guarantee is usually outstanding for its full amount from the date of award or contract signature until the end of the maintenance period. However, a performance bond may be converted into a maintenance bond upon completion of the works. In Exhibit 1008, it is assumed that the conversion takes place for a higher percentage.

    iii. The advance payment guarantee is issued and outstanding for its full value upon contract award but reduces to nil on completion.

    iv. The retention money guarantee builds up to an agreed percentage by completion date and can then be converted into a maintenance bond until the end of the maintenance period, or can be extended under its own name of retention money bond during the same maintenance period. An alternative way of charting the guarantee outstandings build-up is presented in Exhibit 1009 (with a maintenance bond issuance for only 5%).

Exhibit 1008: Contract guarantees, structure

Example of bond structure, for a two and a half year construction period and one year maintenance period. Assumptions: 2% bid bond; 5% performance bond; 10% APG; 5% RMB; 10% maintenance bond.

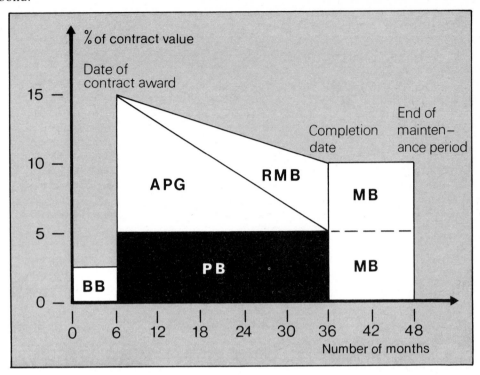

Exhibit 1009: Contract guarantees, alternative presentation

Example of bond structure. Assumptions: two and a half year construction period; one year maintenance period; 2% bid bond; 10% performance bond; 5% retention money guarantee; 10% APG; 10% maintenance bond.

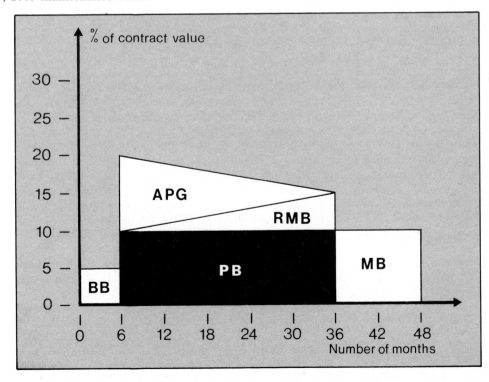

4.2. Other forms of bonds or contract guarantees

4.2.1. Customs bonds

In the world of construction and engineering, customs bonds are often requested to be issued in connection with the importation of equipment. The contractor who is importing the equipment needed for a given project can obtain an exemption from paying import duties or excise duties to the customs authorities of the country involved. However, by the same token, he commits to re-export that equipment upon completion of the project. Should he fail to do so, the customs authorities will claim the applicable customs duties. Usually, these duties are calculated as a fixed percentage of the undepreciated value of the equipment. If the contractor does not make the necessary customs duties payment, the customs authorities will call the customs bond which was issued for that purpose at the time of the importation of the equipment.

Disputes are quite common and can arise when duties are claimed or customs bonds called while the contractor is asserting that he intends to re-export the equipment but has not been able to do so (because of break-down of equipment, non-availability of means of transportation, temporary swap of pieces of equipment or renting to other projects). All these events can occur and may lead to a conflict between the contractor (or importer) and his issuing bank.

Customs bonds are issued for a maturity covering the construction period.[33] For some projects, this period will largely exceed the expected useful life of the equipment. In such cases, the (public authority) employer will usually seek a definite exemption of customs duties for certain types of equipment. This obviates the need for customs bonds and circumvents the nebulous question of whether customs duties are due on pieces of equipment whose useful life has come to an end. However, should the question arise under other circumstances, it is useful to bear in mind that customs bonds are issued primarily to deter the foreign contractor or local importer from selling the imported equipment or capital goods locally. This rationale applies regardless of whether the sale or re-sale takes place before or after full depreciation of the equipment involved.

4.2.2. Crude oil lifting bonds

Recently, the practice of requesting the issuance of bank guarantees or letters of credit relating to the importation of crude oil has gained much ground. Basically, the oil importer is required to cover with the additional strength of a prime bank guarantee his own commitment to come and lift periodically a given quantity of crude oil of a specified quality or gravity, at a contractually-agreed loading point and at an agreed price per barrel. Should the crude importer change his mind, and should his tanker not show up at the expected point in time, or should he object to the specifications of the crude oil which is ready to be pumped on board, the oil exporter may call under the bank guarantee.

At first glance, crude lifting bonds may be looked upon as a lesser risk, as long as they are issued on behalf of importers, traders or oil companies of unquestionable standing, and provided these account parties have a long and well-established track record in the oil world. However, the issuing bank will also have to assess the moral standing and operational capability of the oil exporter involved, to establish whether the exporter is likely to call the crude lifting bond for capricious reasons or whether he has sufficiently developed the necessary oil production technology to qualify as an experienced oil field operator. Most crude lifting bonds are *on demand bonds*. Claims for payment, thus, will be honoured by the issuing bank regardless of disputes between importer and exporter about quality, quantity, price or timing.

Crude lifting bonds call for the payment of a commission to the issuing bank.[34] Usually, this is some fraction of 1% per annum, and almost generally lower than the level of commission due on long-term performance bonds or advance payment bonds issued to guarantee a contractor's completion capability on a major construction project. It is felt that in the case of a crude lifting bond, the performance-related risk element is lower. In addition, the commission or fee level reflects the overall strength and weight of a major oil company's balance sheet and net worth. On the other hand, while evaluating the risks related to a crude lifting bond, bankers will also evaluate the political risks involved depending on where the loading point is located and will be alert for possible conflicting interests such as, for example, where the same bank would have been issuing the crude lifting bonds in favour of the exporter, and would have confirmed a documentary letter of credit in the exporter's country.[35]

---

[33] Requests for extensions occur frequently and in many cases release procedures are onerous. Return or final cancellation can take place well after the project's completion.

[34] See also section 5.2.

[35] See also section 6(4).

Crude lifting bonds can be issued on a case by case basis, producing one guarantee or letter of credit per transaction. They can also be issued as an availment under a revolving, non-cumulative letter of credit facility, whereby the necessary bonding capacity is committed for the total amount of the oil purchase contract, and separate letters of credit are issued and in due time returned as the crude shipments take place.

4.2.3. Transportation bonds

The purpose of a transportation bond is to provide the employer with a guarantee to claim return of an advance payment made to a civil works contractor or turn-key contractor for deliveries of capital goods or materials which are imported into the country but have not yet arrived at the work site. The transportation bond is usually issued for a period starting upon arrival of the goods in the harbour (or, alternatively, at an airport) and ending upon delivery at the work site.[36]

The form of the bond is the same as the form for an advance payment guarantee. By definition, transportation bonds are of short duration and requests for extension, if they occur, should be well substantiated. As is the case for most other construction bonds, the issued bond or bank guarantee is a demand guarantee.

4.2.4. Equipment bonds

Equipment bonds should not be confused with transportation bonds. For most projects, it is common practice to leave the decision on which equipment to buy up to the contractor, who will make the necessary purchase and shipping arrangements with the equipment suppliers. He, too, will make financing arrangements with export credit agencies or other sources of equipment finance. The cost of equipment and plant will be incorporated in the final tender price, either as a lump sum, or more commonly as a *pro rata* portion of the future progress certificates, thus reflecting the depreciation allowances on a given piece of equipment.

However, in some circumstances the employer may prefer to make his own buyer finance arrangements with export credit institutions and the thus established export credit lines will be used for purchases of plant and equipment in accordance with the contractor's needs. The equipment is then made available to the contractor who will actually carry it on his books as an asset. A comparison with a leasing transaction is possible. However, the corresponding liability is not a rental payment obligation but a performance obligation. The involved construction company will have to perform and present work progress payment certificates which include the theoretical lease payment obligation. If the progress certificate is approved and paid, the corresponding rental payment obligation is redeemed. However, the amount of the theoretical lease payment is not a reflection of current market conditions for lease obligations but is based on the expected average life of the equipment and thus corresponds to a depreciation allowance (as if the contractor actually owns the equipment).

In summary, the employer buys the equipment under pre-established export credit lines, makes it available to the contractor, who progressively acquires a theoretical ownership interest through the presentation of progress certificates which include a depreciation allowance for the equipment. The reason and purpose for requesting the issuance of an equipment bond must be seen in the light of the above: whereas the employer is willing to make an advance payment *in kind* to the construction company, i.e., in the form of the use of equipment purchased by the employer, he wants to be sure that this equipment will be used effectively on the worksite, and that all maintenance and repair tasks are handled by the contractor as it were his own equipment. For that reason, the employer will request the equipment bond to be issued for an amount which largely reflects the full acquisition value of the needed equipment. As is the case for an advance payment guarantee, this bond will be outstanding for a declining value, thus reflecting the imputation of annual or monthly depreciation allowances on the initial acquisition value of the equipment.

The maturity of the equipment bond should in principle correspond to the expected useful life of the equipment. However, quite a few areas remain relatively unexplored at this stage. For example, what are the bonding requirements for equipment purchased at the beginning of the works, but actually mothballed for a few years until it is of real use to the project? Can a fully depreciated piece of equipment continue to be used on the project if the overall construction period largely exceeds the useful life of this piece? (The answer presumably is yes.) Is a revolving bonds scheme applicable, as it is foreseeable in large projects of a 10- to 15-year maturity that previously acquired equipment will need to be replaced? To whom do residual economic values accrue, and are there equipment bonding requirements relative to these?

---

[36] For example, transportation bonds were issued for a road construction project in Libya for a period necessary to transport rolling stock, a crusher plant and an asphalt plant over a 350 km. distance.

It is important to look at these issues in the course of the contract negotiation in as far as they determine the conditions upon which an equipment bond can be released. In addition, the contractor may want to limit his eventual liability in case of a call under first demand bonds, such as the equipment bond, by defining the applicable events of default, or by inserting default clauses specifically dealing with deficient maintenance or improper use of the equipment.

4.2.5. Working capital replenishment bonds

Working capital replenishment guarantees (WCRGs) are common features in project finance. However, a variation of the WCRG may show up as a bonding requirement in large construction and turn-key projects. The standard WCRG is an undertaking by an industrial or commercial corporation, not an undertaking by a bank. It is an undertaking, usually by the parent company, to make the necessary liquid funds available to the involved special purpose company, to keep its working capital in times of operational cash shortfalls at a level sufficient to meet loan obligations (principal and interest). The WCRG defined as such is a form of conditional guarantee and the beneficiaries of the WCR guarantee are the special purpose company's project finance lenders.

Exhibit 1010: WCR guarantee structure

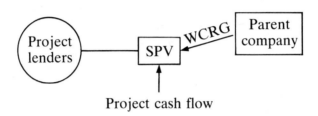

Project cash flow

In the case of WCR guarantees encountered in connection with large infrastructure or process engineering projects, the WCR guarantee is not a corporate guarantee, but a bank guarantee issued in favour of the employer. As is true for equipment bonds, the construction WCRG is a variation on the well-known advance payment guarantee theme. However, unlike the equipment bond, it is *not* an advance *in kind* but in cash. Also, and unlike the standard APG, it is an advance payment *not* on *future* works or deliveries, but on works already performed or goods already delivered.

As such, it is more appropriate to see the underlying transaction as a form of receivables financing, but instead of having a bank making advances to the contractor for proven and certified receivables payable by the employer, it is the employer who is willing to make advances to the contractor, thus *discounting* the receivables payable by himself against an acceptable bank guarantee. Pushing the comparison with other financing techniques one step further, one can see the role of the employer who advances funds to a contractor to bridge-finance payment delays on receivables due by himself, as a banker discounting a banker's acceptance for his customer. The role of the construction WCR bond issued by the contractor's banks can then be compared to the role of central banks or export credit agencies who are willing to re-discount, or to guarantee bankers export drafts drawn by an exporter upon some well-defined conditions.

The advantages to both parties are obvious. The employer does not want to see his contractor run out of cash, for work stoppages would occur. He also does not want his contractor to incur excessive financing costs because they may somehow be passed on to the employer through incorporation in the progress certificate. At the same time, he does not want to create the appearance of accepting the submitted progress certificate when he has not yet been able to fully satisfy himself with the quality of the works, or with the amount of the requested progress payment. Hence, the employer will make available some of his own financing sources while not foresaking the right to question all items listed in the progress certificate.

The construction WCR bond is not a very common form of guarantee. In one case at present under discussion, the working capital replenishment facility is expected to be made available for an amount covering two- or three-monthly progress payments. It is unclear whether in this case the employer can immediately draw on the WCR bond if defects in the works or valuation mistakes in the progress certificate are uncovered. It seems preferable to limit claims under WCR bonds to those instances where the employer first claimed the appropriate amount back from the contractor but did not obtain reimbursement. In the latter case, the bank's WCR bond takes the form of a back-stop financial guarantee, providing additional protection for the employer should he be unable to recover unearned working capital replenishment advances from the contractor.

Exhibit 1011: WCR bond structure

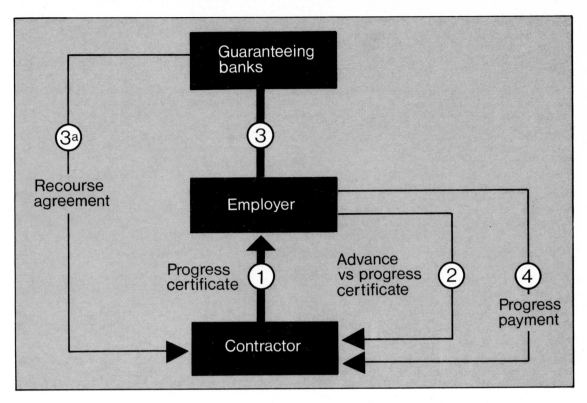

Whichever the interpretation, the WCR bond will have the form of a bank guarantee covering a revolving long-term credit facility made available directly or indirectly by the employer. As such, it is a financial guarantee instrument rather than a performance-related letter of credit or bond. Whereas drawdowns under the WCR facility are related to the progress of the works and actual outstandings under the WCR facility will trigger corresponding WCR bond outstandings, a claim under the WCR bond is no longer performance related but is conditioned by the contractor's ability to return the unearned WCR advances to the employer.

It is possible to establish a WCR facility for amounts reflecting anticipated fluctuations in future progress certificates. The required WCR bond can then also be structured as a flexible or revolving WCR bonding line on which a financial guarantee commission is payable. Release and return of the WCR bond will take place upon final completion of the project, or simply when the employer decides to cancel the underlying WCR credit facility.

4.2.6. Completion bonds and completion guarantees

Completion guarantees—another familiar feature in project finance schemes—are another form of corporate guarantee. They can be expressed either in operational terms or in financial terms. In the latter form, a bank may issue its financial guarantee on behalf of a corporate customer, but the underlying completion obligation will be well-defined in terms of quantity, quality, duration and respect of original deadlines compared to the agreed completion time and production schedule.

A detailed discussion of completion guarantees would lead too far outside the scope of this chapter. However, as mentioned in section 4.1.2 there are recent cases of a construction company or turn-key contractor not only committed to construct but also committed to *operate* and, more importantly, to operate *successfully*, and this during a previously agreed period of time during which the bank's performance (or completion?) guarantee remains outstanding and effective. It may appear from such precedents that performance bonds, while issued as unconditional demand guarantees, may have the appearance of *blank cheques*,[37] because the possibility of having a call under the bond is drawn out over a much greater period of time.

---

[37] As they were called by a court in California in the *Watkins Johnson Co.* vs. *Wells Fargo Bank* case (N.D. Cal., Jan. 22, 1979, C79–0121).

5. Costs and documentation

5.1. Documentation

There are basically two documents which will appear in all guarantee issuances, regardless of the degree of complexity of the issuance: the proper guarantee document, and the recourse document. If the size of the transaction warrants syndication, or if the guarantees for an international contract need to be advised through the local banking system, additional documentation requirements arise. The most common additional forms are: (i) syndication agreement, (ii) counter-guarantees, (iii) agency agreements.

5.1.1. The guarantee document

The guarantee document can be remitted directly by the contractor/exporter or by a local bank or branch acting as an agent for the contractor. Often, it is advantageous to have one and the same bank involved at both ends: transmission of documents will be faster, the risk of communication problems is limited, and coordination is usually smoother on critical matters such as extension, release or return of the guarantee documents. In several countries where the issued bank guarantees need to be advised through a bank resident in that country, the obligations of the advising bank are defined by law or local statute.[38] Four questions which arise at the issuance stage are:

    i. Which is the applicable law, and which would be the competent court?
    ii. Is the guarantee issuance fully covered and matched by the terms of the recourse document?
    iii. Will the guarantee be delivered on time, knowing that the underlying contract documents often impose short deadlines? For example, to be required to issue and to remit a performance bond within 10 days of the formal contract award date is not unusual.
    iv. Will the wording of the guarantee be acceptable to the beneficiary?

In this context, it is in the interest of the contractor or exporter to use the services of a bank which has built up extensive experience with beneficiaries located in a given country. It would be sad to see a bid rejected or a contract award revoked because the issuing bank did not issue the bid or performance bond in the required format.

Exhibit 1012

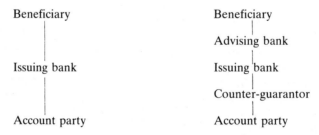

5.1.2. The recourse document or letter of credit opening application

When dealing with their customers, banks can lend them their *money* as well as their *credit*. In the former case, the repayment and security arrangements are recorded in a loan agreement. In the latter case, these terms are recorded in the recourse agreement. Recently, it has become more common to document the bank's and the customer's rights and obligations in two separate documents: (i) a *commitment letter*, addressed by the bank to the customer, whereby the bank states the terms upon which it is committed to issue a guarantee; (ii) if the customer accepts the bank's commitment terms (usually by returning a signed copy prior to a specified date), he will then proceed to the signing of a recourse agreement or *L/C application*.

Regardless of whether one or several documents are used, the following clauses or paragraphs will usually appear: (i) a request to issue a guarantee or letter of credit, i.e., the L/C application; (ii) an agreement with the guarantor on the terms of reimbursement for all expenses, disbursements, costs, etc. incurred by the guarantor as a result of the guarantee issuance; (iii) confirmation of agreed payment and extension procedures; (iv) an agreement on *security* or *support* clauses. Often,

---

[38] For Saudi Arabia, the relevant instructions are contained in the Saudi Arabia Monetary Agency Circular of August 15, 1976.

166

an application form or recourse document will also contain a reference to some paragraphs or articles of local law or general business conditions.

Depending on the guarantee's amount, maturity, payment terms and other risk factors, the security clauses will contain a more or less elaborate set of triggers (events of default), remedies (the proper security requirements) and sanctions (i.e., the consequences of an unremedied event of default).

Triggers and events of default. Similarly to term loan agreements, a recourse agreement (or a bank's commitment letter) can state a number of financial and/or operational covenants or ratios, the breach of which may constitute an event of default. For example, the issuer may be entitled to obtain additional security if the account party's liquidity, as covenanted under an agreed current-ratio-level, deteriorates or when delays in the works exceed a previously agreed grace period. Another way of monitoring the account party's obligation is to insert the equivalent of a material adverse change clause.

Security requirements. There are basically two categories of security requirements: (i) security which must be obtained prior to or at the moment of the guarantee issuance; and (ii) security which may be obtained some time in the future. In the former case, the guarantee issuance is fully or partly secured. In the latter case, the guarantee is issued on an unsecured basis but the occurrence of an event of default may trigger a request for obtaining security. Apart from making the above-mentioned distinction as to *when* security is obtained, we can also broadly identify *which* type of security is common in guarantee issuances. The following categories can be listed, in order of declining effectiveness and strength: (i) collateral cash, mortgages, third party guarantees or any other form of tangible security; (ii) undertaking to provide a mortgage, or cash collateral or third party guarantees etc.; (iii) undertaking to provide acceptable security; and (iv) assignment of underlying contract rights and payments.

The difference between *cash collateral clauses, cash substitution clauses* and *security clauses* should be mentioned. A *security clause* grants the issuing bank the right to obtain some form of acceptable security when the right thereto is triggered by the occurrence of a previously agreed event of default. A *cash collateral* clause is akin to a security clause but defines the type of security which must be obtained, i.e., collateralized cash. Both clauses appear in the recourse document, both are an agreement between account party and issuing bank and both clauses, at least in the context of this study, are interpreted as granting a conditional right in the future (as opposed to security which is obtained at the time of the guarantee issuance). A *cash substitution* clause is agreed between the issuing bank and the beneficiary, and grants the issuer of the guarantee the right to substitute his guarantee with an equivalent amount of cash. Although eventually the cash payment will have to be repaid by the account party, the cash substitution clause will appear in the guarantee document rather than in the recourse document. The consequences for the customer are the same, as far as the reimbursement obligations are concerned, but in the case of an actualization of the cash substitution clause, the guarantee obligation is considered to be terminated. It is easy to see why in many countries employers/beneficiaries refuse the insertion of a cash substitution clause. They usually want to reserve for themselves the right to call the guarantee and obtain cash. In addition, issuing banks may also have reservations about cash substitution clauses, because an ill-timed substitution of their guarantee with cash may lead to litigation, the consequences of which are usually not assessable at the time of the cash substitution.

Exhibit 1013

Clause	Parties	Involved document	Form of security	Cash remitted
Cash substition clause	Guarantor and beneficiary	Guarantee	n/a	To beneficiary
Cash collateral clause	Guarantor and account party	Recourse document	Defined	To guarantor
Security clause	Guarantor and account party	Recourse document	Not defined	n/a

Sanctions. The sanctions following a breach of covenants are again comparable to those in a case of an unremedied breach of term loan covenants. However, there is limited scope for action unless the beneficiary has agreed to a cash substitution clause, or unless the account party's obligations are cross-defaulted, and thus could trigger a default under other obligations to the issuing bank or other banks.

5.1.3. Conclusion

The guarantee document and the recourse document are the two basic instruments in a guarantee issuance. Simplicity and clarity are prime requirements for either document. Particular attention should be paid to consistency. There is great scope for conflict and misunderstanding when the recourse document contains a weaker commitment than the issued demand guarantee, or when the security provisions become effective following a contractor's default under the underlying contract provisions. The same guideline remains applicable: to minimize interpretation problems and to avoid litigious situations, the unconditional first demand character of the guarantee should be properly covered by reimbursement provisions as well as security provisions of unequivocal, matching strength.

5.1.4. Other documents concerning syndicated guarantee issuances

There is no firm or universally accepted terminology for a number of documents used in large, more complex guarantee issuances. But it is important to be familiar with the functions fulfilled by these additional documents. This may be best illustrated by briefly describing a case of a large-ticket guarantee issuance.

Case

Assumptions: — $210 million performance bond;
— covering a $2,100 million construction contract;
— consortium of three partners, each from a different country;
— bond must be advised through local banking system;
— one of the three partners wants the management role for his house bank;
— the three partners agree to appoint one international bank as the agent;
— partners want to be only severally liable to their banks.

In a case such as this one, the distinction will be made between agent banks, issuing banks and risk-taking banks. Often, the role of issuing and risk-taking banks is combined by large banks. However, it is quite common to see a number of banks appearing as risk-taking, i.e., counter-guaranteeing banks when, for country exposure or regulatory reasons, they prefer not to appear as issuing banks. At the same time, beneficiaries usually prefer to work with a limited number of issuing banks, and often require that no more than one co-signed guarantee document be remitted.

In this example (see Exhibit 1014), four banks are appearing as issuing banks for $40 million, $70 million, $60 million and $40 million. The three joint venture partners have each signed a recourse document for a total of $70 million. Recourse rights accrue as follows: (a) for partner one: to banks F, A, B and D; (b) for partner two: to banks A, B and C; (c) for partner three: to banks A, C, D and E. Banks F and E are only counter-guaranteeing banks. Bank A is issuing bank and risk-taking bank for the same amount of $40 million. Bank B issues $70 million but takes risk for $60 million. Bank C issues $60 million and takes risk for $50 million and bank D issues $40 million and takes a $30 million risk.

The syndication manager will have an inter-bank agreement signed by all participating banks. For practical reasons, it is preferable to have one and the same agent bank assuming the coordination role at every involved level: at issuing level, at risk-taking or counter-guaranteeing level and at partners level.[39] The agent and syndication manager will then list everyone's rights and obligations (see Exhibit 1015) and will further handle all documentation and accounting matters.

In large syndicated guarantee issuances, the recourse agreement is sometimes called *facility agreement* or *credit agreement*, and contains all the necessary clauses with respect to the account party's indemnity—issuance and extension procedure, partial and total calls, conditions precedent, representation and warranties, events of default or other triggers, security arrangements, agent responsibilities, applicable law, and reference to appendices.

5.2. Costs

In principle, for every involvement of an extra party, costs will be incurred and fees will be payable. This means that if the addition of extra intermediaries can be eliminated, a cost-savings factor will come into play. The usual fees payable are: (i) an advising fee, payable to the advising bank for their administrative services; (ii) an agent fee or management fee, payable to the agent bank for their syndication, coordination, documentation and book-keeping work during the life of the guarantees; (iii) a guarantee commission, payable to the issuing bank; (iv) a second commission, payable to those banks issuing counter-guarantees in favour of issuing banks. Obviously, if no counter-guaranteeing banks are involved, this extra fee is not due. Also, the issuing banks usually charge a

---

[39] It is obvious that many alternatives are possible. For a good description see F. O. Crawford, "The tools and techniques of sharing the risk," Gulf Banking Survey, *Euromoney*, 1978, and the previously quoted *CIG Information Memorandum*, pp. 26–8.

Exhibit 1014
Example of a syndicated guarantee structure.

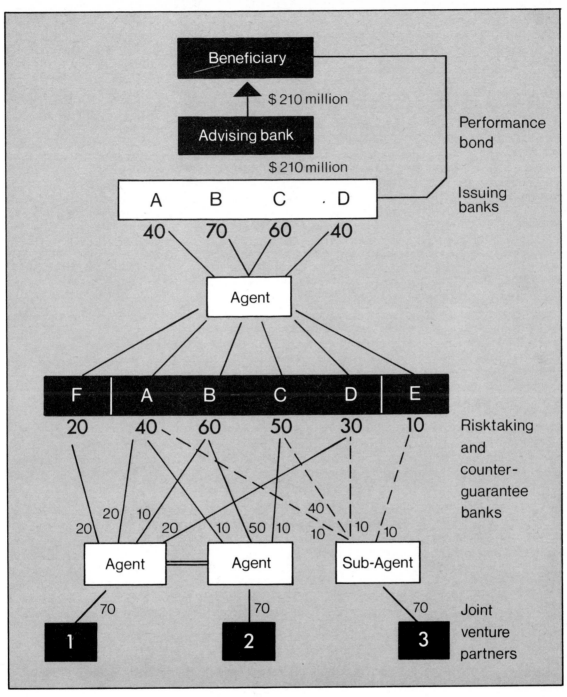

Exhibit 1015

Partners	1	2	3	Total
Banks				
A	20	10	10	40
B	10	50	—	60
C	—	10	40	50
D	20	—	10	30
E	—	—	10	10
F	20	—	—	20
Total	70	70	70	210

lower commission on the counter-guaranteed portion; (v) in some cases, additional management fees are payable if the number of agent and/or sub-agents is increased. In some cases the structure of a guarantee package was coordinated by one (or two) large international banks, thereby eliminating the need for additional sub-agents and also producing cost-savings effects at advising bank level.

Different pricing rules are applicable on so-called *umbrella* bonding lines. Whereas at first glance these syndicated bonding lines would allow a contractor to bid on large projects with the assurance that the necessary bonding capacity will be readily available when his bid is successful, this type of facility is not necessarily cost advantageous and is not as open-ended as the terminology may lead to believe. The main additional cost factor in this case is the commitment fee which is payable on the unused portion of the committed bonding line, and which usually ranges from 0·25% to 0·5% per annum.

Exhibit 1016: Contract guarantees, issuance costs

Beneficiary	Costs	Remarks
Beneficiary		1. Actual level of fees and commissions depends on account party's credit standing and transaction related project and country risk.
Advising bank	Advising fee	
Agent bank	Agent fee	2. Not all listed fees and commissions are charged cumulatively.
Issuing bank(s)	Guarantee commission	
Sub-agent	Sub-agent fee	
Counter-guaranteeing banks	Risk-taking fee	
Syndication manager(s)	Management fee	

6. Concluding remarks

Almost by definition, change and novelty are continuously attempted and aimed at in international trade, and particularly in the world of international construction and engineering. It should therefore not be surprising to see the demand for related financial services in a continuous state of development and adaptation to new needs. A few such features recently received a lot of detailed attention in banking, construction and exporting circles:

(1) Requests for *a commitment to issue all project-related follow-up bonds*. Information about a project is available in limited quantity and quality at bid stage. The bank(s) may want to wait until the contract is awarded, so that security terms, structure and pricing can reflect truly up-to-date market conditions and related country risks. On the other hand, the customer wants to be sure that the necessary bonding capacity is committed. Banks are willing to consider such requests favourably for prime name customers upon acceptance of a previously agreed set of conditions. A variation of this feature occurs when the customer wants a managing bank to firm up a best-effort syndication commitment to a genuine underwriting commitment.

(2) Bank guarantees for *subcontractor's obligations*. The banks issuing the contract bonds on behalf of the main contractor(s), may want to reserve the right to obtain an assignment of subcontractors' bank guarantees as additional security. Occasionally, though, banks are approached with a request to substitute their recourse on the main contractor with a recourse on the subcontractors' banks up to the amount of the subcontractors' guarantees. It is obvious that this entails additional degrees of risk for the issuing banks, the main contractors and for the involved subcontractors (whose consent is required anyway). It also raises a number of delicate legal questions[40] and makes the guarantee documentation considerably more complex.

(3) Assignment of *political risk insurance policies*. It is becoming common for banks to be willing to issue their first demand guarantees and letters of credit only when the exporter or contractor has obtained political risk cover from an acceptable public or private insurance company, and this for a sufficient amount and realistic set of events. Whether

---

[40] H. Harfield, *op. cit.*, Chapter 11: "Assignments and Transfers", pp. 191–2.

the issuing bank will also require a direct assignment of the insurance policy depends on the project risks, the customer's credit standing and the terms of the political risk cover. In some European countries, two publicly sponsored export insurance systems are encountered: (a) The account party subscribes to an insurance policy covering his net asset exposure (comprising the undepreciated value of the equipment, receivables and liabilities under bonds). The proceeds of payments related to the latter are then assigned to the issuing bank; (b) Insurance cover is obtained directly by the guarantor, who thus becomes a direct beneficiary of the export insurance policy. This system may gain more ground but practical and legal difficulties are slowing down progress in several countries.[41]

(4) *Bond issuances and documentary commercial letters of credit.* The issuance of contract guarantees and the confirmation of a commercial L/C for one and the same transaction and by one and the same bank warrants a word of special caution. This situation occurs when a contractor or exporter wants to obtain progress payments against presentation or documents under a commercial letter of credit opened on behalf of the importer or overseas employer by a local bank. Usually, the exporter wants a bank located in his home country to confirm this commercial letter of credit. However, if the confirming bank is the same as the bank that issued the contract guarantees, it is conceivable that the exporter presents documents for payment (and obtains payment from his bank), but that the shipment or progress payment is refused for plausible or capricious reasons by the importer or employer. In extreme cases, this could lead to a call of the performance bond and consequently the bank who combined the L/C confirmation role with the bond issuance role could be out of funds at both ends of the transaction.

It is obvious that in recent years international banks have considerably increased the volume of their contract guarantee business, thus assisting customers in their efforts to effectively expand international trade and obtain lucrative contracts abroad. Untested waters have been charted and practices have become firmer on many, but not all important points. Recent experiences in court, following political upheavals in Iran and Iraq, have not always added to the gradual build-up of consistent guidelines, although the obtained judgements have confirmed the unconditional, independent nature of the first demand guarantee. The message from these political events, as well as from the regularly recurring operational difficulties is clear: issuing banks and contract parties should be aware that neither the legal nature of a contract guarantee nor a customer's operational track record can be the *sole* basis for the issuance of a demand letter of credit or first demand contract guarantee.

The analogy with a term loan commitment should be repeated here and emphasized. The strength of a corporate credit and its ability to respond to a demand for reimbursement should guide the customer and his bank when entering into a term loan commitment or when issuing a demand letter of credit.[42] The customer as well as the bank must be aware that often the guarantor is bound by all subsequent amendments and usually no alternations in the terms of the contract or in the extent or the nature of the work to be performed can discharge or release the guarantor. In addition, often neither the customer nor his guaranteeing bank have control over extensions and expiry dates, and in some cases employers are considering the issuance of contract guarantees for escalating amounts, whereby the contingent liability assumed by the underlying corporate credit weighs heavier, regardless of the account party's good performance record on the involved project. All this may lead to the conclusion that the prudent *banker* will have to apply credit standards at least as high as those applied in documentary letter of credit transactions or in loans of the same maturity, and that the conscientious and demanding *contractor and exporter* will select as contract guarantee issuers banks that can be trusted in their judgement of the quality and the viability of a corporate credit and are known for their familiarity with the documentation, security and payment provisions of contract guarantee issuances.

---

[41] Y. Poullet, "Garanties Contractuelles", in *Droit et Pratique du Commerce International*, Sept. 1979, pp. 433–4.

[42] H. Harfield, *op. cit.*, p. 165: ". . . If the banker, in the exercise of his informed credit judgment, decides that this customer will be capable of making a money payment at a particular time and in particular amount, then the banker is justified in undertaking to make that payment on behalf of the customer, and it is of almost no moment whether the commitment is in the form of a present advance of funds, an undertaking by way of an unconditional commitment to lend to the customer, or by way of a commitment to third parties to make the payment on behalf of the customer at the time and in the amounts specified. If, on the other hand, the banker assumes the role of a surety and makes a commitment on the assumption that this customer's mercantile capacity is such that the banker's commitment will not be called upon, that is neither sound nor appropriate banking practice."

171

CHAPTER ELEVEN
Legal issues

Rhodri Davies and Anthony Grabiner

Rather than give a complete summary and legal analysis of the law of the various types of export financing discussed in this book, this chapter looks at four topics which, recent litigation has shown, gives rise to problems.

These topics are:

    i. Forfaiting.
    ii. When is an issuing or confirming bank entitled to refuse payment of a letter of credit?
    iii. Can an issuing or confirming bank be precluded from later relying on a defect in the documents, or other defence, which it does not raise at the time of rejection?
    iv. The transfer and assignment of rights deriving from letters of credit.

Three of these topics relate to letters of credit, although performance bonds are briefly mentioned since they are governed by principles identical to those which govern letters of credit.

The analysis offered here is based on English law.

1. Forfaiting

The background to a forfaiting transaction is most frequently an export of goods where the exporter has agreed to accept deferred payment from his importer. The most usual form of payment is by promissory notes or bills of exchange. Consequently, the law relating to forfaiting is very often only a particular application of the law of negotiable instruments, although many of the general principles apply to the forfaiting of all obligations. It is the forfaiting of negotiable instruments which is primarily considered here.

The exporter having obtained, for instance, bills of exchange accepted by the importer and maturing at some future date, may well wish to sell them for immediate payment. Accordingly, he will approach a bank or other financial institution (the forfaiter), offering the bills for sale. At this point the special characteristics of forfaiting which distinguish it from a normal factoring or discounting operation become clear. For, having once sold the bills, the exporter will not wish to be later reminded of them should they be dishonoured. He, therefore, wishes to sell *without recourse* to himself if the bills are not honoured on maturity. The precise extent of the protection which the without-recourse term provides for the exporter and for others is a vital question in forfaiting. The forfaiter will, of course, require a higher discount in a forfaiting transaction with its without recourse term than he would in an ordinary discounting transaction. However, almost invariably he will also require the liability on the bills of a party of undoubted financial standing, or a guarantee from such a party. The importer's liability on the bills will, therefore, usually be supported by the undertaking of his bank. This undertaking will very often take the form of an indorsement *per aval*, which is the forfaiter's preferred form of security. The aval, although recognized in many jurisdictions, creates considerable difficulties in English law.

If the original forfaiter does not wish to retain for himself the whole of the transaction and the whole of the risk, he will, in his turn, sell the bills on to other forfaiting houses without recourse to himself or to the exporter. An important distinction emerges here between what may be called the *primary market* and the *secondary market*. The primary market is that in which the exporter first sells bills to a forfaiter, often his own bank, who may be called the first forfaiter. The secondary market is that in which the first forfaiter sells the bills on to other forfaiting houses. The vital difference between these two markets lies in the extent to which the buyer of the bills can be expected to investigate the background from which they come.

1.1. The legal structure of forfaiting

It is important to identify the parties who will have a legal relationship in a typical forfaiting transaction. Exhibit 1101 illustrates a forfaiting transaction involving bills of exchange. The bills

Exhibit 1101: A forfaiting transaction

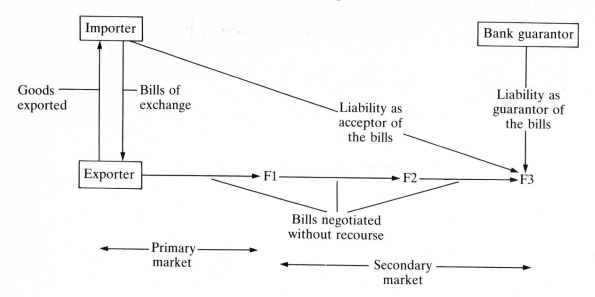

have been drawn by the exporter on the importer and accepted by him; they have also been guaranteed by a bank guarantor. Almost certainly there will be an indemnity agreement between the bank guarantor and the importer, but this does not concern the forfaiter. The bills have been negotiated without recourse three times in the forfaiting market. The first transaction between the exporter and the first forfaiter (F1) took place in the primary market, the later transactions between the first and second forfaiters (F1 and F2), and the second and third forfaiters (F2 and F3) took place in the secondary market.

Many of the liabilities of the parties to these transactions are defined by the law relating to negotiable instruments. In particular, the relationships between the holder of the instruments (F3) and the parties liable on them (the bank guarantor and the importer) are governed solely by the general law of negotiable instruments (together with the general law applicable to the guarantee if it is in a separate document). Indeed, the only factor which in a purely legal sense is particularly characteristic of forfaiting is the negotiation of the bills without recourse.

For purposes of analysis, a forfaiting transaction concerning negotiable instruments is best regarded as creating two contracts. First, there is the negotiation of the instrument; this contract conveys or transfers the title to the instrument. It takes the form of an indorsement for an instrument payable to order, or simple delivery for an instrument payable to bearer. The legal requirements and consequences of this contract are determined entirely by the law applicable to negotiable instruments, both with respect to the immediate parties to the transaction, and also with respect to all other parties to the instrument. Thus, if the requirements for negotiation of the instrument are not fulfilled, the forfaiter will not be able to maintain a valid claim against the bank guarantor or the importer, since he will not have a good title to the instrument. Equally, an indorser must accept the normal consequences of his indorsement as against all other parties to the instrument. As between the immediate parties to the transaction, however, the position may be modified by the second contract. This is the contract of sale of the instrument. It may contain terms or warranties adding to or restricting those in the first contract, but it can only affect its immediate parties.

This division into two separate contracts is, strictly, too extreme; liabilities on the instrument and on the sale are only aspects of one transaction, but for purposes of exposition it is convenient to treat them separately, below. However, in considering them, it is useful to bear in mind the various risks attendant on a forfaiting transaction and these will be identified next.

1.2. The risks

The forfaiter will look first to the bank guarantor and the importer for payment. It is helpful to identify those events which may result in his not receiving payment as expected, and turning to others for satisfaction. For legal purposes these events, or the risk of their occurrence, may be categorized as follows:

i. The insolvency of the bank guarantor and the importer.
ii. The failure of the bank guarantor and the importer to pay for political reasons.
iii. The refusal of the bank guarantor and the importer to pay on the valid ground that the obligation is not binding on them due to defect apparent on its face, e.g., a bill of exchange is not for a sum certain in money as required by section 3 (1) of the Bills of Exchange Act, 1882.
iv. The refusal of the bank guarantor and the importer to pay on the valid ground that the instrument is not binding on them due to some hidden defect, e.g., forgery.
v. The refusal of the bank guarantor and the importer to pay without any valid legal ground.

The last of these does not strictly deserve a place in a legal list, but it is included as, in practice, it is almost as important as the others.

The risk of all or any of these events occurring may be larger than the forfaiter originally estimated, if he decided to purchase the obligation on the basis of, or partly on the basis of, a statement of fact made by his seller which later turns out to be untrue. This point raises the questions of misrepresentation and breach of warranty.

1.3. The contract of negotiation

The first object of every seller of obligations in a forfaiting transaction, whether in the primary or the secondary market, is to ensure that he does not become liable on the instrument forfaited. In English law, sections 16 and 58 of the Bills of Exchange Act 1882, make this object easy to achieve. Section 16 provides:

"16. The drawer of a bill and any indorser may insert therein an express stipulation—
(1) negativing or limiting his own liability to the holder."

This section allows a holder of a bill of exchange or a promissory note payable to his order to indorse it in blank so as to make it payable to bearer, while expressly negativing his liability as indorser by the use of the words "without recourse", or others to the same effect. Similarly, an exporter may draw a bill of exchange on an importer while at the same time expressly negativing his liability as drawer.

Once the instrument is payable to bearer, and consequently may be negotiated by delivery without indorsement, section 58 of the Act comes into play. Section 58 provides:

"58. (1) Where the holder of a bill payable to bearer negotiates it by delivery without indorsing it, he is called a 'transferor by delivery'.
(2) A transferor by delivery is not liable on the instrument.
(3) . . ."

The combination of these two sections makes it possible to ensure that the only parties liable on the instrument itself are the importer and the bank guarantor.

The position is not quite so straightforward under Annex I to the Geneva Convention providing a Uniform Law for Bills of Exchange and Promissory Notes, 1930, to which many countries are parties, although the U.K. is not. Under Article 9 of the Annex the drawer of a bill of exchange cannot exclude his liability as guarantor of payment, and stipulations to this end are "deemed not to be written". However, under Article 15, an indorser of a bill or note can exclude all his liability. Consequently, promissory notes are often preferred in the forfaiting market, as they will not be drawn by the exporter, but the importer and the exporter may indorse them without recourse to himself. This point is an example of the many ways in which English law on negotiable instruments, contained principally in the Bills of Exchange Act 1882 (the Act) differs from Annex I to the Convention.

1.4. The contract of sale

Although the seller in a forfaiting transaction does not become liable on the instrument itself, he will usually undertake certain liabilities under the sale. It should be noted that such liabilities are only owed to the buyer, whereas liabilities on the instrument are owed to all subsequent parties to it. Where the instrument is negotiated by delivery alone, subsection (3) of section 58 provides:

"(3) A transferor by delivery who negotiates a bill thereby warrants to his immediate transferee being a holder for value that the bill is what it purports to be, that he has a right to transfer it, and that at the time of transfer he is not aware of any fact which renders it valueless."

Section 58 does not in terms apply where an instrument is negotiated by an indorsement which excludes the indorser's liability, but it is submitted that in such a case a court should and would apply the same rules.

The instrument forfaited will usually purport to constitute a genuine and legally enforceable obligation. In warranting that it is what it purports to be, the seller, therefore, warrants that it is enforceable; thus, for instance, he warrants that the signatures are not forged and that it is free from any other hidden defects. He does not warrant that what it purports to be is of any legal effect, for instance that it does not require stamping to render it enforceable (see *Hamilton Finance Co. Ltd.* v. *Coverley Westray* (1969) 1 Lloyd's 53, at p. 71). This is a question of law, and each side is equally well placed to spot defects on the face of the instrument. However, if the instrument is governed by a foreign legal system, as a matter of English law the seller might be held to warrant that it was legally valid under that system. The last phrase of subsection (3) provides an exception to the general rule that the seller does not guarantee that the instrument will be paid; the exception is that the seller does warrant that at the date of the sale he does not know that, for instance, the acceptor is insolvent. If he did have such knowledge and he sold without disclosing it, his conduct might well be fraudulent.

As an alternative to a claim for damages for breach of any of these warranties, the forfaiter might contend that there has been a total failure of consideration, as his seller has not delivered the obligations which he agreed to buy, and that, accordingly, he is entitled to the return of the price he paid. This would be a claim for restitution of what has been paid, as opposed to a claim for damages for loss. The difference between the two is that in order to assess damages, all the circumstances of the transaction must be taken into account to ascertain the size of the claimant's loss; if he was going to make a profit on the transaction, that approach will favour the claimant. However, in a restitutionary claim for the return of the price, the claimant can recover only what he has actually paid.

It is now possible to discover who bears each of the risks set out in section 1.2. It is clear that the seller is not liable in the case of risks (i), (ii) and (v), that is to say insolvency, political reasons, and an unjustified failure to pay. This is the result one would expect, for these are the risks the forfaiter intends to take and for which he charges a higher discount than he would for a with recourse discounting transaction. On the other hand, the forfaiter does not expect to bear risk (iv), that of non-payment on an obligation which is unenforceable due to some defect which is hidden from him. In such a case, the forfaiter has a breach of warranty claim against his seller, who will no doubt in turn make a breach of warranty claim against his seller, the loss being thus passed down the line until it reaches the first forfaiter, who bought in the primary market and had the best opportunity to discover hidden defects. As for defects on the face of the instrument—risk (iii)—when checking the documentation offered to him, amongst other matters the forfaiter must satisfy himself that the obligation appears to be valid: *caveat emptor.*

These results may, however, be altered by express or implied agreement between the immediate parties to the sale (*MacDonald* v. *Whitfield* (1883) 8 A.C. 733, at 745, P.C.). Subsection (3) of section 58 is a slightly unusual provision in that, unlike most of the Act, it is not concerned with liability on the instrument but only with the contract of sale. In principle, however, there is no reason why the parties should not be entitled to contract out of the warranties set out in subsection (3) if they should wish to; equally they could, if they desired, impose wider obligations.

The proper function and significance of the words "without recourse" should be mentioned here. Their object is to ensure that no liability arises on an indorsement. If there is no indorsement, they are not strictly necessary at all, since there will be no liability on the instrument in any event, and in a forfaiting transaction the contract of sale will not give rise to any liability apart from the warranties. However, the words without recourse are often used in the context of the contract of sale, and it has been suggested that they provide a defence to breach of warranty claims. This approach is misconceived; the sole function of a without recourse provision is to make it clear that the seller is not guaranteeing that those liable on the instruments can, or will, pay; it does not relieve him from the obligation to deliver instruments which comply with the warranties he has given. In short, he must still perform his contract.

1.5. Untrue statements of fact

In entering into a forfaiting transaction the forfaiter is acting very much like an insurer; he must assess the risk and calculate the discount he will offer on the basis of the information supplied to him by his seller. If this information turns out to be inaccurate, the forfaiter's position is unacceptably different from that which he could reasonably have expected, and in the event of loss he will naturally turn to his seller for compensation.

As a matter of law, a claim based on a precontractual statement which turns out to be untrue may be formulated as a claim for misrepresentation or for breach of warranty, or for both. To establish a claim for misrepresentation a plaintiff must show that the representation is false, that reasonable men would regard it as material to their decision to enter into the transaction, and that he in fact relied on it in making that decision, although he may also have been influenced by other matters. The remedies for misrepresentation are either damages or rescission of the contract, that is to say the undoing of the contract on terms that each side returns to the other what it has received. In a forfaiting transaction, this means the return of the obligations in exchange for the price. A plaintiff who rescinds may also be entitled to recover an indemnity for some of his costs. The rules which decide whether a plaintiff is entitled to damages or rescission are a matter of general law and are not set out here.

To establish a warranty, the plaintiff must show that the statement was of such importance that it is a reasonable inference that the parties intended it to have legal effect. In such a case, the statement becomes a term of the contract of sale and the maker is liable in damages for breach.

In a recent case in London, misrepresentations and breaches of warranties were alleged in an area of particular importance for forfaiting. The case may be called the ADCA case after the leading plaintiffs and largest participators in the transaction, Allgemeine Deutsche Credit-Anstalt. Its facts are set out in an article entitled "The Case of the Phantom Cranes" by Donal Curtin in *Euromoney*, August 1980. It is not necessary to repeat them here, save to say that the case included, or appeared to include, many of the typical elements of a forfaiting transaction. Unfortunately for the curiosity of many, the case settled after five days in the Commercial Court in London. The opportunity for a judgement deciding many of the issues in this area was, therefore, lost. Nonetheless, the ADCA case had the beneficial effect of concentrating the minds of lawyers and bankers on the potential problems of forfaiting.

One of the claims made by the plaintiffs was for misrepresentation and/or breach of warranty in that they had each been told that, underlying the bills of exchange which they bought, there was an export transaction concerning cranes. It was eventually conceded on all sides that there was, in fact, no underlying transaction at all. To establish that the statement that there was an underlying export transaction was material, that they were likely to have relied on it, and that it was of sufficient importance to be a warranty, the plaintiffs obtained reports from independent banking experts. ADCA went to Charles Gmür of Finanz AG Zurich, and his views were generally accepted by the other banking experts as a definitive statement of forfaiting practice. The following points of particular importance emerged:

i. There is a vital distinction in forfaiting between trade obligations and finance obligations. This is because long experience has shown bankers that obligations arising out of a trading transactions are more likely to be met than those whose object is simply to raise money.

ii. A forfaiter buying obligations direct from the exporter (the first forfaiter) should satisfy himself as to the nature and validity of the underlying transaction and the obligations.

iii. A forfaiter buying in the secondary market is not expected to repeat the detailed investigations of the first forfaiter (and, indeed, it would be difficult for him to do so), but he is entitled to rely on a short statement from his seller that the obligations are trade obligations arising out of, for example, an export of machinery from France to Poland.

It should be emphasized that these are points of practice not law, and any individual transaction may depart from them.

The without recourse point requires a mention again here. It is clear that a without recourse provision does not relieve a seller of the obligation to deliver instruments which justify his representations about them and their provenance, any more than it excuses him from making good the warranties he has given.

1.6. The aval in English law

The aval is not a recognized form of guarantee in English law. This is not to say that, in deciding a case where a foreign legal system was to be applied, an English court would not give effect to an aval; it undoubtedly would. Furthermore, the use of an aval would in itself be some indication that the parties intended their transaction to be governed by a legal system which recognizes avals. However, if an English court was faced with an aval in a case undoubtedly governed by English law, it would be in considerable difficulty. The difficulty might be resolved by the application of section 56 of the Act which provides:

"56. Where a person signs a bill otherwise than as drawer or acceptor, he thereby incurs the liabilities of an indorser to a holder in due course."

This section only applies in favour of a holder in due course. Most forfaiters will, however, fulfil the necessary requirements to be holders in due course.

An alternative approach would be to argue that, in principle, there is no reason why a guarantee should not be placed on the back of a negotiable instrument, and that the obligations imposed by an aval are clearly defined by commercial usage and foreign legal systems. Such an argument would have to overcome two hurdles in particular. First, section 4 of the Statute of Frauds, 1677, requires that, to be enforceable, an agreement which constitutes a guarantee must be in writing, and it may be that an aval would not sufficiently state the terms of the agreement. Secondly, the concept of a guarantee which is in effect negotiable would be a novel one in English law. There is no reason why it should not be introduced though, particularly in the context of negotiable instruments where the law is much influenced by mercantile practice. It might further be argued that the terms of section 56 of the Act do not allow effect to be given to an aval other than as a simple indorsement. This problem might be overcome by arguing that section 16 allows the indorser to define the scope of his liability.

It is unfortunate that English law does not recognize the aval since it is well established in many other legal systems, where it plays a useful role. For example, it is recognized in Articles 30–32 of Annex I to the Geneva Convention. There is no doubt that an English court would struggle hard to find means to give effect to an aval, and it might well succeed, but until the position is clarified a prudent forfaiter contemplating an instrument which is, or may be, governed by English law would be well advised to take his security in some form more familiar to English lawyers. Resolving uncertainties in the law is fascinating for lawyers but expensive for their clients.

1.7. Conclusions on forfaiting

This discussion of forfaiting may be summarized by saying that in the normal case:

    i. In the absence of any misrepresentation or breach of warranty, the forfaiter bears the following risks without recourse to any other party:
        (a) the insolvency of the bank guarantor and the importer;
        (b) the failure of the bank guarantor and the importer to pay for political reasons;
        (c) the purchase of an obligation which is not binding due to a defect apparent on its face;
        (d) the refusal of the bank guarantor and the importer to pay without any valid legal grounds.
    ii. If the obligation purchased is not valid and enforceable due to a hidden defect, the forfaiter has a good claim against his seller for breach of warranty, and a without recourse provision is no defence to such a claim.
    iii. If the forfaiter has purchased an obligation on the basis of a statement of fact made by his seller which turns out to be untrue, he may have a good claim against his seller for misrepresentation and/or breach of warranty. Again, a without recourse provision is no defence to such a claim. A statement in the secondary market that there is an underlying trading transaction when there is not, will generally constitute an actionable misrepresentation and/or breach of warranty.

It must be stressed that these principles are those of an archetypal transaction; almost any individual transaction may depart from them in practice or raise aspects of the law which have not been discussed here.

2. Letters of credit

In this section, three aspects of the law relating to bankers' commercial letters of credit are considered:

    1. When is an issuing or confirming bank entitled to refuse to pay?
    2. Can an issuing or confirming bank be precluded from later relying on a defect in the documents, or other defence, which it does not raise at the time of rejection?
    3. The transfer and assignment of rights deriving from letters of credit.

These questions may conveniently be considered in that order, since much of the real importance of the third lies in the extent to which the bank's obligation to pay is narrowed or widened by a transfer or assignment of rights under the credit.

A letter of credit constitutes a direct contractual obligation owed by the bank which issues it to the beneficiary. This obligation is separate and independent from the contract of sale between the beneficiary as seller and the applicant for the credit as buyer. It comes into existence when the beneficiary receives the advice of the credit from the issuing bank or its agent. If the advising bank adds its *confirmation* to the credit, it undertakes an obligation identical to that of the issuing bank.

The precise extent of the issuing bank's obligation is defined by the terms of the credit. Essentially, it is that, if the beneficiary satisfies the conditions in the credit, i.e., if he presents the required documents prior to the expiry date, the bank is obliged to pay; if he does not, the bank has no obligation to pay. The bank's obligation is thus an all or nothing one.

Whether the conditions precedent to the bank's obligation to pay are satisfied depends largely on whether the correct documents are presented. The documents presented must be completely in order for the bank's obligation to arise. This is because: "In documentary credit operations all parties concerned deal in documents and not in goods" (Uniform Customs & Practice for Documentary Credits, 1974 Revision (hereafter, the UCP), Article 8a). Banks frequently pay out very large sums of money under letters of credit which they then debit to their customer's (applicant's) account. In such circumstances, it is not for the bank to pay out on documents which are not in perfect order: "There is no room for documents which are almost the same, or which will do just as well," (*Equitable Trust Co. of New York* v. *Dawson Partners* (1927) 27 Lloyd's 49, at p. 52, H.L., per Viscount Sumner).

The UCP is drawn up and published by the International Chamber of Commerce. It is expressly incorporated in virtually all letters of credit. Its legal effect depends on this incorporation, by which its provisions become terms of the contract formed by the letter of credit. Thus, its legal significance depends on its standing as having been agreed to by the parties; it does not have the same weight as rules of law such as those contained in statutes. In some cases, this may restrict its effect since there are limits, although generous ones, to what the law will allow parties to contracts to agree to, although none of them are likely to apply to letter of credit transactions.

2.1. When is an issuing or confirming bank entitled to refuse to pay?

There are five situations which must be considered here:

    i. when it is apparent that the documents presented do not meet the requirements of the credit;
    ii. when there is fraud in the presentation;
    iii. when false or fraudulent documents which appear to meet the requirements of the credit are presented by an innocent presentor;
    iv. when the applicant (buyer) is entitled to restrain the bank from making payment;
    v. set-off.

However, there may be circumstances other than these in which a bank would be entitled to refuse to pay. An example might be a credit which, to the beneficiary's knowledge, was opened solely to finance an illegal transaction in which he was involved.

2.1.1. When the documents presented do not meet the requirements of the credit

It follows, inevitably, from the general principles set out above that, in these circumstances, the bank is not obliged to pay. However, it is always open to the applicant to expressly agree to payment on documents which are defective; if the bank then pays, it will of course be entitled to an indemnity from the applicant. Alternatively, the beneficiary may agree to accept payment subject to an obligation to repay the bank if it later emerges that he should not have been paid.

2.1.2. When there is fraud in the presentation

It is necessary to begin here by defining *fraud*. In English law, it is well established (apart from specific statutory contexts) that fraud requires an intention to defraud, i.e., actual dishonesty (*Derry* v. *Peek* (1889) 14 A.C. 337, H.L.). Thus, in order for there to be fraud in the presentation, the presentor must present false or fraudulent documents, knowing that they are false or fraudulent, or knowing that they may be so and without any belief in their genuineness. Documents are false for these purposes when, although made by the person by whom they purport to be made, they contain statements of fact which are demonstrably untrue: for instance, a statement in a bill of lading that 20,000 tons of steel has been loaded, when in fact only 10,000 tons has been loaded.

A statement of opinion from which others might reasonably differ, for instance, as to the quality of goods, cannot be false so long as it is in fact the opinion of the person whose name it bears. The expression *fraudulent documents* will be used here to mean both documents which are technically forged, i.e., which purport to be made by someone other than the true author, and those which are made by the party whose name they bear but which are made dishonestly, e.g., are known to be untrue when made.

If the bank discovers in time that the documents are false or fraudulent, it is of course entitled to refuse to pay (*Sztejn* v. *Henry Schroder Banking Corporation* (1941) 31 N.Y. Supp. (2d) 631). If it only discovers the truth after it has already paid, it is entitled to recover back the payment as money paid under a mistake of fact. A presentation is, nonetheless, fraudulent if the documents are presented through the medium of an innocent agent acting for a fraudulent principal.

If the applicant applies to the court for an injunction to prevent the beneficiary presenting documents under the credit, or to prevent the bank making payment, the court will apply a stiff test requiring clear proof of fraud before granting an injunction:

> ". . . it is certainly not enough to allege fraud; it must be 'established', and in such circumstances I should say very clearly established."
> (*Edward Owen Engineering Ltd.* v. *Barclays Bank International Ltd.* (1978) 1 Q.B. 159 C.A. per Browne L. J.)

If an applicant does not apply to the court but still wishes the bank not to pay, the bank could not be criticized if it applied the same test as the court would apply. However, it is always open to the bank, if it wishes, to take the risk of not paying where fraud is not clearly established, in the hope, or belief, that proper evidence of fraud will become available, and in order to protect the applicant. For once the bank pays, the applicant will have to indemnify it first and then endeavour to pursue its claims against the beneficiary.

2.1.3. When false or fraudulent documents which appear to meet the requirements of the credit are presented by an innocent presentor

This situation may be quite distinct from the question of fraud in the presentation. It is quite possible to have an innocent presentor of false or fraudulent documents; indeed that is what happened in *United City Merchant (Investments) Ltd. and another* v. *Royal Bank of Canada and another, "the American Accord"* [1979] 1 Lloyd's 267, where shipment of the goods was required to be on or before December 15, 1976, and amongst the documents which had to be presented under the credit were a full set of clean on board ocean bills of lading. The court found that the goods were only shipped on December 16, and that the bill of lading, which bore a notation stating that the goods were on board, had been fraudulently dated December 15 by an employee of the shipping lines' loading brokers. However, the beneficiary was not a party to the fraud and presented the bill of lading innocently. The bank declined to pay on the grounds that, amongst other things, the date of the bill of lading was false. On these facts Mr. Justice Mocatta held that the beneficiary was entitled to succeed, since the documents had been in order on their faces and the beneficiary was not implicated in the fraud.

The current state of the law, therefore, is that even fraudulent inaccuracies in the documents do not justify the bank in refusing to pay, unless there is fraud in the presentation, or possibly in the transaction. This state of affairs is open to strong criticism. The point may be made by reference to another recent case. In *Kydon Compania Naviera S.A.* v. *National Westminster Bank Ltd. and others* [1980] Com. L.R.12, the beneficiaries of the credit sold a vessel for scrap. They failed in an action against the confirming bank for non-payment, due to defects on the face of the documents.

Mr. Justice Parker did not decide the question we are concerned with here, although he did say he would be inclined to follow the decision in *the American Accord*. However, one of the documents required by the credit was a certificate from the Greek registrar that the vessel was free of encumbrances, and at the end of his judgement the judge said:

> "It is of the greatest importance that banks should, in the absence of very special circumstances such as fraud on the part of the beneficiary, not be concerned with the proof or otherwise of the factual situation behind the documents. It may be that the circumstances where they can be so concerned are subject to exceptions other than fraud. If, for example, in the case of the Greek registrar's certificate in the present case the bank had received from the Greek registrar a letter stating that, since signing the certificate he had discovered that he had mistakenly overlooked a particular encumbrance, it might be that this would justify rejecting the certificate. Where, however, as here, the alleged inaccuracies relate to matters in dispute between the buyer and seller, it is in my judgment not a matter with which the bank can be concerned."

The learned judge's proposition with regard to the registrar's certificate is plainly correct, but the distinction between matters which are in dispute between buyer and seller and those which are not is, it is respectfully submitted, incorrect. Any point of importance will form a focus of dispute if the transaction breaks down.

A distinction is sometimes suggested between documents which are fraudulent and those which are false due to error or carelessness. So long as the presentor is not a party to the fraud, it is difficult to see why this should make any difference; the important point is that the documents are false, not how they came to be so.

An example of the difficulties which may be caused by the present rule can be seen by considering back-to-back credits. The banker in the middle of a back-to-back credit transaction must pay on the presentation of documents under the credit issued by him, and then himself present the same documents for payment under the original credit. If he knows or believes the documents are false, or fraudulent, and presents them under the original credit, he will be committing fraud. Yet, if he is not entitled to refuse payment of false documents under his own credit, he is placed in an impossible position. The solution must be that he is not obliged to pay on his own credit until documents which are correct on their face and genuine are presented to him.

The reason a letter of credit requires the presentation of certain documents is that the applicant-buyer intends that the seller-beneficiary should be paid when, and only when, the events represented to have happened by the documents have, in fact, happened. In short, the object of stipulating for the documents in the credit is that they should reflect the truth; if they demonstrably fail to do so, the bank should be entitled to reject them, for it is a pre-condition of the beneficiary's entitlement to be paid that he should present documents which meet the requirements of the credit. The credit, impliedly at least, requires genuine documents. Thus, a beneficiary is not entitled to be paid if he innocently presents documents which are not genuine. This is not because his good faith is in any way disputed, but simply because he has not performed the pre-condition to his entitlement to be paid.

It is, therefore, submitted that the law ought to be that the bank is entitled to reject documents which it knows to be false or fraudulent when it would be entitled to reject if the true position was apparent on the face of the documents, as indeed it ought to be (see A. G. Davis, *The Law Relating to Bankers' Commercial Letters of Credit*, 3rd ed., 1963, pp. 145–56). This can hardly be said to be unfair to the beneficiary, for it is his responsibility to present genuine documents, and it should be within his power to ensure that the documents are genuine. However, an exception must be made in favour of bona fide holders of drafts and documents under negotiation credits; this point is discussed below, when dealing with negotiation credits.

If the bank does have the right to reject false documents, it does not follow that it has any duty to investigate the genuineness of documents presented to it, any more than it must look for fraud in every presentation. The position is simply that, if the bank is provided by the buyer or some other third party with evidence which clearly establishes (applying the same test as for fraud) that the documents are false, it should be entitled to act on such evidence. Of course, clear evidence of falsity in a matter wholly within the control of the beneficiary will, in itself, give rise to a strong inference of fraud.

It must be said on this question, though, that the present state of the law is represented by the decision in *the American Accord*. That case is going to the Court of Appeal where no doubt the point will be fully considered. It is, perhaps, unfortunate that the falsity in that case only concerned 24 hours; a larger discrepancy between the truth and the document might have raised the issue more starkly.

2.1.4. When the buyer (applicant) is entitled to restrain the bank from making payment on the ground that there is fraud in the transaction

The word *transaction* is used here to describe the sale contract under which the price is to be paid by letter of credit, together with any misrepresentations or collateral warranties that may be associated with it. It hardly needs to be said that, normally, the bank has no interest in the sale contract, and even less concern with misrepresentations or warranties associated with it. Such matters are not relevant to the contract contained in the credit, and the bank is not entitled to raise them against the beneficiary. However, if the seller-beneficiary is engaged in a fraud, the object and culmination of his scheme will be obtaining payment from the bank. In such circumstances, although the bank could not refuse to pay of its own motion, the court will not stand idly by if the buyer-applicant, who would otherwise pay the price of the fraud, applies to it for injunctions to restrain the beneficiary from presenting and the bank from paying. It might be argued that where the only fraud is in the transaction, it is too far removed from the credit, but "fraud unravels all", and a court will not allow a fraudulent seller to rely on legal principle to perfect his fraud.

The bank is only justified in refusing to pay, on the grounds of fraud in the transaction alone, by an order of the court, and the court will only make such an order on clear proof of fraud.

2.1.5. Set-off

On general principles a debtor may defend a claim by his creditor on the grounds that his creditor owes him money, and the two debts or claims should be set-off against one another. There is no reason why a bank should not be entitled to use set-off as a ground for not paying under a letter of credit.

3. Can an issuing or confirming bank be precluded from later relying on a defect in the documents, or other defence, not raised at the time of rejection?

To take first the simple case of fraud; if fraud can be proved, the fraudsman can scarcely rely on the fact that it could not be proved earlier. Leaving aside fraud then, this point is raised most acutely when the beneficiary would have been able to correct all defects in the documents prior to the expiry of the credit, had they been drawn to its attention on the occasion when the documents were first rejected. If a defect could not have been corrected in any event, then the beneficiary could only have been entitled to payment if the credit had been amended, and no act by the bank, short of amending the credit, can entitle the beneficiary to claim payment when it could never have met the requirements of the credit.

In *Kydon Compania Naviera S.A.* v. *National Westminster Bank Ltd.* (referred to above), where the defects first raised at the trial could have been corrected in time, if they had been drawn to the attention of the beneficiary before the credit expired, the beneficiary argued that the bank was precluded from relying on such defects. This argument was put in two ways, and it failed on both of them. First, it was said that the provisions of the UCP impose a duty on the bank, which it owes to the beneficiary, to specify all defects; therefore, if the bank does not specify a defect at the time of rejection, it is in breach of its duty, and it cannot take advantage of such a breach by raising the defect later, when it cannot be corrected. The articles of the UCP in question are Articles 7 and 8(c) and (e). Article 7 provides:

> "Banks must examine all documents with reasonable care to ascertain that they appear on their face to be in accordance with the terms and conditions of the credit . . ."

In dealing with the argument that this duty was owed to the beneficiary, Mr. Justice Parker said:

> "[Article 7] is in my judgment directed to the duty owed by the issuing bank to his customer and perhaps by a bank authorized to negotiate to the issuing bank. It is certainly so treated in Gutteridge and Megrah. To treat the duty as being owed to the beneficiary appears to me unreal. The issuing bank is contractually obliged to pay if the documents are in order, but if it pays when the documents are not in order and it has been wholly careless about examining then, it offends common sense to say that it is in breach of duty to the beneficiary. It has simply paid when it need not have done."

Parts (c) and (e) of Article 8 state:

> "(c) If, upon receipt of the documents, the issuing bank considers that they appear on their face not to be in accordance with the terms and conditions of the credit, that bank must determine, on the basis of the documents alone, whether to claim that payment, acceptance or negotiation was not effected in accordance with the terms and conditions of the credit."
> "(e) If such claim is to be made, notice to that effect, stating the reasons therefore, must, without delay, be given by cable or other expeditious means to the Bank from which the documents have been received . . ."

These provisions seem to be intended to govern relations between the issuing bank and a bank which has acquired documents either by negotiation under a negotiation credit, or because it is specifically nominated in the credit as authorized to accept, pay, or negotiate under it (see UCP General Provisions and Definitions, e.). They cannot assist the original beneficiary or any other party who does not fall within their contemplation. Even in the case of those within the contemplation of Article 8, it is submitted that there is no duty imposed which supersedes the ordinary legal position.

The second way in which the argument was put in the *Kydon case* was on the basis of the ordinary legal concepts of estoppel by representation and promissory estoppel. The basis of these concepts is that if A makes a representation or promise in circumstances such that B reasonably relies on it, A will not later be entitled to go back on his representation, or promise, as the case may be. Each case turns on its own facts, but there are three reasons why it would normally be very difficult to establish that either of the concepts applied to the rejection of documents by a bank. First, the practical circumstances in which letters of credit operate do not naturally give rise to any inference that the bank is making any representation or promise when it rejects documents. To quote again from Mr. Justice Parker:

> "Having found what, at the particular times, they considered to be good and sufficient reasons for rejection the . . . bank specified them. To hold that they thereby made any representation [that there were no other defects or that they would pay if those specified were corrected] would in my view involve a radical departure from the accepted legal position and would seriously undermine the whole system of documentary credits, for banks would be obliged, for their own protection and the protection of their customers, always to scrutinise with the utmost care every document presented from beginning to end

notwithstanding that they may find in the first few lines of the first document at which they looked one or more good and sufficient reasons for refusal to pay.

"It is for the beneficiary to see that the documents are all in order and he has no cause for complaint if the bank rejects as soon as they find one or more defects or, if they reject again on finding further defects and so on."

Secondly, the question of whether the documents conform to the requirements of the credit is a pure question of law. It is a general principle of English law that a person is assumed to know the law; consequently, it cannot be said that the beneficiary reasonably relied on a statement by the bank that there were no other defects, since that is a question of law, the answer to which the beneficiary is assumed to know as well as the bank. The application of this principle here is not as odd as it sometimes is, since the beneficiary can reasonably be expected to consult his own legal advisers on such matters, as indeed the beneficiary in the *Kydon case* did.

This leads on to the third point, which is that often it will not be reasonable for the beneficiary to rely on representations by the bank; he should rely on his own judgement and his own advisers.

An example of a case where, despite these points, a bank would be precluded from relying on a defect might be where a bank rejects documents specifying defects X and Y, and stating that it will pay if defect X is corrected, regardless of defect Y. If the beneficiary, in reliance on this promise, took no steps to correct defect Y, the bank could not raise it again later.

3.1. Performance bonds

Performance bonds are mentioned here only to say that the principles which determine when the bank can refuse to pay on them, and how far it is precluded from relying on later defences which have not been raised at the time of rejection, are identical to those applicable to letters of credit. Indeed, several of the cases which are accepted as laying down the law on letters of credit concerned performance bonds.

4. The transfer and assignment of rights deriving from letters of credit*

There are in principle four, or possibly five, ways in which rights deriving from a letter of credit may be transferred from their original owner to a new owner:

    i. novation;

    ii. negotiation under a negotiation credit;

    iii. transfer under Article 46 UCP (Uniform Customs and Practice for Documentary Credits);

    iv. assignment;

    v. assignment of proceeds of the credit.

4.1. Novation

A novation is not strictly a transfer of rights; a novation takes place where one contract is discharged and another is substituted between different parties but with the same terms. For example, there would be a novation of a letter of credit where A and B agreed with an issuing bank that the bank should cancel a letter of credit in favour of A and replace it by a new letter of credit, of which the beneficiary would be B. The effect of this is that there are no continuing contractual relations between A and the bank; A drops out.

Novations have some advantages over other methods of transfer, most of which arise because a novation is not a transfer at all. Thus, when rights are transferred, the transferee, B, will often find that his rights against the bank are closely affected by, and limited by, the transferor's, A's, conduct and legal relations with the bank; if B wishes to sue the bank, he may well have to join A as a party to the litigation. In the case of a novation, however, B has his own contract with the bank to which A is not, and never has been, a party, and B need concern himself only with ensuring that the terms of that contract are complied with. Thus, he must present documents which meet the requirements of the credit, but fraud in the transaction by A can be no defence to a claim by B, and the bank cannot set-off as against B any claims it may have against A.

However, novations are unusual, no doubt because they require the full and active co-operation of the issuing bank, and they do not allow the transfer of some, but not all, of the rights arising under a letter of credit.

---

* The need to consider carefully this area of the law has recently been highlighted by the case of *Singer & Friedlander* v. *Creditanstalt-Bankverein* Vienna Commercial Court, Aug. 13, 1980.

4.2. Negotiation under a negotiation credit

A letter of credit is not a negotiable instrument. However, negotiation under a negotiation credit combines some of the advantages of letters of credit with those of negotiable instruments, particularly the security of a bank's obligation provided by a letter of credit, and the independence from defences available against prior holders, which is the perquisite of a holder in due course of a negotiable instrument. Most negotiation credits contain a standard clause taken from the Standard Forms for the Issuing of Documentary Credits of the International Chamber of Commerce (Brochure No. 268), Form No. 2A:

> "We hereby engage with drawers and/or bona fide holders that drafts drawn and negotiated in conformity with the terms of this credit will be duly honoured on presentation and that drafts accepted within the terms of this credit will be duly honoured at maturity."

A clause in this form constitutes an offer by the issuing bank to anybody who cares to take it up. This offer is accepted by the conduct of the holder when he accepts negotiation of the draft and the documents (see *In Re. Agra and Masterman's Bank* (1867) L.R. 2 Ch. App. 391, per Cairns L. J.). Negotiation under a negotiation credit, therefore, creates a direct contract between the holder and the issuing bank. It is not a case of the transfer or assignment of rights which once belonged to the original beneficiary, but of the creation of a new contract. Neither is it a case of liability on a negotiable instrument, since although the draft is drawn on the issuing bank, it is not a party to it, never having signed it.

It follows from these principles that a bank's rights to refuse payment to a bona fide holder of drafts and documents after negotiation under a negotiation credit are as follows:

i. The bank can, of course, reject for defects on the face of the documents.
ii. The bank may also reject if negotiation has not been effected in accordance with the terms of the credit, e.g., the credit will often require the draft to be marked "drawn under documentary credit no. 1234 of X Bank Limited", and details of drafts and negotiations to be indorsed on its back.
iii. The bank may reject for fraud in the presentation.
iv. The bank cannot reject for false or fraudulent documents which are in order on their faces. Bona fide holders of the documents cannot be expected to take any responsibility for their genuineness, and the issuing bank accepts this risk when it issues a negotiation credit.
v. The applicant for the credit will not be entitled to restrain the bank from making payment to a bona fide holder of drafts and documents on the ground of fraud in the transaction. This is because the right to such restraint depends on the circumstance that payment would otherwise be made to a party directly involved in the fraud.
vi. The bank is not entitled to set-off against the holder any rights it may have against the original beneficiary (*In Re. Agra and Masterman's Bank,* supra).

Thus, a bank accepting negotiation of a draft under a credit must be scrupulous to satisfy itself that the documents appear to meet the requirements of the credit, and that negotiation is effected in accordance with the terms of the credit. If these conditions are met, and it is bona fide, it will be secure.

A brief mention should be made of credits available by acceptance. In a credit available by acceptance, the bank's undertaking to accept drafts is usually addressed solely to the original beneficiary. Consequently, the bank has no liability to third parties as it has no contract with them under the credit, and until it accepts it the bank is not a party to the draft. However, once the draft is accepted by the bank, upon its presentation together with the required documents, the letter of credit becomes discharged and the bank is liable, on its acceptance, to holders of the draft according to the normal principles of the law of negotiable instruments.

4.3. Transfer under Article 46

Article 46 of the UCP makes provision for a limited right for a beneficiary to transfer his rights under a letter of credit. Article 46 is an unsatisfactory and contradictory provision. Its provisions include:

> "(d) A credit can be transferred only if it is expressly designated as 'transferable' by the issuing bank. Terms such as 'divisible', 'fractionable', 'assignable', and transmissible' add nothing to the meaning of the term 'transferable' and shall not be used."
> "(a) A transferable credit is a credit under which the beneficiary has the right to give instructions to the bank called upon to effect payment or acceptance or to any bank entitled to effect negotiation to make the credit available in whole or in part to one or more third parties . . ."

"(b) The bank requested to effect the transfer, whether it has confirmed the credit or not, shall be under no obligation to effect such transfer except to the extent and in the manner expressly consented to by such bank . . ."

Insofar as they suggest that the right of a beneficiary of a transferable credit to have the credit transferred is subject to the discretion of the bank, these provisions are very unsatisfactory. Credits should be simply transferable or not transferable, and the decision whether or not to transfer a transferable credit should be that of the beneficiary, not the bank. If a bank does not wish to have its liability transferred, it should not issue a transferable credit.

Article 46 further states:

"(e) A transferable credit can be transferred once only. Fractions of a transferable credit (not exceeding in the aggregate the amount of the credit) can be transferred separately, provided partial shipments are not prohibited, and the aggregate of such transfers will be considered as constituting only one transfer of the credit . . ."

The most satisfactory legal analysis of a transfer under Article 46 is that it creates a direct contract between the issuing bank, and the confirming bank if there is one, and the transferee deriving from the advice of the transfer sent to the transferee, in the same way as an ordinary letter of credit contract is created by the advice of the credit. Thus, the bank enters into a new contract with the transferee while maintaining its contract with the transferor, although its liability to the transferor will be reduced by the amount of the liability it assumes to the transferee.

It has been suggested that transfer under Article 46 should be regarded as either a novation or an equitable assignment (see Gutteridge and Megrah, *The Law of Bankers' Commercial Credits*, 6th ed., 1979, pp. 167–70). Both these are unsatisfactory solutions. The first, because the transferred letter of credit is unlikely to be in the same terms as the original; for instance, the amount is often lower, and the first beneficiary will almost certainly retain rights against the bank and not drop out completely. The second, because if there was an equitable assignment the bank would normally be entitled to set-off against the assignee (transferee) any claims it had against the assignor (original beneficiary) before it had notice of the assignment, which in the case of a transfer would be at the time of the transfer, and indeed any later claim closely related to the letter of credit contract. The assignee would also not be entitled to sue the bank in its own name, but would have to join the assignor (original beneficiary) as a party to the litigation. The reality of the situation is, therefore, better reflected by giving the transferee a full legal right and not just an equitable interest.

The bank's rights to refuse payment to a transferee are, therefore, the same as those it has against any other original beneficiary, or the new beneficiary under a novation. Accordingly, the general discussion above, of when a bank can refuse payment, applies. The bank cannot set-off against the transferee any claims it has against the transferor, since a transfer is not a true assignment, and neither can the applicant restrain payment on the ground of fraud in the transaction by the transferor.

4.4. Assignment

This concerns assignment on ordinary legal principles rather than any particular mechanism established by the UCP. The first question must be whether there is any place for assignment of rights under a credit governed by the UCP, other than as expressly provided for by Articles 46 and 47. Article 46(d), which provides that a letter of credit is only to be transferable if it is expressly stated to be so, and decrees that the word "assignable", amongst others, adds nothing to "transferable" and shall not be used, has been quoted above. Article 47 provides:

"The fact that a credit is not stated to be transferable shall not affect the beneficiary's rights to assign the proceeds of such credit in accordance with the provisions of the applicable law."

The clear implication of these provisions, and especially the procription of the word "assignable", is that the UCP does not contemplate any transfer of rights under letters of credit except as is expressly provided under Articles 46 and 47 (assignment under Article 47 is discussed below). The right of transfer under Article 46 is a limited one, in particular the credit; allowing for fractions, this may only be transferred once. As a matter of law, an express or implied provision in an obligation, which prohibits or limits its assignability, will probably be effective in these circumstances (see Halsbury's *Laws of England*, 4th ed., vol. 6, title "Choses in Action", para. 89). It is, therefore, submitted that a purported assignment of rights under a letter of credit governed by the UCP is ineffective to confer on the assignee any rights against an issuing or confirming bank, unless it can be brought within Article 46 or Article 47 (see A. G. Davis, *op. cit.*, pp. 110–14).*

---

* It was so held in Vienna in the *Creditanstalt* case (*op cit.*) on principles equally applicable in England.

However, since there is no English decision on this point and Gutteridge and Megrah (*op cit.*, pp. 170–7) consider that it is possible to assign "the whole benefit of a credit" contrary to what is suggested above, some further consideration must be given to it. In English law, an assignment may be of the legal title to property under section 136 of the Law of Property Act 1925, or only of the equitable interest. For an assignment to be effective under section 136:

 i. the assignment should be of the whole of the assignor's rights; and
 ii. the assignment should be in writing and signed by the assignor; and
 iii. express notice in writing of the assignment must be given to the obligor.

If these conditions are satisfied, the assignee will acquire from the date of the notice all the assignor's rights against the obligor, including the right to sue in his own name, subject to any set-off available to the obligor against the assignor at the date of the notice, and any defences which later arise out of a transaction inseparably connected with the obligation assigned. It is, therefore, clear that the assignee takes subject to any defences open to the bank on the documents and subject to any set-off available to the bank at the time it receives notice of the assignment.

However, the question of fraud in the transaction poses a problem here. If the fraud is quite unconnected with the contract contained in the letter of credit, the only ground on which the buyer (applicant) can restrain payment is that payment would otherwise be made to the fraudsman; if the assignee is innocent, there would seem to be no ground in such a case for refusing to pay. The case of *Stoddart* v. *Union Trust Ltd.* (1912) 1 K.B. 181, provides a useful illustration, although it has nothing to do with letters of credit. The Union Trust bought a newspaper from one Price on the basis of fraudulent misrepresentations as to its circulation and advertising revenue. Price assigned the right to receive £800 of the purchase price to Stoddart, who sued the Union Trust for it. The Court of Appeal held that as the Union Trust had not sought to set aside the contract or alleged a breach of it, and their fraud claim was personal to Price, they had no defence against Stoddart. The decision has been heavily criticized but the principle would be stronger in a letter of credit case, where the right to payment rests on a contract in the credit that is quite separate from the contract of sale, and even more removed from any fraud which is preliminary to the contract of sale.

This example provides a further argument against the assignability of letters of credit. It would be an unpleasant surprise to an applicant, who had ensured that the credit issued was not transferable under the UCP, to find that his fraudulent seller had assigned the rights under the credit to an assignee who was entitled to be paid.

If an assignment does not comply with section 136, for instance, if it is only an assignment of some of the rights under the credit, and it is made for value, it will probably take effect as an equitable assignment. The principal difference between an equitable assignment and a legal assignment for present purposes is procedural, in that the assignee must make the assignor a party to any proceedings he wishes to bring.

It should be repeated, however, that very probably a letter of credit governed by the UCP is not assignable at all. If an issuing bank wishes to ensure that this is the position, it would be well advised to provide expressly that its credits are not to be transferable under the UCP, or assignable at law or in equity.

4.5. Assignment of proceeds—Article 47

Article 47 has been quoted above; the position under it is quite simple. It is open to the beneficiary to assign the right to receive payment under the credit, and no more. To be effective and binding on the bank, such an assignment must be for value, and notice must be given to the bank. Such an assignment is one of future property since the property—the right to payment—does not come into existence until the original beneficiary (the assignor) would be, but for the assignment, entitled to payment from the bank. Thus the bank need only concern itself with whether it is obliged to pay the original beneficiary. But if it is, it must actually make payment to the assignee. The case of *Singer & Friedlander* v. *Creditanstalt-Bankverein*, which is being fought in Vienna, is an example of the assignment of proceeds; Creditanstalt-Bankverein have now won the first round.

There seems to be, at present, a growing willingness, on the part of bankers, to litigate their disputes when for one reason or another it has not proved possible to arrive at an amicable out-of-court solution. The reason may be that the amounts of money involved in these transactions are so enormous and the points or principle so important that the more traditional approach of not resorting to lawyers and the courts has now been overtaken.

Authors' Biographies

Charles J. Gmür has practiced with international banks in the German, French and Italian part of Switzerland as well as in Spain, France, Sweden and Canada. He has held various posts including Foreign Exchange Trader, Credit Officer, Branch Supervisor and Inspector. Mr. Gmür is a Senior Vice President and Manager of Crédit Suisse, Zurich, and since 1967 has been head of the special financing division. He is also Managing Director of Finanz AG Zurich, CS Leasing Ltd., Chairman of CS Factoring Ltd., CS Leasing Immobilier SA., and Finanz AG London, affiliates of Crédit Suisse which he has built up. He is a board member of several industrial and trading companies.

Lode Beckers was born in Belgium and graduated from Louvain University as Doctor of Law and M.A. Political Sciences. He joined Citibank in Brussels in 1969 and was head of the London Oil and Mining Department until 1976. After an assignment with Citibank's World Corporation Group in New York, he was transferred to Paris in September 1978 where he set up Citibank's specialized banking department for European construction and engineering customers operating in Africa, the Middle East and other overseas markets. Lode Beckers is a Vice President of Citibank and has contributed to *Euromoney*, the *Investor's Chronicle* and various publications in his home country. **Giles Clarke** is a Manager of Credit Suisse First Boston. He advises U.K. corporations about financing their external activities and in arranging merger and acquisition business in Europe, the Middle East and the Far East. He holds an honours degree from Oxford University in Persian and Arabic and has a degree in Arabic from Damascus University. He spent a number of years working in the Middle East prior to joining CSFB in 1976.

Rhodri Davies obtained a B.A. in law from Downing College, Cambridge, and is a practising barrister.

Anthony Grabiner obtained an LL.B. and LL.M. from the London School of Economics. Sometime lecturer in law at London University. He is a practising barrister and a standing junior counsel to the U.K. Department of Trade, Export Credits Guarantee Department.

Robert H. Miller M.A. (Cantab.) began his career in domestic banking in one of the regional branches of Crédit Suisse in Switzerland. He later moved to the International Division in Zurich where he joined Finanz AG Zurich, a wholly owned subsidiary of Crédit Suisse. He has been in London for the past four years where he was Manager of Finanz AG London until Dec. 31, 1980.

Paul O'Hanlon was educated at the London School of Economics and the London Graduate School of Business Studies. He worked as a solicitor before joining Citibank N.A. in 1975, where he is now a Vice President and head of the London branch's unit concerned with the finance of commodity merchants.

Christine E. Raemy-Dirks is an Assistant Vice President with Crédit Suisse, Zurich, where she heads the barter and compensation department. She holds a degree in economics from the University of Frankfurt/Main and a post graduate certificate in the field of European economics from the College of Europe, Belgium. After two years of professional academic work at the University of Frankfurt/Main she joined the World Bank in Washington in 1976. Since 1978 she has worked for Crédit Suisse, Zurich, in the division of special financing.

Nikolas P. Soskin was educated at Eton after which he worked at Brinckmann Wirtz and Co., in Hamburg and Banque de Paris et des Pays-Bas in Paris before joining S. G. Warburg & Co. Ltd., in London. He joined Gillett Brothers Discount Co. Ltd. in 1972 and spent 18 months in Singapore where he participated in the creation of the Singapore Discount market as first Managing Director of the Discount Company of Singapore. He became a Managing Director of Gillett in January, 1974.

Thomas Teichman was educated at the London School of Economics and University College, London (B.Sc. (Econ.) Hons). He has worked for a major U.S. commercial bank, a British Accepting House and from 1975 until 1979 in the Crédit Suisse Group as Manager of Finanz AG London Limited. Since 1976 Mr. Teichman has also been a Vice President of Crédit Suisse in its London Branch and is now Advisor to Finanz AG London Limited and a Director of Finanz AG Middle East Associates Ltd. He has acted as an external consultant to the Economist Intelligence Unit, London.

Index